Z

D1631398

TAKING FRESH
GUARD

TAKING FRESH GUARD

A memoir

Tony Lewis

headline

First published in 2003
by HEADLINE BOOK PUBLISHING

10 9 8 7 6 5 4 3 2 1

Every effort has been made to fulfil requirements with regard to reproducing
copyright material. The author and publisher will be glad to rectify any
omissions at the earliest opportunity.

Thanks to Patti Wallis for her administrative help.

Cataloguing in Publication Data is
available from the British Library

ISBN 0 7472 7598 X

Typeset in AGaramond by
Letterpart Limited, Reigate, Surrey

Designed by Letterpart

Printed and bound in Great Britain by
Mackays of Chatham plc, Chatham, Kent

HEADLINE BOOK PUBLISHING
A division of Hodder Headline
338 Euston Road
LONDON NW1 3BH

www.headline.co.uk
www.hodderheadline.com

To my girls,
Joanie, Joanna and Anabel

CONTENTS

CHAPTER 1

TO BEGIN AT THE BEGINNING

I begin with an unexceptional tale of family chaos during the Second World War. I was born in 1938 at the Swansea home of my mother's parents. We stayed on there after 1939 along with all non-combatant members of the large Flower family. Gone to the war were my mother's brother, Leslie Flower, and two sons-in-law, Elvet Thomas and my father, Wilfrid Llewellyn Lewis. No doubt we were herded under one roof for safekeeping. The numbers of inmates grew as, every so often, a soldier returned to procreate with urgency. My sister Heather was born there in 1941, and cousin Geoffrey soon after.

The large terraced house, Sunnybank, coped without a bulge, and even today looks solid on Glanmor Road as it winds up out of the Uplands. This was Dylan Thomas territory. Round the corner was his birthplace in Cwmdonkin Drive, behind us the park where we played with the very same chained cup as the 'solitary mister', his 'Hunchback in the Park', and below us all life passed the Uplands Hotel where he was known to take a drink.

The sounds accompanying my earliest days were the cheeping and chirruping of Uncle David's canaries and budgerigars in the home-made aviary outside the back door, the constant clatter of porcelain as my grandmother, a prolific cooker of sponge cakes, prepared to feed the masses and the whine of Uncle David's lathe from his workshop in the roof. He had been struck down with polio in his teenage years yet he turned himself into a master craftsman in the close company of his father. The night sounds were, and are still, the droning bombers, the wailing, soaring sirens of air-raid warnings, big bangs and the shrill whistles of the Home Guard or of Air Raid Precaution units. Windows had to be blacked out while the grown-ups continued a marathon of Monopoly. I somehow recall going high up in the three-storeyed house with my grandfather to watch the searchlights criss-cross over Swansea, no doubt desperately trying to pinpoint a German plane. To me it was exciting, not dangerous. Everyone believed that the Germans were trying to bomb Llandarcy oil works, situated between Swansea and Neath, but the facts are otherwise. They made a mess of our town and changed our lives. Between 1940 and 1943, there were forty-four raids on Swansea, which killed 369 people. During the famous three nights blitz in February 1941, forty-one acres of the town's trading heart were blown up. Fires spread through narrow streets, as the Luftwaffe dropped 800 high-explosive bombs and 300 incendiaries. More than 300 shops were destroyed. Four of them were owned by my grand-father, H.W. Flower, Tobacconist and Confectioner. He was left with only one, a couple of doors along from the Swansea Empire Theatre in Oxford Street. 'Swansea Aflame' the old newspapers read and as raids continued, the town was declared an evacuation area.

Family anecdotes are colourful. On the nights of the blitz, 19, 20, 21 February, apparently my grandfather, fearing the worst, walked to the centre of Swansea to check on his shops. Each night he set off long before the 'all clear' had sounded, down the long Walter Road. On the very night his businesses were demolished he was stopped at a police barrier as he made his sad way home. The top of Walter Road, he was informed, was impassable because there was a bomb buried in it that had not exploded. It was the same stretch of road he had just walked down. He must have whistled his way past the crater on the other side of the road. He had so nearly gone up with the shops.

I have also been told that evacuation was the least painful experience the Sunnybank commune had in mind for me. I was a menace during air-raid warnings when everyone in the house made a dash through the kitchen to the cellar. At the cellar door, however, stood a tiny bus conductor who would step aside and let 'passengers' proceed only if they came up with a pretending penny in exchange for one of his pretending tickets, rolled from the machine attached to a shoulder-strap. So, fleeing for their lives, they had to queue at the top of the stairs while I lisped, 'Ticketh pleathe, ticketh pleathe. Full upstairs, room downstairs. Ticketh pleathe.' As far as the females were concerned, I was a part of the Nazi war effort that crumbled with a clip round the ear. For the men, my grandfather and Uncle David, I was a helpful assistant because in the cellar was a small snooker table. Each time the black went into the top pocket I was called in with my small stool, to step up, remove the ball and replace it on its spot. My first job in sport, I reckon.

Soon my mother, Marjorie, decided to try evacuation as recommended by the government and in a sensational dash for safety landed us in Neath, a town all of eight miles from Swansea, positioned nearly the same number of miles from the Llandarcy oil refinery but on the other side. Well, I guess seven miles inland to the north-east was a long way in those days.

We rented a small house and I started at the Gnoll Infants School, but the war dragged on and we were towed back to Swansea where I briefly attended Brynmill School. By 1946 we were back in Neath. One day, Heather and I were scrubbed up to go to the railway station. I was eight and the man in army uniform standing in front of us on the platform was reintroduced as our father. It was the man who had stayed with us before, the one with the Sam Browne, the revolver and the sweets. Captain Lewis was home from Germany forever, and moved promptly into civvy street as the manager of the London and Manchester Insurance Company, perched in a small office above the Dolcis shoe shop at the junction of Green Street and Wind Street with Orchard Street and New Street. He quickly opened up unofficial branch offices at a table in the MC Café, run by the brothers Moruzzi, and at the bar of the Liberal Club, depending on the time of day.

Neath it was then.

CHAPTER 2

MY HOME TOWN

Bracken Road, in the Llantwit area of Neath, was a modern cul
de sac when the Lewis family moved there, short, straight and
with a turning circle at the end for horses and carts, delivery
vans and for the one car, a Wolsley, owned by Mr Stevens in number
seven. Round the circle were five buildings housing ten families in
small, semi-detached, pebble-dashed replicas, fronted by knee-high
brick walls and privet hedges of varying health and strength. Iron loops
that had once held ornamental, drooping chains were still fixed to the
wooden posts. The chains themselves had long gone to the war effort
for ammunition, possibly down to the 'Japan' Tinplate Decorating
works at Melyn Crythan, under 'the Arches' in Neath town, where over
four hundred people fashioned various wartime supplies for the
Ministry of Munitions.

Llantwit means church of Illtyd, the Christian saint, but the word that
all Neath people put automatically alongside Llantwit is 'cemetery',
making it the dead end of town. Just after the Second World War, Neath
spread in that direction. One year the limit of the town was the Neath
rugby and cricket ground called The Gnoll, and the next it had spawned
Bracken Road, Hazelwood and Oakwood, Glen Road, Illtyd Street,
Leonard Street and a steep hill of council houses called Ivy Avenue.

In Bracken Road, the houses provided modest but clean family living away from the town centre. On these limits of built-up Neath, the back gardens of the houses opposite us led up the sloping allotments to the ruined Gnoll House on top of the hill. The Gnoll woods were a 12,000-acre estate no longer in private ownership, a natural playground of ponds and glades and council soccer pitches. It was cover for courting couples, peeping toms and, in the autumn, a conker kingdom that fuelled the playground battles of the schools below, Alderman Davies's Church School and the Gnoll School. 'Gnoll' was the password for our daily lives, attached as it was to Gnoll Avenue, Gnoll Drive, Gnoll Park Road and Gnoll Road Congregational Chapel. The Neath Cricket Club was behind the garden of number seven Bracken Road, and we could see, through the high, spiked railings, a broken-down pavilion, nets and roller. The main sporting arena, however, for timeless cricket Tests and for rugby internationals where no whistles blew was the dead-end road itself. A street lamp at the neck of the turning circle end was the rugby post. The crossbar below the gaslight, on which the lamplighter used to rest his ladder, was our bar; in our imaginations it stretched right across the width of the road for all penalties, conversions and drop kicks. At the other end of the road, near the main Harle Street, the lintel above the Harris's side door was the level over which all scoring kicks had to pass.

In Bracken Road, the dividing wall between adjoining semis was thin. 'Do you want more toast, Wilf?' my mother would call out to my father from the small kitchen, and Tom Morgan from next door would reply that he was full, thank you, and couldn't eat any more. It was massive good luck that the Morgans in number nine listened to the same wireless programmes as the Lewises in number ten. When the 'Coronation Scot' signature tune drifted in through the wallpaper above the fireplace on a Sunday evening, we rushed for the 'Light Programme' to tune in to Paul Temple and Steve. One dark, silent night a loud and desperate wail shook the wall, followed by a crash, we thought of furniture. My father looked up from his *Telegraph* crossword to remark, 'I knew those accountancy exams were getting on top of him. Too much pressure on the poor boy.' Peter Morgan, older than

I was by a few years, was wading through a swamp of cost accountancy. He had just gone under, taking the tablecloth, cups and saucers with him. At least, that was the Lewis theory.

Pleasant people, the Morgans. Old Tom Morgan liked his garden and made the most of two tiny parcels of land that went with the home, grass to the front, vegetables at the back. My father, on the other hand, was naturally unskilled as a handyman and had a serious aversion to physical toil. If pressed by my mother, he would leave his armchair, groaning, advance without hope to take up a screwdriver, gouge a lump out of his hand, scratch the paintwork and end up taking a hammer to a screw. When my mother took to the toolbox, everything worked and my father took cover, but outside the house, the garden for this handsome man was simply a sod too far. It was a no-go area; he became ill at the rumble of the lawnmower that my mother was pushing. Whenever he heard gardening activity he used to take his frown to the box of family papers in the corner of the living room and sigh as if high duty had called. Out would come the major documents – the bills for rent, for gas, for water and for electricity. He loaded the writing of four cheques on the living-room table with the gravitas of running a major department of the Treasury. His body and mind were simply out of sympathy with the outdoors, and so the only words he ever addressed to nature's deities were 'Oh God! I hate gardening.' In fact, a horticultural triumph did come his way by a cunning plot. Without telling my mother, he let the back garden to a neighbour, Mr Birch, who, instead of paying rent, grew our fruit and vegetables. My mother recognised deceit when she saw it, but Dad could go to the cricket club and tell everyone round the bar how his new potatoes melted in the mouth and that his raspberries were far chubbier than last year.

I am not sure how quickly he settled into our semi after the army. The officers' mess must have been another world. What now should he do with his five O-levels from Dynevor Grammar School in Swansea? His mind was outstanding, his handwriting elegant and orderly and he was conscientious, though a serious worrier. If he had stayed with the London and Manchester I know he would have made a commercial success, but instead of running with the ball, he kicked it to touch and

I guess it was for the regular salary that would keep his kids fed and clothed through their education. At the age of thirty-five he entered the Civil Service, the Ministry of Health and National Insurance, later Social Security, where time-serving mattered. This meant a limit to his ultimate advancement but he saw Heather through to a fine music degree at Cardiff University and me through National Service and Cambridge.

I suspect, too, that he was influenced by my mother. She was a natural homemaker who refused to believe that wholesome life existed outside the family, or even away from Swansea. She was a Swansea girl; Neath never suited her. The daughter of a successful retailer, she was the practical lady who knocked up a shelf or two, played the piano by ear, and kept her husband injury-free. As a handyman, I was to prove his natural successor.

There was relief that times had steadied. My father, especially, told vivid stories of the tough days of the 1920s depression. Bracken Road was gently post-war, happily noisy with young boys and girls shouting and clanging their way through late-evening games of kick-the-tin that brought Mrs Morgan scolding to her window. We sneaked through her hedge on to the road to boot the empty can while she was drawn by rustle or whistle in another direction. Otherwise darkness brought silence and from my window in the front of the house I studied the lamp-man replacing another broken pane of glass or putting in new gas mantles. Often in summer, after my bedroom curtains had been officially drawn, I used to part them again. I would stand and stare for an age to see whether the black carthorse, the grey or the bay, all turned out for the night in the field above us in front of the Gnoll woods, would graze his or her way first to the imaginary winning post at the far end of the field. At the same time Heather, younger and competi- tively studious, was in bed after practising a Chopin ballade, flipping through her trigonometry and polishing off her library book. I was slower; some teachers suggested through indolence, others took note of a plodding mechanism, which was taking me, albeit as slowly as one of my carthorses, in a forward direction.

If Neath was famous it was for the Hollywood film star called

Raymond Jones who took the name of an area of Neath known as the Millands. The name Milland might have lifted him to the stars but it never caught on in Neath. With that small-town devotion to over-familiarity that keeps a gossipy town alive, the whisper would go round the pubs – 'Raymond Jones is home.' C.F. Walters was an England cricket captain, Wil Roberts and Andrew Vicari artists. The name of Jock Harston was good Neath gossip, too, because he was the first Trotskyist to contest a British parliamentary seat. He collected real support in the Neath by-election of 1945. Sir David Evans Bevan was placed above all because his brewery provided jobs and the produce was bitter beer. Every growing boy, post-war, was reared on pints of bitter – straight glass, of course.

My Neath, however, began on Bracken Road. I was washed away in an endless flow of rugby on the road, day and night. The names on the programme never changed – Waverley Doughty from number four, Micky Williams five, Robert Stevens seven, Alan Jordan an occasional, eight, Peter Morgan rarely, nine, and me. The regulars from the main Harle Street were Peter Jenkins, Tudor Thomas, Clive Harris and Tony Randall. Play was interrupted by two horse-and-cart merchants, Hopkins the Milk and Arthur the Oil; by two lorries, the coalman and the Our Boys pop lorry; and by Mr Stevens's Wolsley, smelling of real leather and engine oil in the turning circle at the dead-end of the road.

The games we played were born of fantasy. Tony Lewis never played at all – he was Viv Evans, the Neath full-back. No one wanted to play for Wales; only the black jersey with the white Maltese cross of Neath would ever do. I once asked for a Neath jersey for Christmas and was shattered to unwrap a black and amber hooped jersey, rather like Newport's. I was ahead of my time – replica team shirts were another forty years coming.

When we played as a team, say against Oakwood Road or Hazelwood, we would make our entrance on to the road from my front garden, which was as near to the halfway line as any. For very big games we would stand to attention near the manhole cover, where we could stand up an oval ball or a stuffed school cap for the kick-off, and sing the national anthem. Sometimes, probably just after Christmas, we had a new leather ball. 'We'll only pass it,' the boys would say, but soon the bald patches popped, the bladder bulged and it was off to Halford's for the inner tube repair kit.

We never got around to touch-rugby and so Bracken Road was usually awash with blood from wounds, bodies were coloured by bruises and Elastoplast and reeking of iodine and TCP. You had to be clever to sell a dummy. Along the high wall from Harle Street you risked a shoulder charge that would slam you into bricks and mortar. Further on, fifty yards from the lamp-post, where the low walls fronted numbers one to ten, a push would see you either with a face full of privet on one side or clean into the front garden on the other. Either way the razor-sharp top edge of the low wall would score a blood mark on your leg. An ankle tap from behind was always persuasion to get rid of the ball smartly but the sliding fall left flesh on the road. It could be worse. You could hang on and knock-on. Unforgivable! These pen pictures explain why everyone on that road could side-step infield and hand-off a defender. The side-step begat the dropped goal with either foot; nor was elusiveness the reserve of the few talented boys. A side-step, a hand-off and a drop goal were life's three main requirements for staying alive in South Wales in the years after the war. Micky Williams, a big boy, had a thumping hand-off while Clive Harris, who practised many black arts in his back garden, such as frying spiders alive and firing pellets from his airgun into the space between Janice Barnes's head and the top of her school hat, specialised in secondary or late tackling.

On reflection, there was huge merit in learning to play the game of rugby football in rough conditions. Not for us the formality of playing with backs or forwards. In this twenty-first century, when the best rugby teams in the world aim for their perfect fifteen-man game, they might well do worse than play without a referee on a Neath road. And we had pavements on each side, too!

To play rugby in those distant days was second nature, almost compulsory. Soccer was an occasional option on the road or in the schoolyard but this would only be when the rugby bladder was under repair or the stuffed cap had exploded and no one's mum was in to stitch it up. Rugby was clearly a rich part of a South Walian identity. We watched every ball kicked on the Gnoll: Neath, Neath Athletic, the grammar school's big matches and all sorts of West Wales league and cup games. Amman United and Loughor drew so many President's Shield finals there at the end of one season that they continued – toe to toe with 0–0 or 3–3 – through the first month of the next. Cricket was strong but it still lived in rugby's shadow. Almost every cricket ground in South Wales had rugby posts at the other end of the ground.

The town of Neath was almost self-contained. It was a river port and municipal borough with 33,000 inhabitants. Its antiquities included a Roman settlement and castle as well as an abbey that, like many others, was a victim of Henry VIII's act of dissolution and the follow-through of his collector of wealth, Thomas Cromwell. Men found heavy work in coal, copper, tin and steel but when I grew up, coalmines were closing and there was a rush for jobs with the Steel Company of Wales at Margam, Trostre and Felindre; also for the building of the Briton Ferry Bridge, opened in 1955 to spare Neath all A48 traffic. The Neath Canal was joined by an aqueduct in Aberdulais to the Tennant Canal, which in turn joined the River Tawe taking goods to the docks at Port Tennant in Swansea. There was a revival of river trade although the majority of Neath people in the 1950s did not suspect it. New wharves were built to serve the petro-chemical works at Baglan Bay and the Albion Works. In fact, by the 1970s, there was coal traffic coming out of Neath Abbey, with many cargo vessels bobbing back and forth to Common Market destinations in Scandinavia.

As for cricket, our version on the road did not look quite like the sepia pictures I have seen of poor kids playing against three chalked stumps on a wall. That was what we did in school but not on our special oval. You could play across the turning circle using the narrow gap between the gateposts of number four and number five as the wickets. Alternatively, you could come in off a Harold Larwood run down the centre of the road and attack the gateposts between numbers six and seven. Major matches, that is Test matches against Oakwood Road and Hazelwood combined, perhaps with Glen Road thrown in, were two-innings affairs down the middle of the road, with plenty of fielders, and were staged with the advantage of three wooden stumps set in a heavy wooden block, which one of the parents had made. The ball had to be kept on the ground; hits over gardens were out. A tennis ball was the usual ammunition and some of the boys could make it swerve and turn. Micky Williams drifted off-cutters and spun them back; Waverley Doughty with his slinging action was the first reverse-swing bowler I ever saw; Tony Randall was a clever, flighty left-arm slow bowler; and Robert Stevens, a good ball player, was the length bowler others were not. Clive Harris could twist off-spinners quite sharply but, on the whole, preferred shooting girls. He could always get a bowl when he wanted; after all, he was the one with the gun.

There was huge merit in learning cricket on the road, too, especially on one that was fairly flat with rough worn patches. Take the batting. For the short games, across the turning circle, you stood on the pavement, bat tucked neatly behind the feet, and either stayed where you were to play off the back foot, or played forward on to the road to meet the ball with the front foot three inches below the back. It can be argued that this bred the English vices of the lunging forward stroke and the rather static back-foot prod, but the essence of playing well was to make up your mind. Once down at the road level it was nearly impossible to regain the upper ground. As for bowling from a standing start, there was real momentum to be gained in the step down off the pavement and it truly persuaded the best to keep the front leg straight, as Alec Bedser did in the *Boys' Book of Cricket*. No bowler could afford the bent front leg; compounded by the pavement drop, he could lose a whole twelve inches at delivery. This all sounds heavy in theory but not a bit of it: Bracken Road was the nursery of natural response to testing conditions.

All I can claim is that we made it work and I believe that our footwork and ball control were better developed because of the difficulties. The bowler with the wet tennis ball was always to be feared because not only did the ball skid on quickly but also it directed a spray of muddy water at the batsman's eyes. For real, major matches against the other roads we used a cork ball. There were no pads of course. Rain never stopped play because our front room was always available. Playing on the floor, the bowler would twist a marble a couple of yards at small wooden stumps and the batsman would try to stroke one through the field of eleven cigarette cards. The scorer sat on the sofa with his hand inside an old shoebox, adapted as a scoreboard, waving to acknowledge the umpire's signals and pulling round paper loops of figures. I was nearly always Gilbert Parkhouse with the bat, or sometimes Denis Compton or Len Hutton and Alec Bedser with the ball. When I bowled I made changes to the fielding side: my wicket-keeper was Les Ames and the slips alongside were Hammond, Compton and Hutton. Fielding at point was E.W. Dawson of Cambridge University and Leicestershire (I liked his write-up on the back of the card) with Jack Hobbs at cover. Hedley Verity fiddled around at mid-off and Allan Watkins was at backward short-leg where he stood for Glamorgan. Tom Goddard and Harold Larwood spread out.

There is a postscript to cricket on the road. Through the long, tall spiked railings in the Stevens's garden we could see Neath Cricket Club and all the practice and play there. One of the dads sawed through the bottom of a spike so that we could lift it out of its cast-iron frame giving us space to sneak through. We took net practice in the off-season but were always chased away by a watchman. Soon my father had made me a junior member of Neath rugby and of the cricket, too; that was seeing the gates to heaven open all at once. I was fifty yards from Roy John's lineout jumping and from the languid, left-arm loop of Stan Trick's spin bowling.

We were short of municipal amenities but there were a few council-owned rugby and football pitches. Our swimming pool was the Gnoll Pond, a natural pool in the woods of the Gnoll Estate, which had a lifeguard, a diving board and a million tadpoles. There were changing cubicles and organised swimming galas but, truthfully, this was Tarzan country. Cricketers, with no time for being beach boys, did not swim very well and my biology master, Mr Rogers, used to warn against death by drowning from the weight of aquatic larva.

New tennis courts appeared at Dyfed Road, next to the cricket ground, and slowly through the 1950s the town council did a fine job in creating choice. Day-to-day life for the inhabitants of Neath, however, was mostly centred on school, the rugby and cricket fields, the pub, the street and chapel, home of God and weekend shop window of non-conformist crumpet.

My mother sent me to the Gnoll School in Neath because I did not have to cross the road to get there: down Harle Street, turn left along Gnoll Park Road and in through the gates. The senior school was at the front; the infants school at the back across a large shared yard. It is interesting to record that when my sister's turn came to go to school, my mother had no hesitation in sending her a little further into Neath town to attend Alderman Davies's Church School. The Gnoll inmates included the good, the bad and the ugly; Alderman Davies's omitted the bad and the ugly. There was a strong whiff of social superiority about them. Maybe it was St David's Church and their uniform that gave them the saintly glow, whereas at the Gnoll it was imperative to be skilled at advanced marble games, cigarette card 'flicks' and 'blows', and fighting.

Most teachers were women up to the scholarship examinations, which was the eleven-plus for the grammar school, but there were a couple of men who had gone underground in the pit during the war and had retrained as schoolteachers. One year the woodwork teacher reported that every one of the school chisels had disappeared. Thieving was popular in spite of heavy punishments. He solved it the following year by announcing a special offer – if there were any fathers at home who needed their chisels sharpening free of charge, they could bring them in and the master would be pleased to oblige. Back they came, fifteen chisels with the faint lettering on the wooden handles – Gnoll School Property.

Every playtime in the yard there was football or cricket or maybe a piece of supervised gym. If you have seen film of airmen in captivity, you will easily set the scene in the Gnoll school yard: cigarette cards being traded, pop swigged, marbles or half bottles of vinegar to harden the conkers exchanging hands.

Once, a mother clad in green overalls stormed into our classroom with the loud intention of closing the schoolmistress's eye if she ever again swished a cane across 'my boy Robert's arse'.

Morning hymns were sung in the main hall in Welsh, which almost none of us could speak. Welsh words in white chalk were unfurled on black charts while Miss Thomas patrolled the lines, eager to correct mispronunciations with a swish here and a swish there. John Redwood, in later days Secretary of State for Wales, who honourably essayed the Welsh national anthem at a rugby international, would have been cut to ribbons.

The girls' school was just a gap in the wall away and my future wife was at large there – we even sat the scholarship examination for the grammar school in the same hall – but what are facts if you are ignorant of them at the time? My brother-in-law Glyn was a few years ahead of me in the Gnoll. Whenever we meet now for a pint in the pub, the Gnoll stories keep us laughing.

It was after school one day when we were kicking around in the yard that a whistle blew and a thin teacher with a moustache, Mr Ivor Habbakuk Jones, was crooking a finger at me. 'How old are you, boy?'

'Nine, Sir.'

'You are in the school team to play Cwrt Sart, away, on Thursday, the Under-fifteens.' I thought rugby. 'You appear to bat all day on the yard so you can open the batting.' Cricket!

In huge, heavy buckskin cricket boots borrowed by my father, cut-down whites and a cable-stitch sweater than my mother had knitted years before, I made my cricket debut on a real pitch at the Briton Ferry Town Cricket Club.

Without doubt, my father joined in my love of ball games although he had the good sense to follow, not push. He had been a hockey player for Swansea and Bridgend but, for me, he settled for the non-stop bash of rugby on the road and occasionally up in the Gnoll woods. It was an inspirational move to take me to see Wales play rugby for the first time when I was eleven years old. The game was against Ireland at Swansea, and I remember walking down Harle Street in pouring rain wondering if they would cancel the match. 'There are breaks in the cloud,' my father kept saying. 'It will be fine later.' And so it was. By the time of the kick-off I was tucked in between him and a barrier near the front of the big bank on the Bryn Road side of St Helens. They always said that rugby internationals were taken away from Swansea because there were 40,000 spectators and only two toilets. True or not, it was a crush and men were peeing all round us. We were at the bottom of the terrace and having to cope with high tide. During the match the railing collapsed at the front, not twenty yards from us, but without injuries. Part of the crowd spilled out on to the field and had an even closer view. I wondered why so many of the backs were from Cardiff – Trott, the full-back, Matthews, Williams, Cook, Cleaver and Tanner. My father kept saying, 'Now you just watch Hadyn Tanner and keep an eye on Bleddyn Williams for the side-step, and Jack Matthews, and if Ken Jones, the sprinter, gets the ball, no one will catch him.' I recognised one forward, Rees Stephens of Neath, the lock, or what is called Number Eight today. Well, this bundle of Welsh fireworks never ignited. Ireland scored a try in the first half a long way from us on the other side: a kick inside from someone called Jack Kyle, whom everyone appeared to recognise, and a jump and dive over by a red-headed forward called Jim McCarthy. Norton of Bective converted and Ireland won the match 5–0 and with it the Triple Crown. Everyone near me blamed the referee. They thought that McCarthy was offside. We looked in the programme to check the referee's name and saw it was Tom Pearce, an Englishman. I joined in the booing every time he came near. A dozen years later I met Tom Pearce, the former Essex cricket captain and organiser of the Scarborough Cricket Festival in which I was playing. 'I suppose you were another one of those blind Welshmen booing me at Swansea in forty-nine,' he said, but it was kindly rather than aggressive. For shocking openers it did not match my first handshake on the same day with Brian Sellars, the Yorkshire chairman – 'Na' then, you little Welsh bastard . . .'

An influential experience of my childhood was being taken to watch Glamorgan's annual county championship match on the Gnoll. To see for the first time the giant Wilf Wooller lead out his men was one of the most exciting moments of life to date, 1949. The Glamorgan team included Emrys Davies, Hadyn Davies, Willie Jones, Gilbert Parkhouse, Allan Watkins, J.C. Clay, Len Muncer, Jim McConnon and, in some of the local matches, our own amateur left-arm spinner Stan Trick. Just to see the yellow daffodils was enough to send us racing back to the road to start another timeless Test.

One Sunday morning in Gnoll Road Congregational Church the whisper was that some Somerset cricketers were in the congregation; there was no play on Sundays in those days. It was June, I was ten years old and I collected the autographs of M. Cope, H.T.F. Base, J. Lawrence and H.L. Hazell. Those were not the days for presenting first names to strangers.

A fortnight earlier at Swansea, two pieces of play entered my soul forever. Emrys Davies, pillar of Glamorgan's batting, a left-hander, so gentlemanly, so expert in his craft, took first strike in the second innings against Middlesex. He hooked, but down at the foot of the big terrace was Jim Sims to catch him. My father and I had rushed from home to the match by three buses, taking the best part of two hours, and 'The Rock' was gone. I decided to hate Middlesex and the bowler, Mr G.O. Allen, an amateur. Many years later, I reminded Gubby of that tiny event in his career. All he could come out with was, 'I wasn't so quick in those days, either. You should have seen me before the war.'

Middlesex were set 266 to win after a Glamorgan declaration at 183–7 and my father explained how Len Muncer, once of Middlesex but now our off-spinner, and Stan Trick, spinning the ball away from the bat, would bowl us to victory over the Londoners. What a superb action Stan Trick had! It was rhythmical, even elegant, but with bite in the delivery and tricky flight. S.M. Brown was out and also H. Brearley, father of Mike, but then came a Middlesex batsman who appeared not to be playing his eye in, as we were taught. He played a shot I had never seen before, and against Stan Trick, too: leaning on to a half-extended left leg he swept the ball from almost an upright position with a straightish bat, down to fine leg for four.

Rain ended the match. Middlesex were 139–2 and D.C.S. Compton was 67 not out. I was there! And importantly, so was my father. What a delight it must have been for him after the war.

CHAPTER 3

MUSIC OR CRICKET

The scholarship examination was passed and my parents were relieved. In September 1949 I arrived for my first day at Neath Boys Grammar School, a solid red-brick building overlooking a couple of rugby pitches and a small cricket square. Clearly, one fine day early in the twentieth century, a town planner had decided to create an advanced educational centre on the outskirts of town, over the river bridge, at Dwr-y-Felin (watermill), because the Neath Technical College stood next door to us and across Dwr-y-Felin Road was the Grammar School for Girls. In our senior school years, we would peer hopefully over the high wall into the female world of long grey socks and navy blue knickers, crisply pressed white blouses and school ties, or green candy-striped summer dresses with statutory sandals. I was not old enough yet.

Splitting up friends at the age of eleven on the evidence of a day's examination was harsh but fitted the drive for education that was shared by the whole of South Wales. Pass the exams and stay out of the coal mine; go to university and be free of the tough industrial realities of South Wales. Teach or preach, do law or accountancy, but whatever you do, said our parents whose families had survived the general strike in 1926 and all the wrath of the overcrowded coalmining industry, shut the door of the front room, do your homework and pass your exams.

So many of my friends can tell of fathers who threw down a miner's helmet and lamp on the kitchen table alongside the school books to show the choice – study or dig coal. Not that going underground was altogether frowned upon. Young boys in the mining valleys longed to follow father and grandfather down the pit. It was the culture; it was the manly, honourable road ahead.

Those raised in one of the many mining villages in the Neath Valley were usually tough and spoke Welsh. To come from the town, down at the mouth of the River Neath, was to be soft and anglicised. The valley boys descended from the hills every day to the grammar school by special train along the Neath and Brecon line and it was amazing to witness how a simple, harmless railway carriage could become an armament factory. Into school they would come with a window strap severed so that the rolled-up leather at the top could become a cosh for shoulder blades. The luggage rack, made of strong netting, had gladiatorial possibilities, held high in the left hand to entrap the enemy's lunge before whopping him in the ribs with the armrest of a third-class compartment.

On the first day at Neath Grammar School you were thrown a rugby ball to see how you caught it and your voice was tested. Within a week you were in possession of a musical instrument. Rugby was compulsory, not an option, but for the choir you had to be in tune. The diviner of talent was music master John Hopkin Jones, known to the school as 'Hoppy'. 'Come with me, boy,' you would hear and then you would see a thin, frail man whose physique did not match his deep voice, leading a new boy by the strap of his new satchel into the main hall. There, alongside the piano, the terrified novice had to find enough voice to complete a scale. 'Pitch this, boy. Doh. Good, good, now Ray, boy. Ray. Good. Now go through that door and ask Mr Herbert for, let me see, a cello I think. Yes, tell him you would like to learn the cello.' Having completed my second day at school I was to be seen walking home with the soprano part of the Mozart Gloria and a cello in a brown canvas cover, a satchel and my gym kit. It was not that Hoppy had spotted any special aptitude but that he was desperately short of cellists and sopranos for his big concert of the year. Within a week, I had swapped the cello for a violin and soon I was in the back desk of the second fiddles of the school orchestra. Another team game.

The annual dream of John Hopkins Jones was to pull off ten leg-side stumpings and conduct a concert in the town's Gwyn Hall with four-part choir and full orchestra. It was a shock to see a music teacher (so physically vulnerable that he wore fur-lined boots to school in the summer to keep out the cold) slip his hands into a pair of wicket-keeping gloves and stand up to fast bowling for hour after hour. To him, however, cricket was both art and theatre. He tried to cram in as much keeping as possible and would stride across the field to the nets, completely kitted out in red and white quartered cap, his own large gauntlets, considerable pads, white spiked boots, and chewing, to convey his readiness for heroic action, like an air ace shaken from his sleep by the call to 'Scramble'. For him, the bravura take down the leg side and the removal of the bails in one rhythmical action was as a swoop of Barbirolli's baton. There was style and surprise. It was a cheat that someone who played Bach on the piano with such dramatic simplicity should be so short of nature's breath to play a long innings in life, which he did not.

So the massed chorus of the full school would crowd into the hall for lunchtime rehearsals of 'Zadok the Priest'. It would take Hoppy half an hour to organise everyone into four parts and get the orchestra tuned. That done, he retreated halfway back down the hall to his rostrum, an upright wooden chair, and peeled off the first of many sweaters. The preamble to Zadok is lengthy and for one reason or another the orchestra usually tripped up along the way so there were restarts. Hoppy would get frustrated but still concentrated on conveying tempo and the slow but sure arrival of the Queen of Sheba by reducing his own movement to a minimum. He made Klemperer look busy. On a good day, we would reach the choir's first deep intake of breath; Hoppy would leap into action and drill the point of his baton through the very heart of his choir. Zadok the Priest and Nathan the Prophet anointed Solomon King and ding-a-ling, ding-a-ling – the school bell crashed in to announce the end of the lunchtime and the beginning of lessons. Poor Hoppy, overrun by fleeing pupils, was left sitting on his chair, discarded sweaters and sheets of music lying round him on the floor, tie round the back of his neck and sweating through his shirt. We never got to the Gwyn Hall with Zadok, not in my whole time at the school.

There are always key teachers. Sam Evans was one. A Welsh-speaking Rhondda man, he could always be seen and heard on the rugby fields, blasting on the whistle and shouting, 'Free kick, boy. Dull play.' He was in charge of the Under-fourteens when I first encountered him. I sold a dummy in the centre, ignoring the winger outside, and sprinted for a try under the posts. The whistle was shrill, his voice taut and high. 'Come here, show-pony. A man outside you and you sold a dummy. You're a show-pony, boy. Take a spell on the touchline for five minutes and remember rugby football is a team game.' I could not believe it and, as I wandered off, looked back to frown. The whistle blasted again and he trotted over.

'Right, boy, stay off for ten minutes and learn a bigger lesson. D'y know what it is?'

'No, sir.'

'It's this, Lewis. Life is frequently unfair.' He blew again and was gone.

Our paths crossed again when I decided to study history in the sixth form. Sam Evans was the senior history master. Within weeks he built in me a love of history that I have always retained. He was the first to explain that the study of history centred on asking the right questions, not squeezing facts into my head.

He was positive about my rugby, deciding that I was a scrum-half. After a couple of seasons being kicked about at the base of the lineout, I moved to centre and first made the school team in that position. Speed, or rather the lack of it, was my problem and so I took the advice of the new rugger master Roy Bish, the Aberavon centre, and retreated to full-back where I felt completely at ease for the remainder of my playing days. We were lucky to have such an analyst of the game as Roy. After he had finished playing, he became one of the foremost coaches in Europe, ahead of his time in the analysis of the game.

To give you an idea of the precedence rugby took at Neath Grammar School, I must relate the story of Walter Thomas, the senior French master. 'Waller' was a big man with a love of literature and a strong way with words. His brother Gwyn Thomas, author, playwright and broadcaster, was a deal more famous, but Waller lacked nothing of Gwyn's sharp eye and shattering phrase.

One day he prepared to conduct a lesson with the upper sixth in Room Five, which overlooked the rugby pitch. '*Les Fleurs du Mal*,' he announced, noisily clearing his nostrils; he suffered from sinusitis. 'Baudelaire.' He flipped open the textbook. 'Turn to "La Charogne", the dying carcass. Filthy stuff but compulsory.' Then, glancing sideways, he saw one of our tiniest school sides taking the field against local opposition – a proper match.

'Who are they and who are they playing?' Waller inquired.

'The Under-thirteens, sir, playing the technical college from next door.'

He raised his index finger. 'Come.' He walked out of the room indicating that we should follow. A dozen of us trailed along the corridor not knowing where we were going. Just at the end of the building Waller turned into the senior lavatories, marched smartly across to the window and lit a cigarette.

'Right,' he proclaimed. 'We will remain here in the senior bogs for the next two periods where you and that dirty sod Baudelaire will be far more at home, and I can witness the delights of the Under-thirteens.'

I kept playing rugby because that is what you did in Neath. It was rugby football more than anything that brought together those young boys who had been split up by the scholarship examination, some going to the grammar school, some to the technical college and others staying where they were in the Gnoll or elsewhere. In this regard, the whole town owed a huge debt to Rees Stephens, the Welsh rugby captain, who was the driving force in founding the Neath Athletic Rugby Club. Everyone in the town was brought together by 'the Athletic'. I would often play for the school in the morning and for one of the many Athletic teams in the afternoon. The YMCA was our base. From 1996 to 1999, although no longer living in Neath, I was proud to be the club's president. Rugby players in my Neath were the heroes, cricketers came second; violinists were definitely part of a fey fringe.

Now, as I look back, I can see that one of the most inspired programmes of the post-war Labour government was to fill state schools with musical instruments. It was easily possible to be a prop forward and a flautist. Orchestras were formed. In my part of Wales, a place in the school orchestra could lead to the West Glamorgan Youth Orchestra. By audition, that could lead to the Glamorgan Youth Orchestra and that might send you to the stars to take a place in the mighty National Youth Orchestra of Wales.

My mother played the piano by ear in safe key signatures, but the serious musicianship in our family was on the Lewis side in the form of two aunts, both Welsh-speaking. Eirlys, small and pretty, was a trilling coloratura from Fairfach near Llandeilo; Kathleen was a powerful contralto who lived in Eaton Socon in Huntingdonshire where she ran a small private school. Rarely did a cup clink when Eirlys sang 'Clychau Aberdyfi' after Sunday tea in Bracken Road, but no one dared even a sip when Kathleen took up her stance alongside our upright piano, a steadying arm on the top as she directed her solo from Handel's Samson at the outside wall – 'Oh God, Oh God, Oh God of Hosts, Behold thy Servant in distress'. Bracken Road shook.

Soon, Heather was the star and it was no surprise to see her go on to Cardiff University to take her music to a pinnacle, laying the basis for a career in playing and examining that lasted for all her working life. It was in the music department at Cardiff University that she met her future husband, Dr Peter James, later to be Warden of the Royal Academy of Music in London. Once I got going on the violin, Heather and I would shut ourselves in the front room of number ten and play violin and piano sonatas every day of our lives. My mother would bustle in and chide, 'If you two don't come out and eat something today, you won't have the strength to play a note tomorrow.' We never asked the Morgans in number nine if they liked music.

I went on to lead the school orchestra and the West Glamorgan Youth Orchestra and trotted up to the front desk of the Glamorgan Youth. A place in the 'Glam' meant holiday courses spent in the school camp at Ogmore-by-Sea, which ended with a few concerts round the county. The Ogmore camp was a collection of huts and fields on a slope down to the Bristol Channel, overrun by sheep.

Life in Ogmore offered adventure, romance and a musical education for a lifetime. Adventure? I remember waking up one morning in one of the old huts we called a dormitory, looking along the line of beds and seeing hoary heads and every top blanket white with fine snow that had drifted in through the eaves overnight. Naked electric light bulbs swung slowly on single flexes. It was Zhivago-like. After breakfast, we were locked into a full rehearsal and then the sectionals. A little play, more practice and then, after supper, dancing! Was it the violin or was it the lure of the girl piccolo player? Boys were trying to impress girls who were seeking to impress boys. My eyes could drift from the top of the music stand to the ruby lips of a viola player or to the shapely legs in the front desk of the cellos. Neil Kinnock, former leader of the Labour party, was on the Glam courses in the sixties and has written fondly of female players: 'cool, crisp in school uniform or late fifties starched petticoats. Exotic creatures who were a four hours each way bus journey from my home town of Tredegar – out of reach for fifty weeks of the year, and, in the other two weeks, hard to catch.' It was that age. We needed the heavy snow to cool us down.

Romance? We were make-believe professional players. Our sheet music bore the fingering and bowing marks of experts. My father had bought me my own violin from a member of the Swansea Empire theatre orchestra. I moved among fiddlers whose instruments were polished with Hydersol liquid and were wrapped in soft yellow dusters. Perched on the tailpiece were adjusters, fitted to all four strings, but gone were the strings of gut. Gut was expensively chrome spun for luscious tone. A Cathedral gut string cost three shillings, a Pirastro, four shillings and six pence. I looked in the mirror, impatiently waiting for hard skin to develop under my chin, the badge of a true inhabitant of the world of two bows, rosin, Menuhin chinrest and wide vibrato. I attempted to tune the violin without removing it from the vice-like grip of chin and shoulder, turning a peg with only the left hand as the note wavered above and below the required intonation until perfection arrived. Without doubt, I was a poser.

We played the roles by day we dreamed of all night. Brass players Vaselined lips and blew out spittle from their valves; the woodwind boys and girls bound reeds while the timpanists counted a hundred bars for the first time in their lives without tapping a shoe or counting out loud. We were proper players. I went to bed as Heifetz and found it a helluva disappointment to wake up as Tony Lewis. The sounds of that orchestra playing on dark winter evenings at Ogmore are still with me. Muted strings play the 'Death of Ase' from the Peer Gynt suite. When I came to travel the world, playing or reporting cricket, and felt homesick, I spun up a picture image of the first three golf holes along the seashore at Royal Porthcawl, and the music would always be the opening statement of Beethoven's Piano Concerto Number Four – stylish holes, noble music, a major hope for a great round and good to be alive.

Music and cricket clashed in my teenage years. My private violin teacher, Miss Nest Saunders, informed me that I was arriving out of breath and that my vibrato was getting faster and tenser and we would have to do something about it. Miss Saunders, daughter of a work colleague of my father, was not many years out of university and taught during the week at Christ's College, Brecon, but fitted me in to her weekend with lessons on Saturday nights. Saturday nights!

'Why is your left hand so stiff? Have you been in the garden? Playing rugby? Your finger work is tense.' One summer she got it. The problem was called batting. I explained how the left hand, the top hand, controlled the bat and was the immovable one. On Saturday evenings, however, it had to become the flexible one on the violin fingerboard. She announced that my lessons were to be extended by half an hour so that I could spend time loosening up. She directed me to stand in front of the fireplace of her small front room, place the fingertips of my left hand on the mantelpiece and then slowly withdraw them so that the split-second they were unsupported they would flop into a vacuum, pointing towards the floor: the ultimate relaxed, fiddling fingers.

I had a fascinating conversation on this subject forty-seven years later when I was president of MCC and entertaining guests at a Test match. Peter Skellern, professional singer, composer, pianist and entertainer, with whom my connection was the Lord's Taverners, told the story of his daily journeys to the Guildhall School of Music when he was a student. He admitted that he could not bring himself to play the piano if he had been carrying his briefcase on the London tube. 'My hands would have tensed up. I was often seen shambling strangely through the streets of London with my briefcase and other bits under my armpits.'

Miss Saunders fitted the old description of firm but fair and the lesson sunk in deeply. Even now, standing at a cricket-club bar, I can be caught flopping my fingers to a state of perfect relaxation as if any moment she will be reincarnated and ask me to unleash a Kreutzer study.

To be strictly accurate, there was another reason why my vibrato was becoming feverish at the age of sixteen. I had met Joan Pritchard, smallish, athletic, with big black eyes. I wanted to see her swing a tennis racquet at the Dyfed Road public courts and watch her dash down the right wing of the hockey field with speed and power before whacking a cross in front of the goalmouth. I wanted to . . . well, talk to her a lot, which I usually accomplished after church and in Berni's coffee bar at the top of Queen Street. On Saturday evenings when I was with Nest Saunders, I wanted to be with Joan Pritchard at the Gnoll Road Congregational Church Good Companions Youth Club, getting to grips with her.

Gnoll Road Church, like Bracken Road and the grammar school, was one of my life's academies. In choir practice on Tuesday evenings we learned the most high-church music under the baton of the organist and choirmaster Gwilym Bevan. I think he imagined he was in St Paul's but I was happy to widen my musical knowledge among the basses. He was a would-be Anglican making music in a Congregational chapel. We chanted psalms and it took just one rehearsal of 'God So Loved the World' unaccompanied to realise the rough voices would soon be sitting it out with the folk below. We youngsters spoke knowledgeably of Purcell's 'Bell Anthem' and hummed the harmonies of Wood's 'Expectans Expectori' or drifted with the wonders of 'Thou Wilt Keep Him in Perfect Peace' by S.S. Wesley. When Heather and I were on dishwashing duties after Sunday lunch, we balanced the red anthem book on the kitchen windowledge and performed. The days of thundering 'Aberystwyth' or 'Praise My Soul' were over.

Gwilym, understandably, was not enamoured of the Whitsun march, which was an annual march through the streets of Neath by churches and chapels singing their Christian witness, each under its own banner, and each to its stirring anthem. Ours was 'Onward. Forward. Shouting out Hosanna.' Over and over we sang it, never stopping to ask why the Neath Council decided to roll out new tar on the roads every Whitsun holiday. Our Reverend Samuel marched for half a mile, as far as the Victoria Gardens. Under his mackintosh he was carrying a packet of sandwiches, a current *Wisden* and a Glamorgan Cricket Club season ticket. He would slip on to the N & C, Neath to Cardiff, luxury coach in the twinkling of an eye, and by the time we had retreated to the Whitsun field to eat sandwiches and have races in well-tarred shoes, he would be revelling in the sight of Willie Jones, Glamorgan's little left-hander whom he most admired, square-cutting the tourists for delicious fours at Cardiff Arms Park.

On Friday and Saturday evenings the church schoolrooms at the back of Gnoll Road Church became a nightclub, with dancing to a record player at a darkened end of the big room and table tennis and snooker elsewhere. The Good Companions played in the Neath and District Table Tennis League, and I was in the team, turning out against other youth clubs in the Neath area. I tried the life of Howard Jacobson's 'Mighty Waltzer' in the world of Barna versus Leach of penholder grips against orthodox, of sponge against pimples. On Saturdays, after school rugby, I was on my way up Skewen Hill to change in Len Williams's house into the yellow and gold number nine centre-forward shirt for the St Mary's league match played on the dog track. In the church schoolroom we played jazz records, John Lewis and the Modern Jazz Quartet, Bix Beiderbecke, Gerry Mulligan and Chris Barber. Have you read . . . was the question – Steinbeck, Lawrence or Spick and Span with the boobs and bums. Kissing girls began to advance from the process of lip-swelling friction to one of red-hot tongue combustion. As Reverend Samuel locked up on freezing winter nights there was a rush for premium necking locations behind the church buttresses. He gave us five minutes before waving us out of cover with his torch.

It took nine years to make an honest girl of Joan Pritchard. We were married in Gnoll Road by the same Reverend W.J. Samuel in 1962, both aged twenty-four. We prospered and so did the minister who went on to be the Congregational Moderator for Wales and a lifelong fan of Glamorgan cricket.

I was sixteen when my violin playing took a leap forward. I was lucky to have Heather at home to accompany me in so much sonata work. We had books of Mozart, Beethoven, Handel, Corelli and Vivaldi. Nest Saunders started me on the concerto trail with Mendelssohn while Hopkin Jones declared himself prepared to stay behind after school hours to work on the two concertos of Bach. Fred Herbert, the school's violin teacher, drew me into his chamber music group at lunchtimes and I was becoming a cerebral fiddler – all shape, phrase, fingering and a serious bow. Finally, Nest Saunders, in a few minutes of blinding revelation, made me think I would be forever wrapped round a fiddle. After a lesson one Saturday night we retreated to her family sitting room where she placed a shiny record on the radiogram.

'Psh!' she said. 'Just listen.'

I had never heard the Beethoven concerto before but, more to the point, I had never been so mesmerised as I was by the sound of the violin's first entry in the first movement when it soared in octaves out of the long orchestral introduction: isolated, noble, flying but under beautiful control.

Nest Saunders sat, legs curled up on the sofa.

'Did you like that?' I nodded. 'Always remember that it was Joseph Szigeti who first made the violin speak to you, and Beethoven, of course.' We heard it all again.

Listening to Szigeti was a defining moment. Does everyone have one? So asked Neville Cardus, who went on to write:

. . . in 1908 on December 3rd, I stood at the back of the Free Trade Hall in Manchester and heard the first performance of the A flat symphony of Elgar. I was one of the many who listened with excitement as the long opening melody marched before us, treading its way over a slow, steady bass, broad as the back of Hans Richter, then conductor of the Hallé orchestra . . . I did not listen to a composition in A flat, I entered the world of it.

Head crowded with roseate notions, I prepared for an audition for the National Youth Orchestra of Wales, conductor, Clarence Raybould. The summer concerts of 1955 would be concluded with a performance at the Edinburgh Festival. The letter came inviting me to join the orchestra. Nest Saunders and I began work on what I was now calling, like an old pro, the band parts.

However, I was a cricketer, too, and gradually dreams of a fiddling future came up against the rapid progress of that other life, one spent wearing Len Hutton autographed brown sausage batting gloves. I should begin cricket talk with the fact that only two Welshmen have captained England in Tests and both were from Neath Grammar School and Neath Cricket Club. C.F. Walters was an amateur with Worcestershire when he played his eleven matches for England and his one game as captain happened in 1934 at Trent Bridge when R.E.S. Wyatt, the series captain, was unfit. Cyril's photograph still hangs on the wall of the Neath pavilion. I never saw Cyril Walters play, but those who did always put him forward as a model batsman of skill and elegance.

A.R. Lewis was indeed the second Welshman to captain England in Test matches. By the age of eleven, I had played two games on grass for the Gnoll School, and yet a few weeks after my seventeenth birthday, appeared in the county championship for Glamorgan. It was fast-moving stuff. Young Neath boys who want to follow Walters and Lewis in the twenty-first century have even less help than we had. There is no grammar school and no school cricket field. The Neath Cricket Club is the main hope.

In the 1940s and 1950s I was lucky. Everyone who could turn an arm over played cricket and there was a battle for places in the teams. The Neath Schools Under-fifteen side was selected from a highly competitive network and there was a scrap between South Wales towns for the Dewar Shield. I once played in a South Wales schoolboys side against London and the Home Counties. There were trials for the Glamorgan Secondary Schools and for the Welsh team. The Welsh Secondary Schools played against Glamorgan Colts and this was a serious dust-up for advancement towards the professional ranks. A place in the Glamorgan second team would bring you into contact with well-known professional players. In fact, the first ball I faced in the County Second XI competition in 1953 was bowled by one of my cigarette cards, T.W. Goddard of Gloucestershire. He was a giant of a man with a long, rather gaunt face. On that day, he bowled his off-spin from round the wicket and let out a distracting grunt as he let the ball go. I saw a half-volley first ball and drove it through the covers for four. 'You'll never do that again, son,' whined the wicket-keeper. He was right. Brazenly trying to drive the next ball to the covers, I saw a flash of leather disappear under my right armpit on its way over the top of leg stump. Tom Goddard, by the way, was fifty-three years old at the time and leading the Gloucestershire second team as an amateur. A young cricketer's life in South Wales focused on getting into teams and staying there.

Youngsters were welcome in the Neath club, junior members were coached and matches organised. The grammar school played every Saturday of the summer term under the supervision of Ronnie Williams, the sports master. Ronnie had been a useful rugby player who ended up having to wear elastic supports round both knees, which he used to adjust during his history lessons. On reflection, as a referee and an umpire, he was a 'homer'. If we were locked in a tough match against the best schools such as Cardiff High School, Cowbridge or Gowerton, it was always a good decision to bat first. Even better, when I was captain, I realised that matches could swing very suddenly in our favour after 4 p.m. on a Saturday; it was the clever moment to come on to bowl my erratic leg-spin. No matter how far the ball pitched outside leg stump, if I made clean contact with the batsman's body, he was out. The reason for Ronnie's alacrity with the business finger was not only bias, but also he had to go shopping with his wife. Instead of staying to shake hands with the visiting schoolmaster, he could be seen clambering over the gate at the corner of the field to sprint for the James bus to Gwaun-cae-Gurwen, which stopped outside the girls' school. By now, I had white leather sausage gloves and a Wally Hammond autographed bat. I was posing again.

I played first against the English Secondary Schools in 1953 at Worcester. Our captain was a North Wales public schoolboy from Ruthin named R.W. Barber. I remember that his kit was carried in a big leather bag, just like the county stars, and he had two bats, enough to put him in a different class from the rest of us. He was the only North Walian in the Welsh team and he had never met any of us before but, of course, our paths would cross again as his cricket career continued with Cambridge University, Lancashire, Warwickshire and England. It was impossible to understand at that early stage, especially of an older boy and my captain, what a wonderfully independent person Bob was. It was the strength of his game later on because after a hard time captaining and grafting at Lancashire, he turned up at Warwickshire and threw the bat around, blasting his way into the England side. Famously, he flayed Australia in Sydney in 1966, scoring 185 in 255 balls with 19 fours, and on the first day of the Test match. His leg-spin, too, was deceptive and skilful, with a quick wrist action. His impact on the game was enough to persuade many to wonder if they would be far more successful if they copied his thumping approach. One day we looked up and Barber, the businessman, had gone to live elsewhere in Europe. He had never committed heart, mind and body to a career in the game but his skill and athleticism were a real adornment.

The Welsh Secondary Schools appearance was the pinnacle of our season. I was once invited to play for The Rest against the Southern Schools, a match, I was told, that could lead to a game at Lord's. Wales also had a fixture so I refused and stuck to the red cap with the Prince of Wales feathers. Our dream was to play for Glamorgan and some of us made it. Alan Rees, from Port Talbot, was my opening partner. He not only became a fine cricketer but also won rugby caps for Wales at outside-half. Peter Gatehouse, of Caerphilly Grammar School, was a lively left-arm bowler who could truly bend the new ball back into the right-handed batsmen. Graham Reynolds of Newport was a school-master who played occasionally in the professional game.

In 1950, aged twelve, I saw my first Test match. I was travelling by train with my father to my aunt's home in Huntingdonshire when he decided to call in to a Test match at The Oval between England and the West Indies. We sat on the grass on the gasholder side on a sunny day. Only one wicket fell before we had to leave in the late afternoon – Stollmeyer was lbw to Bailey. I thought it was high and, thirty years later, Jeff Stollmeyer agreed with me. Trevor Bailey, when challenged, simply screwed up his nose, closed his eyes and puckered his lips, which, to those who knew him, forever meant 'don't be ridiculous'. The delight of that first day of the fourth Test was a wonderful demonstration of patience and elegance bursting into searing cover drives from F.M.M. Worrell who was well on the way to scoring a brilliant century.

In 1951 I was at St Helens in Swansea to see Glamorgan spin South Africa to defeat. Muncer and McConnon, our off-spinners, became household names. The scores were tied on 111 after the first innings and Glamorgan spun out the tourists second time around to win by 64 runs. The crowd sang the national anthem, a collection was taken for the players and amazing scenes confirmed St Helens' status as a real theatre with its steeply sloping terraces and the most dramatic walk to the field down what we used to call 'the eighty-nine steps'. There were sixty-nine in fact. If anyone had told me then that I would be playing for Glamorgan alongside Wooller, Clift, Pleass, Hedges, Shepherd, Hadyn Davies, W.E. Jones, Watkins and Parkhouse in four years' time, I would have laughed at them.

How did I learn to play straight, go back, go forward, drive or late-cut? I had a mentor in the Neath club, a former captain, Cyril Michael. He was a local headmaster and a fine club player in his day. He had cricket wisdom. In later days I read a passage in Imran

Khan's book that almost exactly replicated some coaching given me by Cyril Michael. Imran described as 'a watershed in my career' the stricture delivered by the games superintendent at Aitchison College in Lahore, Naseer Ahmed, concerning when to play back and when forward. 'He said he didn't mind how long I stayed at the crease or how slowly I scored as long as I followed the two basics of batting – playing back to the ball pitched short and forward to the delivery that was pitched up.' All this sounds elementary but it is essential to create this habit for a lifetime. It is a reminder, too, that batting is a simple process. I know well that the barrage of fast head-high bowling that came out of the West Indies from the late 1970s drove batsmen on to the back foot, often shuffling across the stumps, but the fine players never mistook the ball of full length. Graham Gooch was a wonderful example of a player who was upright, balanced and solid on his feet, who was always ready to get on the front foot to drive the ball in textbook fashion however rare the half-volley. Australia's Steve Waugh consistently scores runs in Test cricket. His determination and cussedness as an opponent are part of it, but right at the heart of his technique is the understanding that you play right forward to meet the ball of full length and right back to cope with anything shorter. Simply add the ingredient of playing straight down the line of the flight of the ball and you have a recipe for every beginner that will apply throughout a whole career.

Vivian Richards has told of the importance of learning to play cricket on rough ground although he admits the surfaces in Antigua were dangerous, full of hoof marks after the boys had pushed off cattle. He acknowledges that he played a lot of strokes across the line, such as the cut and the hook, but it bred in him the natural facility for split-second adjustment.

Back in the 1950s, however, the modern cricket academy did not exist. The best young players in South Wales were taken in to the Glamorgan coaching schemes. On Tuesday evenings in winter, from the ages of thirteen to eighteen, I used to miss a double period of Spanish at school and take an hour's train trip to Cardiff. Our indoor 'school' was the second-floor corridor of the North Stand at Cardiff

Arms Park. We tugged netting and white tarpaulin into position and helped lay twenty-two yards of ship's linoleum for two pitches. There was no heating and no running water; it was a three-sweater job in December. One dark winter's afternoon I plodded through snow from Cardiff Station with the lads from the west, who would have included my constant companion in future Glamorgan days, Alan Jones, and found the whole place in darkness. Practice was bound to be off. We entered the innards of the big, black monster of a grandstand, eventually coming to a light and the sound of coach George Lavis's immaculate diction, 'Come. Get changed in five minutes.' Blazered and in cream flannels with a cream cravat for style, George was stoking a couple of charcoal braziers. Our breath was freezing fog an inch from our mouths. On went the lights and we played.

At the start of a new millennium, can the conditions in which we learned cricket in South Wales be replicated? Cricket on the street is impossible because you would get knocked over by cars. Cricket in the state schools is not the mad passion it once was and just does not happen unless a teacher has a special interest, and a field on which to play. On the other hand, the Welsh Secondary Schools persist and it should be noted by those who denigrate schools in their current cricket efforts that when Glamorgan won the county championship in 1997, only fourteen cricketers played for the team and eleven of those had played for the Welsh Schools. The Sports Council for Wales now deploys five development officers throughout Wales and conditions for practice are far superior to my days.

For me the moment came in that summer of 1955, a few weeks after my seventeenth birthday and just two days before I was due to set off to join the National Youth Orchestra of Wales. I came down to breakfast to find a letter on my plate. I opened it, saw an embossed yellow daffodil at the top and knew it was from Glamorgan County Cricket Club. The man whom the whole of Wales called 'The Skipper' had signed it. Wilf Wooller was a colossus. His eighteen Welsh rugby caps were a passport to immortality. Rugby folk thought that his cricket was just a piece of summer eccentricity, but he was a formidable all-rounder.

Dear Tony,

I have been delighted to hear of your good form with the bat and would like you to play for Glamorgan in the last two County Championship matches of the season – Leicestershire at Cardiff and Warwickshire at Neath.

A couple of hours later I had decided. The violin went into its case and the band parts were placed in a large envelope addressed to the Welsh Joint Education Board. I had fallen in love with my bat and my violin. It was hard to choose because to advance at either now meant absolute concentration, blinkers in fact.

C H A P T E R   4

THE LITTLE GREEN DIARY

I discovered recently a small, green, soft-covered pocket diary for 1958 in a brown box, under loose papers, on the high shelf of a cupboard in a room we use for storing and ironing.

This diary belongs to – Anthony Robert Lewis, 10 Bracken Road, Neath, Glam.
  Telephone No. – Don't have one.
  In the event of accident please notify – Mr W.L. Lewis of above address.

When I found it, it occurred to me immediately that this diary had not been having much fun. Its practical life began promisingly on 1 January, four months into my National Service as a non-commissioned aircraftman, but was sustained for weeks with just one initial entry – 1 January: 609 days to go! Thereafter it became the victim of an owner who treated it merely as a jotter in which travel expenses were kept alongside bus and train times with an occasional note of a batting average. For example, a true young diarist might have greeted his or her twentieth birthday with a trumpet in red ink, but the entry for mine, on 6 July 1958, is in biro as follows:

Travel to Andover: train – 9s 3d; meal 5s; Andover to Euston 10s; London to Manchester £1 2s 0d; taxi 2s 6d; laundry 5s 6d; meal on train 10s 0d.

Manchester to Gloucester 19s 7d; meal on train 10s 0d; taxi back to camp 12s.

These arrangements refer to a journey I was to make a week later to play a one-day cricket match for the RAF against Hampshire at Andover, followed by a three-day game for the Combined Services against Lancashire at Old Trafford. There is not a private thought or a conversation or a pip of sentiment preserved in this diary. On reflection, it could be the most accurate reflection of two years spent among the final intake of National Servicemen. Those of us who were recruited without the prospect of war to sharpen our minds and bodies put our thinking machines into neutral. We did wriggle alongside a Bren gun, changing the magazine to trigger short bursts for the defence of Queen and country. 'Mag on, mag off. Move it, move it,' the instructor still yells in my ear. 'Too late, Lewis, you're dead. We're all bleedin' dead. What a bleedin' shower you are.' I would never complain, however, that National Service was a complete waste of time. I can argue that my academic progress was halted and that my cricket needed the professional game in order to develop, but we were all made aware of those who had given more than two years of their time to their country during the Second World War. That conflict was not far behind us. And if I wanted to argue the cricket point, I would have to concede that many fine players lost the sunny mornings of their careers – for example, Len Hutton, Denis Compton, Jim Laker – and still brightened our lives in the afternoons and evenings of their play. Some did not come back at all. Yes, I did meet excellent people in the Air Force, some of them still friends, and only in retrospect is it hard to ignore the lack of personal progress during formative years.

My green diary spent forty-three years buried in a wooden box, a blind passenger on eleven house moves. Now it revealed only the trivia of my Air Force life. For example, on Saturday, 1 November, after playing full-back for Gloucester at Leicester, I took the 10.36 p.m.

train from Leicester on a journey of many changes, arriving at Neath General Station by 7.10 a.m. Sunday, 2 November, I note, is a one-word day – Joan – followed by the riveting information that my train departed Neath at 9.18 p.m. and arrived at Gloucester at 11.25 p.m. Joan Pritchard held my constant love and attention, but there was no mention of the rugby match itself in which I recall I produced an effective tackle on Tony O'Reilly, the Tigers' Irish international left-wing. Our whole Gloucester side was kicked out of the clubhouse after consuming many jugs of beer because one of our lads flipped a Jacky-Jumper firework along the floor to land under the skirt of Mrs Swan, wife of Ian, the Scottish international. Snap! Crackle! Pop! Some incidents you can remember without the benefit of a Letts 11K Diary.

What persuaded me, then, on Saturday, 20 December, to write 'Buy Christmas card for Joan'? We wrote to each other almost every day. How was I ever going to forget a Christmas card? Joan, once of Neath Grammar School for Girls, Glamorgan Training College, Barry, and now of the Laban Art of Movement Studio in Addlestone, Surrey, was the lust of my life out of uniform. We wrote so often that she eventually gave me a present of my own personalised notepaper – Senior Aircraftman Lewis A.R., 1/10 B Squadron, Royal Air Force, Records Office, Gloucester. I was an A/C, one of twenty resident in a billet. I was a nobody and yet I sent letters out as if the replies would return to a brass-plated address and personal post box rather than be included in a pile of envelopes, bound by a rubber band and tossed on the centre table once a day. It was unheard of. Well, as the Hindu believes, if you are only a road-sweeper, be the best road-sweeper in the world. You might come back as an Air Marshal!

December, I note, came without the usual cash-flow crisis. In pencil it is noted on 15 November 1958 that RAF Savings Account No. 498386 is worth £19 5s 0d. As for the batting average, L/A/C Lewis had compiled 898 runs, which divided by 22 innings and allowing for not-outs, made an average of 40.8. This, in short, is the diary of a stoical time-server on twenty-four shillings a week.

Why did I choose the Royal Air Force? In fact, I had written first to the Army but the captain-secretary of the Glamorgan County Cricket Club,

Wilfred Wooller, had instructed, 'Don't be a bloody fool. I'll talk to Alan Shireff. Join the Air Force, then you can nip off and play for Glamorgan whenever we want you.' Squadron Leader Shireff was a distinguished Air Force cricketer who had first-class experience with Cambridge University, Hampshire, Kent and Somerset. There were times, right from the start of my service, I wondered when this guardian squadron leader might show up. I thought of him while I sweated in the cookhouse 'tin-room' at RAF Cardington, my Reception Unit. Up to the elbows in boiling water, my hands groped in deep zinc tanks for the large cooking trays, and with wire wool attempted to scrub away the congealed cold grease of departed fried sausages and bacon. I looked up through the wall of steam at the cookhouse sergeant. No sign of Shireff.

The trouble with first base is that you were neither in the Air Force nor in civvy street. We were in possession of new bibles with the Royal Air Force insignia on the front and the motto 'Per Ardua ad Astra' to set the noble purpose, but the stores never had enough kit in all the required sizes to clothe every new recruit immediately. It required a fair slice of 'Dad's Army' experience to appear ready for war dressed in a working blue beret, blue service shirt with detached collar, working blue trousers and socks, check sports coat with leather patches on the elbows and suede chukka boots. ''Eft, 'ight, 'eft, 'ight. Chin in, chest art. Swing those arms, Airman. Squaaad to the right, right turn.' After ten days of this, however, with the kitbag now full, I was off to West Kirby for three months of square-bashing.

'Yes, I am Welsh, Corporal. Yes, I like music, Corporal.'

'Then get down the NAAFI and move the bleedin' piano, Airman.'

'Tell me a new one, Corporal,' (muttered).

West Kirby was marching, saluting, shooting and reeling before the deafening Irish falsetto of Sergeant O'Grady, who delivered the old 'uns with Palace of Varieties timing and thunder – 'Oy'll stick your rifle so far up yer arse, laddie, you'll be using the foresight as a collar stud.' Boom! Boom! 'Oy'll stick this rifle so far up yer arse, laddie, you'll be using the bayonet as a toothpick.' Boom! Boom! At six every morning the station Tannoy bashed out its own shocking reveille – a treble forte burst of the Everly Brothers' recording of 'Wake Up Little Susie'. The enemy may get us, but we would never die of subtlety in Her Majesty's.

If ever I could request a choice of music for a desert island, I would have to go with 'Wake Up Little Susie'. Even if I was as bone-thin as Tom Hanks became in the film 'Cast Away', I would get up in the morning and race to perform what the services termed 'yer ablutions'. At the sound of the first few bars, I would be upright, reaching under the mattress for those working blue trousers, which had been pressed by the weight of my body, and the shirt, warmed overnight for the brutal cold of an early winter morning. As the sun rose on my island, I would be found standing to attention outside – outside anywhere – waiting for the remainder of human life to form around me. To my end, I would still leap from my pit if the Everly Brothers sang, and die standing up, a tombstone to myself.

At West Kirby on the Wirral we were close to Wales where we were transported for simulations of active combat called Reliability and Initiative Training. It was here that I gleaned the information of a lifetime, that in the event of an atomic explosion, I would have five seconds in which to dig a six-foot trench or fall flat on my face. Get ready for the mock explosion we were told by the nice Corporal Bellingham who planned to set off a flare without warning. To be truthful, war was not all that remote. A number of my National Service contemporaries had been drafted to Cyprus to trade real bullets.

There was no moon as we waded in full gear through deep, watery marshland in the Berwyn Mountains. My big pack swung heavily on my back with the 303 rifle, the groundsheet, the water bottle, the 'ammo'. I staggered forward under this mountain of survival luggage while holding the map an inch above the water in my left hand, pointing the torch with my right and clearing the reeds from my face by shaking my head back and forth in the style of the very poor crawl I perform when swimming. It was not a time to lose your hat. Suddenly, there was a bang, and a flash lit up the hillside. The atomic bomb! Five seconds. Most of these heroes a month ago had been sipping a pint in a warm pub, or maybe listening to 'Much Binding in the Marsh' on the wireless in front of the fire. Now we found ourselves in icy, winter mountains, face to face with pretending death. A real death threat might have got us going quicker because by the time we thought, 'That's an atomic bomb,' our five seconds were up. In any case, there was only one option: total immersion with the gear taking us to the bottom.

To a man, we turned out to be cowards. Instead of flopping flat into the water, we crouched hopefully, legs bent, chins floating, eyes peering to left and right for signs of the dreaded corporal. There were frozen giggles. We could get away with this. Corporal Bellingham's voice flew from the hilltop, screeching loudly enough to drive the red kite out of Llanrhaeadr-ym-Mochnant for the next forty years. 'You're dead. The bloody lot of you, dead. Blown to bits. Burnt to bloody cinders. You're all on a charge. One more chance and next time, if I see an arse or a head above water, I'll shoot the bleedin' thing off.' He cracked back the bolt action of a rifle. Half an hour later we were retreating through this same marshland when up went the flare. Down I sank, reeds wrapped around my boots, big pack driving me down under the water, clinging to my 303, my torch, my map, my hat, grabbing out for the bottom. I had taken appropriate action within five seconds but how long was I supposed to stay under? How long is an atomic bomb blast? Where is Squadron Leader Shireff? I am drowning. At least it is Wales. That night I returned to my tent, opened up my little diary, considered the military mayhem of the day and all I noted is this: 'first-class average in the County Championship for Glamorgan since 1955: 199 runs in 11 innings, average 6.2.' Not another word.

I can find no mention, either, of my permanent posting to RAF Upwood. I was told that Upwood was an operational station and I would see a real, working aircraft for the first time in six months. Armed with kitbag, three train warrants and three bus warrants, I set off for this outpost, south of Peterborough, north of Huntingdon, close to Ramsey, that was land far beyond all previous travels. The green bus chugged through Abbots Ripton, Wennington, Little Raveley and Great Waveley to a stop outside the Upwood guardroom. Sport was not a word much used there, certainly not rugby. 'We're operational, y'know,' they all kept saying, as if Biggles was about to loop-the-loop over the NAAFI. The reality was this: I had said goodbye to linseed oil and narrow grained willow, to dubbined Gilbert rugger balls, and to Joan Pritchard's dancing legs. Immediately, I was allocated a vital job for the next eighteen months – Rations Clerk and Typist in the Upwood Orderly Room. I had applied for other roles from the start. When I inquired about a commission, the Careers Officer said there were now no National Service commissions available to non-graduates, but if I signed these forms for three years . . . I shook my head and pushed them back across the desk. What about the band? The Welsh National Youth Orchestra had wanted me. He pushed the forms back towards me. Minimum three years. I pushed them back.

But then, whose hand moved unseen on that sunny first morning at Upwood? A signal arrived with the information that A/C Lewis A.R. 5051643 had been posted in error and was to report to RAF Innsworth in Gloucester. Somewhere, perhaps, a George Smiley was moving the pawns in the interests of national security. Keep Lewis away from machinery and maths would have been the order. Faceless orders had been issued and the words 'rugby' and 'cricket', alien to Upwood, were whispered in the Orderly Room as I collected warrants, two bus and three train.

The diarist, of course, omits to note that his life changed when the cricket season came to his new homes, RAF Innsworth and the RAF Record Office in Gloucester. True, I was mostly absent. I found no difficulty in getting off to play, whether for Innsworth, for Home Command, for the Air Force or Combined Services, or even for Glamorgan Seconds or Neath in the South Wales and Monmouthshire League. No one complained. I simply collected a bundle of travel warrants and returned to camp many days later to collect my back pay. There really was a godfather. Who was it? One day I got a bit of nudge-nudge from Flight Lieutenant Yeadon, the officer in charge of the Orderly Room. He was a large, Yorkshire rugby man who signed the chits to get me off and often referred to my opening partner in the Innsworth cricket side with a wink. This was Group Captain Fred Roberts, a diminutive left-handed batsman, nimble but not young. He was a batsman of real talent who came out of the office once a week to reveal a neat collection of profitable strokes.

One Wednesday afternoon, the Groupie said that long ago he had played a couple of games as an amateur for Glamorgan. No more than that. It was many years later that I read a book about Glamorgan cricket and discovered that J.F. Roberts had been a schoolboy at Pontardawe Grammar, about four miles from my own Neath Grammar, and had played for Glamorgan as an amateur between 1934 and 1936. We therefore had an origin in common. The write-up went on to say that he represented the Air Force and Combined Services, retired to Swansea, retaining sporting interest with golf at Pontardawe, where he was president, and kept in touch with cricket through his membership of MCC. Even later, in 1995, almost forty years after my sudden transfer from RAF Upwood, I looked up the current *Who's Who*. Air Vice-Marshal John Frederick Roberts, CB 1967, CBE 1960 (OBE 1954) had joined the RAF in 1938, served in the Middle East 1942–45 (despatches). The key entry was this: Senior Air Staff Officer, RAF Record Office, Gloucester, 1958–60. He had overlapped the Gloucester days of my little green diary. He ended his Air Force career as Director General of Ground Training (RAF) with appended hobbies of cricket, golf, cabinet making. No mention of protecting young Welsh cricketers from exposure to the real Air Force. Weekly, the more he pushed the ball between fielders for silent singles, the louder the pennies dropped. I was seriously indebted to Fred Roberts of Pontardawe.

I turn the pages of the diary to June. Monday and Tuesday, 9 and 10, are two dates with simple notes: Command Trials (did not bat). It was especially sunny and hot and I can only guess a touch of sunstroke persuaded my pen to write the lie. I did bat – many times. I presented myself at RAF White Waltham for the trials as an automatic choice. I had played county cricket and my name had already been included in selections for the RAF and Combined Services. In fact, I had a getaway plan for the second afternoon, with train connections planned for a journey to Eastbourne so that I could be at the Cavendish Hotel to join the Air Force team for a match against Colonel Stevens's XI on 11 and 12 June. It was shimmering heat at White Waltham by the time I took guard near midday. The first ball, briskly delivered, cut back off the seam and clonked back the leg stump. Later in the afternoon, now fielding at second slip, I missed a fast catch at comfortable height that crashed into my genitals – the sun went all spotty, the sky filled up with creepy crawlies and my lunch appeared in my throat. After a delay, I staggered to the boundary and with help ended up on my back in the camp hospital. My scrotum had swollen to what looked, from my horizontal viewpoint, to be a giant blood-orange. Two female nurses coolly strung up the orange in a sort of designer hammock above my limp body. The officer in charge of the cricket trials called in to deliver what he thought was encouraging news – I could have a long bat on the second day!

Next morning, the walk from sick-quarters to the crease was a John Wayne special – legs wide apart, threatening a fast draw and death in the afternoon – but only so that the orange had space and swinging room. Immediately, I was lbw. The officer, whose name I never knew, had now lost patience, ordering me to stay at the crease so that the Command selectors could see something of my play. A few balls later I was lbw again – 'but stay there, Lewis. Just get some runs. Show us you can bat.' This was said just before I was caught at slip with my body some way from the line of the ball. Generosity departed. 'Off you go, Lewis. You may be picked by the Air Force but you're not in the Command side against Coastal.' There was no doubt that a regular officer would be chosen instead of me and I could not blame them. At Eastbourne I got a hundred, though on loan to Colonel Stevens.

To the surprise of some, I was called up for the Combined Services to play Lancashire at Old Trafford in a three-day match with real first-class runs to be scored. Accommodation for 11, 12, 13 July 1958 was at the Grosvenor Hotel. The weather was dismal. The pitch was green and hard and the fast bowling of Lancashire's Colin Hilton fizzed past the nose, either after a steep bounce or often without bouncing at all. When big Colin clattered his way to the crease, his arm became a sling. If his body was balanced, he could bowl a devastating ball of superb length, high bounce and lateral movement. He could splatter wickets all over Manchester. But there were moments when the arm lost all synchronisation with the legs and body, and he released the ball with a jerk of a fifteenth-century wooden catapult levering a lump of rock at a fortress. The missile would arrive at 90 m.p.h. without bouncing. He was a dreaded bowler of beamers.

That day he felled Officer Cadet G.P.S. Delisle, who was batting at number three. Poor Peter left the field, a bloodied towel held to his head. I walked in next, looked down to mark my guard and saw a crease dappled with blood and dust – not truly encouraging. I hung on in, losing a few partners, one of whom was Second Lieutenant S.J.S. Clarke who was immediately bowled by Hilton without scoring. Next morning the Second Lieutenant came into the dressing room to announce to the skipper, Lieutenant Commander M.L.Y. Ainsworth, 'Sorry, Skip. Can't bat today, I'm afraid. I've pulled a muscle in my shoulder.'

'How did you do that, Simon?'

'Did the damned thing shaving,' responded our hero, losing the support of the suspicious bunch of professionals round the dressing room who were doing their National Service – Peter Parfitt of Middlesex, Graham Atkinson of Somerset, Barry Knight of Essex, Malcolm Scott of Northants and Rodney Pratt of Leicestershire. They had seen fear of fast bowling before and this, they agreed, was the real thing.

'If it was war,' drawled Parf, 'I wouldn't be following that particular officer into action, old boy.'

'You'd have to shoot him, Parf, if it was war,' suggested Barry Knight.

In the early 1960s, when Glamorgan were playing Middlesex at Lord's, Peter Parfitt shared a loud aside with me. From the side of his mouth came the confession, 'Certain events have persuaded me, dear boy, that I was probably wrong about Simon Clarke at Old Trafford in 1958.' He referred to the thirteen caps Simon had won as a gutsy scrum-half for England, which included a couple of rough-and-tumbles against the New Zealand All Blacks. 'D'y' know, old boy, when I watched Simon play rugby, I was forced to admit that it is indeed very possible to pull a muscle while shaving.'

Not surprisingly, the diary carries no account of this Combined Services match but, of course, *Wisden Cricketers' Almanak 1959* does:

Atkinson from Somerset and Lewis (Glamorgan) batted attractively for the Services, whose captain declared when still three
behind. Lancashire responded by declaring after Wharton and
Marner had hit attractively in a fourth wicket stand of 92. Despite
another sound display by Lewis, the Services could not recover in
their second innings from a poor start against the pace of Moore
and C. Hilton, but only seven minutes of extra time remained
when the last wicket fell.

Good game. The diary, without a scrap of modesty, notes my personal
scores, 73 and 62, and the leap in my first-class average to 38.2.
Lancashire won by 86 runs but both sides had declared.

And so it happened, out of this strange medley of Services cricket,
clerking work at the RAF Record Office and overnight picket duties, I
found the path to Lord's. The Combined Services were to play the
Public Schools on 8 and 9 August 1958.

MCC and Lord's had never been part of my life. When I was growing
up in Neath, I rarely went as far as Cardiff let alone London. When I
played cricket with Glamorgan Seconds we did travel to our neighbour-
ing counties regularly, Somerset, Gloucestershire and Worcestershire,
and I had that day at The Oval Test in 1950 and holidays in Huntingdonshire, but, eight years later, this was only my second visit to London.
I was twenty. I played a lot of league cricket for Neath in the 1950s and
there were two players who had sweaters with MCC colours, yellow and
orange, tucked into their kitbags, but I had no idea what MCC was or
did, and Lord's, the ground, was even more remote. I had read how
Wilson of the *Wizard*, a great cricketer in the boys' paper, would ensnare
the whole Australian team in a Lord's Test by placing every fielder on the
leg side and bowling to the off – or was it the other way round? I was not
familiar with important grounds. Neath Grammar School's great
matches were against Cardiff High, Cowbridge, Barry and Gowerton
Grammar Schools, when boys were let out of classes to ramble round
the boundary in support. Cardiff, I remember, had a real cricket
pavilion. In Neath we had a trestle table for the scorer, chairs brought
out from the school hall and, if it was raining, a covered view from the

bike-shed. Club cricket was played on neat grounds surrounded by a circle of low wooden benches. At Cardiff Arms Park, to reach the Glamorgan dressing room you walked up steep stairs through the dark skittle alley and bar, paled by the stench of beer. Lunch was taken by the teams and the administrative staff under the grandstand where two legendary ladies, Elsie and Theresa, boiled hard, green and black potatoes to submission right next to the area where the groundstaff stored and worked on the machinery. It was often joked that old professional cricketers could leave the field at lunchtime with ruddy faces and return after the interval, blanched by the mixed fumes of over-cooked spuds and two-stroke engine oil.

In the seasons leading up to this 1958 Lord's debut, 1955 to 1957, I had played six matches in the English County Championship for Glamorgan. The venues were Cardiff (three), Neath (two) and Worcester. I was still at school and playing as an amateur. We were oblivious of the traditions of the famous public schools that returned to Lord's every season to play old rivals in two-day matches – Eton and Harrow, Clifton and Tonbridge, Haileybury and ISC against Cheltenham, Rugby and Marlborough. We knew nothing of the three-day games between Oxford and Cambridge Universities and the Gentlemen versus the Players. A South Wales grammar schoolboy was in no way jealous of the public school cricketers' lot although I might have been if I had understood the divisions of class and capital a little better. We simply inhabited different worlds and Lord's was no part of my life.

So how did I get to play there in the end? The little green diary records that late on the evening of 7 August, carrying my canvas cricket bag and a holdall, I took the stopping train out of Gloucester bound for London Paddington. It stopped to drop and collect postbags and disperse milk churns, which had been loaded at Fishguard and Carmarthen and were on their way to the many Welsh dairies in the capital city. I looked out of the window to be sure that Graham Atkinson would find me. Graham was a fine opening batsman, currently disguised as A/C Atkinson of RAF Locking. We slept our way to London up on the luggage racks and at approximately 4 a.m. settled for another bed on the benches at Paddington Station.

Drunks were staggering by and being sick; police patrolled with dogs. We had two hours to wait before the Underground opened. When it did, we were on the first train to St John's Wood. We were ready to play for the Combined Services against the Public Schools by 6.45 a.m.

After four hours lurking we presented ourselves for play. It rained all day. We, the 'other ranks', retreated to the Union Jack Club in Waterloo. Of my entire playing career, this was the nightmare digs. Every inmate was cubicled. Lying on your back on the creaky bed, you could look up at the thick wire grill that composed the top two feet of your walls. The floor was hard, brown, shiny linoleum and the faintest noise would echo from floor to floor. Unfortunately, for those trying to sleep after a day in the field, shipments of soldiers, sailors or airmen marched in and out on studded boots at all times of night. 'The Gurkhas moved out at zero three hundred, mate,' would be the morning information from the worn-out cookhouse orderly, trying to balance a greasy egg on his spatula.

In the one-day match that followed, I had a first sight of future friends – David Green of Manchester Grammar, the Nawab of Pataudi from Winchester, David Kirby of St Peter's, York, and David Peck of Wellingborough. The Schools scored 134 (Pataudi 42) and for the Services, only the officers batted – G.G. Tordoff (69 not out), S.J.S. Clarke (45) and M.L.Y. Ainsworth (17 not out) – but I had made my Lord's debut. It did not matter that I did not bat, did not bowl and caught none. And I still had not met Squadron Leader Shireff.

During National Service, my mind was unoccupied and my cricket, which should have been flowering between the ages of nineteen and twenty-one, staggered forward often in unhelpful conditions. Perhaps a more important consideration is this: how ready would I have been for another war? I suppose I had learned to obey and get on with it, whatever it was in whatever conditions. If Sergeant O'Grady had shouted, 'Right, lads, over the top,' I would have gone without question. Vivid in the minds of all Glamorgan cricket supporters was the story of Maurice Turnbull, a former captain, secretary and one of the club's great household gods. He played cricket for England, rugby and hockey for Wales and was thirty-eight years old in August 1944 when he was killed by a sniper's bullet at Montchamp while serving with the Welsh Guards during the Normandy invasion.

Would modern youngsters benefit from National Service? I have not the slightest doubt that they would. I know that it has become the fashion to take a year off after schooldays and learn about life in the raw by travel to far-off places but the messages of discipline and duty remain priceless. Queen and country remain with me as the solid loyalties; nor would I give up the rich anecdotes of the two years. Leslie Thomas's brilliant, funny book *The Virgin Soldiers* happily sets so much of it on record.

By the way, I did meet Alan Shireff but not until 26 April 1996, forty years after taking Wilfred Wooller's original advice. I arrived at the Lord's Banqueting Suite to make a speech at the RAF Cricket Association Reunion Dinner and approached the gallant organiser: 'Squadron Leader Alan Shireff? This is 5051643, Senior Aircraftman Lewis A.R., reporting for duty, Sir. Wilfred Wooller sent me. Sorry I'm late.'

FRESHMAN'S FORTUNE

Recalling a first term at university I know flirts with banality. It proves nothing to write how advanced education changed my life because that is what advanced education is supposed to do. I was not going up to the Cambridge of Brideshead days although there were echoes of it in the small dining and breakfast clubs, in the Pitt Club for the hunters and shooters on Jesus Lane and in the mannered practice of *thé dansant* in mid-afternoon in the Dorothy Café. Cambridge still represented the ultimate education as well as a complimentary view of the slippery slope of class. The Tutor for Admission to my college, Christ's, however, appeared to have taken huge care about the mix of undergraduates. Dr Lucan Pratt believed he had an eye for talented young men who had something special to offer as well as a dedicated academic performance, be it writing verse, playing the guitar, chess or lacrosse. Playing the fool was all right by him as long as you were excellent at it. In games, he particularly embraced rugby footballers, hockey players and association footballers. Donald Steel was our lone golf Blue. He ignored social badges of school, race and family background. He made Christ's a melting pot of old prejudices. I knew this later.

At the beginning, I could hear that a large proportion of

undergraduates had been to a public school. To my South Wales eye, they moved with a striding self-confidence that I envied. They enunciated precisely and loudly whereas I muttered in a fast staccato, Welsh singsong. Former boarders knew how to look after themselves away from home, all appearing to know each other well, breezing confidently into Robert Sayles to buy more crockery and delivering minced 'good mornings' without appearing to move the top lip. They dressed in green corduroy trousers, smooth check sports jackets and brown brogue shoes. The browns and greens of the countryside had never entered my wardrobe. I could look back and write sharp words about class and cash but it would not be a true reflection of this small Cambridge college where what you did far outweighed who you were. The advantages of a grammar school life began to shine through because after the natural reticence that came from feeling inferior came the openness and homeliness. My cups and saucers came from Woolworth's but the kettle was always on the boil. Nothing mattered except academic pursuit and the release of individual talents and abilities. Even the gospel according to my dad was beginning to fade although I recall the outline statement even now – 'D'y know, son, that the higher civil service, not my end, is dominated by the upper class. When I joined in 1949, the ones who won an open entry into the administrative class were seventy-four per cent Oxbridge.' Thereafter followed the sermon against inherited wealth. Historians can get it wrong. I never thought about matters of social inequality. My currencies were sport, books and music, and I lived by the crafty generosity of the manager of the Midland Bank in the Market Square. I was driven but only by the wish to embrace every new experience and widen the horizon. That has been the motivation for the whole of my life. Diversions? Follow them.

During that first Michaelmas term of 1959, I tried to restart a mind numbed by National Service during which my only cerebral contribution had been to work out how a five-day leave pass could be stretched to a fortnight by attaching official leave to a bank holiday weekend and days off in lieu of guard duty; but I would catch up. Within a couple of days at Christ's, I slipped in alongside those intent on spending dark, autumn afternoons crouched earnestly over books in the First Court library while the chill winds whipped through screens outside.

Why Cambridge in the first place? Let me go back three years. The headmaster of Neath Grammar, Dr Glyn John (MA Oxon), used to swoop on sixth formers, asking where they intended to go to university. I replied Manchester.

'Why Manchester, boy? What will you read?'

'Because Neville Cardus lived there, Sir, and to read history, Sir.'

Wholly puzzled, he screwed up his face and scrunched his eyes closed like old man Steptoe, wrapped his gown around him and hurried away down a corridor.

As early as twelve years old, I was a mite that flitted into the golden web of Neville Cardus. I never tried to escape although his reputation for accuracy was later called into question. Around me spun a language that bound music and cricket together. In cricket, I could see bravura passages, and in music, deftness and control. Cardus read Dickens by lamplight on foggy Manchester streets; I read Cardus by gaslight, too, but in the warmth of my bedroom, by the dull yellow glow of the road's gaslamp, late at night.

I was with Cardus at the Old Trafford cricket ground, 'greenest grass in England', and with him on a Salzburg morning of rains and mists when he lunched with Sir Thomas Beecham for the first time. I would see the Count Esterhazy, 'a large moon-faced man, in Tyrolean cape and leather short trousers', coming to inform Beecham that they had no trace of a Mozart symphony in C major, the one that he intended to conduct there. Beecham assured the Count that Mozart had been only three-quarters of a mile away from where they were meeting when he composed it. Wonderful romance.

Next, not for the last time, Wilfred Wooller offered me advice in a language of his own. 'You're a damned cloth-ears. I'll write to my old college in Cambridge. That's where you ought to go.' At well over six feet tall, the Skipper, leader of the county for fifteen years, was not a man you would want to contradict. After surviving the wartime horrors of Changi gaol as a prisoner of war, he returned to Wales to play county cricket to the age of fifty as if intent on staying out of doors on the green cricket fields for the rest of his life. It was an acceptable fantasy that, when playing for the university, he was once warned by an umpire for biting! He was that sort of physical animal. I was just seventeen when the Skipper decided he would prepare me for the county captaincy. The Cambridge experience would be part of the leadership ladder.

Obediently, I followed the Wooller plan while continuing my own approach to Manchester. An aunt had informed me that a relative, Mr Lewis Holme Lewis, had made a name for himself in Manchester as a city engineer by developing water-driven lifts. He had even installed such a lift in Buckingham Palace. That information I considered an omen. I was predestined, nothing less, to walk where Cardus had once walked. A letter came from Christ's College, Cambridge. Well, I would go for an interview anyway.

I made the long trip from Neath to Cambridge by train, via Liverpool Street Station. I had read the college advice and walked down Regent Street to Christ's carrying an overnight bag loaded with a couple of heavy books by two Cambridge history professors, Elton and Plumb, for last-minute swotting. I felt so desperately uneasy among the gowned undergraduates who eased round the courts that I never left my college room for dinner or breakfast. I pretended to study and got in a complete muddle. I heard every chime of the college clock.

Into the misty Third Court at 10 a.m. came the shout of Dr Pratt. 'Come in!' He was smaller than the voice. He wore glasses and had a purple birthmark on his face. As I sat down, I caught sight of an upside-down daffodil on the notepaper in front of him. He followed my glance.

'Yes, we do have a letter from Wilfred Wooller. But I must tell you that it's not necessarily to your benefit. Mr Wooller, I recall, was a very destructive gentleman. He once cut and knotted the cables of a public telephone box in Cambridge. Also, the last time he called to my rooms,' he raised his eyes, 'it was feet first through my half-timbered ceiling, from a party in the room above.' Dr Pratt left a gap. 'What do you hope to read?'

'History, Sir.'

'Any of your relatives been up at the university?'

'My father's second cousin . . . at, er, Caius I think . . .'

As I was mumbling, he turned to lift a large reference book from the shelves behind him. 'Find him in there,' he instructed, tossing the tome straight at me. I caught it. 'Good,' smiled Dr Pratt. 'But don't forget – get behind it, tuck your elbows in and turn your shoulder to the advancing forwards.' Help! I wanted to go home.

Dr J.H. Plumb's rooms were in First Court. At 10.30 a.m. I responded to another 'Come in.' He was sitting in a winged armchair near the window. He did not look up. I observed the bald head and the owl-like spectacles, a short man but a hero of my own history master in Neath Grammar School. This was Plumb – just like his photograph.

After a long silence, and still without looking up, he said, 'You are Lewis the cricketer, are you not?'

'Well . . . er, Sir, I suppose I am.'

Still not looking up he went on, 'Yes. My brother once umpired a match for the Leicestershire second team.'

'Really, Sir,' was all I could come out with. 'I don't think I've ever met him.'

At last he looked at me. 'No, I didn't think you would have, but that's the only thing you and I would have in common for three years.'

I raced away from Christ's, thinking it a delightful place if you were on the inside but, for me, a dream world that would never be. By bus, by train, by London Underground and by train to the down-line platform of Neath General Station I retreated; then past Mayer's the Fish, round to the market to talk to Micky Williams at the fruit, vegetable and gardening stall, opposite Graham Rees, the toy-seller and, as I made my way up Gnoll Park Road, I felt the ground firmer under my feet. My voice returned.

A few days later a letter arrived with a simple message from Dr Pratt that I was accepted, 'but I cannot think why', and after completing National Service I would have a place for the Michaelmas Term of 1959.

And that is how it happened. On a Tuesday in October 1959, I was still clerking and bumping the billet floor with polish right through to the end. By the Friday, I was outside the porter's lodge of Christ's College, Cambridge, identifying my luggage. It was the first trunk I had ever owned, brown, second-hand, roped, labelled and secured by my father for a trip to eternity.

'Are you Mr Lewis?' inquired the large, square-chinned gentleman dressed in dark, striped trousers, short black coat and bowler hat. The college's head porter was a man of authority; he gave firm orders to other porters who wore aprons.

'Yes. That's my trunk.'

'Good. It will be brought to your room, Sir,' he looked down at a list – 'W7 in Third Court, Mr Lewis.'

'Thank you, Mr Philby,' I offered as a polite opener to our future relationship.

He frowned and looked up sternly over his papers. 'No. It's Philby, Sir.'

In those few days, I had been flipped up in the air like one of my cigarette cards in the Gnoll schoolyard in Neath and this time had come down picture up. I was no longer anonymous, no longer number 5051643. I had travelled up from Neath that day by train in the company of another Neath Grammar School boy, an outstanding schoolboy international rugby player who was to read metallurgy with equal aggression and success, Brian Thomas.

To most people in Neath, Cambridge represented both an academic pinnacle and the privileged resort of the few. My history classes at school rang with piercing questions from the master, Sam Evans, on the subject of life's inequalities – 'Between 1946 and 1948, boy, how much of the wealth of Britain was owned by the wealthiest one per cent of individuals?' He would clench a fist and bang it down on some unsuspecting head. 'Fifty per cent, boy. Fifty per cent.' Having stirred the pot of boiling injustice, he would shout on, 'They decided to redistribute wealth, boy, spread it around. But it didn't go very far, did it? A lump of cold butter, it stayed where it was.' For a lifetime, those embryo historians and I in Neath Grammar were left with the indelible statistic that in 1937 five per cent of the population owned seventy-nine per cent of all wealth. Another Sam Evans special was 'Can a nation survive without its language?' and God help you if you informed this Welsh-speaking son of the Rhondda that you believed 'yes it can'. His Welsh had been self-taught in his teenage.

My father was worried that at Cambridge I would not know what to wear and when, not have enough money to keep up, not have enough to eat. I remember him bravely trying to do some research with the help of a Christ's man who came to Neath in 1956 to play a county match, the Lancashire fast bowler C.S. Smith. I was in the Glamorgan side but it rained for almost the whole three days. This gave us the chance to talk with Colin Smith, a William Hulme's Grammar School boy, and a regular Cambridge cricket Blue who had been at Christ's for a few years. Across a trestle table in the Neath indoor school, Colin drawled, 'Don't worry about a thing, Mr Lewis. Tony'll have a wonderful time,' and as he said so, he reached inside the pocket of his jacket, I thought to take out a notebook. Instead, on to the table fell a packet of three condoms. The Cambridge Blue, I am happy to relate, made a seamless recovery, maintaining the intonation of good advice while scooping up the packet with the sangfroid of Raffles pocketing a diamond necklace from under the victim's nose. Now you see it, now you don't.

My dad had done well enough himself when he was a boy in Dynevor Grammar School in Swansea but he had to leave after O-levels to earn a living. He would always pronounce a belief that chances in life revolved around whom you knew. It was all to do with money and class. 'The money is in the hands of too few,' he would announce, as if it was a revelation each time he said it. 'I'm off to the Liberal Club for a pint.' It took me years to appreciate that the money speech was only his regular exit line for a pint. My mother, by contrast, never deviated from her simple view that children should not be pushed to ambition, should not leave their home town to get on in the world. She did not believe in the 'on your bike' theory. She wanted families to weave and spin at home where they were. The family was the only unit that mattered and brothers and sisters should live round the corner from each other. My mother did not mind as long as we were all together, and yet it was no shock when my father one evening declared that my liaison with Joan Pritchard had to stop or else it would ruin my prospects. Stop it did although gloom arrived on the cross currents of this family clash, and took several years to shift.

At Christ's, I was determined not to be involved with any society or sporting club. I was looking for rebirth as a reader of books and writer of thoughtful essays. Then, one afternoon, I looked up from my desk to a tap on the window. I opened it to the college rugby club secretary who said that the college rugby trial that afternoon was short of a full-back and someone had said that I used to play. I told him I had no intention of playing rugby and so had not brought boots or any kit with me. 'Just stand in,' he begged. It was a clear sunny day so I biked up the Huntingdon Road and turned out in soft basketball shoes. Mr and Mrs Bentley, curators of the college sports ground and pavilion, fixed me up with shirt and shorts. The college first XV captain was there and quizzed me after the game. Who had I played for? Why hadn't I put my name on the board? Neath? Gloucester? No wonder you didn't put a foot wrong. So you are a first-class player. He was not amused.

That evening I was sipping a pint at the bar of the tiny college buttery when Dr Pratt walked in. He crooked a finger at me, frowned darkly and asked, 'Who on earth are you? I didn't accept anyone looking like you into Christ's.'

'I'm Lewis, Sir.'

'School?'

'Neath Grammar School, Sir.'

'I never forget a face . . . don't know yours. Anyway, I hear you play a good game of rugby but haven't got any boots.'

'No, Sir.'

'Why?'

'I left them at home so that I could concentrate on my work, Sir.'

He paused, sipping his sherry without a friendly flicker. Then he leaned across the bar and prodded a finger into my chest.

'Write to your mother and ask her to send you your rugger boots immediately.'

'Yes, Sir.'

'And Lewis...' Then came the wicked smile that Pratt could produce in a blink of the eye. '... ask her kindly to send on your violin as well. Remember that you come to Christ's to give all the talents you have, not to take.' There was not a detail of any undergraduate Lucan Pratt did not know.

A week later I was wobbling to lectures on my new bike, carrying a fiddle under my arm, rugger boots lashed to the crossbar and books lodged in a basket at the back. In the mornings I would join eager undergraduates in lectures down at Mill Lane and then hurtle to the playing fields or music rooms.

Over-optimistically, I volunteered for an audition for the university orchestra. I attended the rooms of David Wilcox in King's and performed some gentle Handel sonata before attempting the sight-reading test. I had not played at all for two years and was suddenly hit by a mind-blank, as the left hand was required to make rushed trips to the higher positions on the E string. Wilcox smiled and nodded.

'You can obviously play this instrument very well,' he encouraged, 'but not even Menuhin can manage two years off. I suggest you start in the university's second orchestra for a while.' He was being more than generous. My vibrato, once so wide and deliciously slow, was now like a short burst of machine gun fire. 'The Army?' he inquired. 'Tanks?' he suggested. I retreated from King's to perform thereafter only in my bathroom where the sound was full until I believed I could hear dexterity and tone returning.

The six weeks that followed remoulded my whole life. My one college kick-around had propelled me to the full-back position in the university rugby club and I entered the fierce competition for a Blue. On one trip to play in London I was reunited, after a long separation, with Joan Pritchard who was now a schoolteacher at Finsbury Park Secondary School and collected knuckle-dusters in a tin box before classes could begin each morning. After that, she used to arrive in Cambridge every Friday night, returning to London on Sunday evenings on the train known to undergraduates as the Popsy Express. Party invites increased, the drinking of sherry caught on; it was a whirlwind life played out within the weekly supervisions of my history studies and the disciplines of wearing a gown after dusk and being back in college by eleven o'clock. Girls could be smuggled in but at a huge risk if the 'bedder' had not been bribed. Mrs Tompkins, who cleaned rooms and made beds on the ground floor of W block in the Third Court, announced without a blush, 'I don't mind who I find you in bed with in the morning, Sir, as long as it's not another fella. I've had enough of them, Sir.'

'Thank you very much, Mrs Tompkins. Why don't I give you ten shillings for the term.' It was the going rate. She ever-so politely accepted, and picked up the hairgrips on Monday mornings.

Along the way, I joined the small herd of big men who played rugby at Christ's. Vic Harding was already an England second-row forward and Trevor Wintle would soon play at scrum-half. David MacSweeney had played in the back row for Ireland, Roger Michaelson and Brian Thomas would play for Wales and John Brash for Scotland. There was much disappointment that David Perry, another future England cap, had been sent down after one year. The story went that he took to a theory that information recorded and replayed at night during sleep would conceal itself in the mind and leap out at examination time. So as lights went out each night, he would switch on recorded lectures on Economics Part One. Alas, David fell just short of ten per cent and was shown the door. Fact or fiction, it was a piece of Christ's folklore that kept us at the books.

The richness of Cambridge life that my father had imagined was to do with money did not exist. There were many students like me with leather patches on the elbows of their sports coats scrambling through on state grants. The richness came from the sudden expansion of activities, the variety of new people and the incredible independence of having one's own rooms. The possibilities for study or frivolity, if accompanied by curiosity, widened the world every day. It was not exclusively a Cambridge experience, nor even the reserve of a university or college, but, as I look back, it was all the more exhilarating in that particular cloistered and famous environment.

Heather had chosen Cardiff University for its music. Academically strong, she pursued the practical side with her work on organ and piano and was well set on the way to being a professional player, tutor and examiner. She studied under Alun Hoddinott, the prolific and highly original Welsh composer.

Reunited with my rugger boots, I was suddenly in with a chance of playing in the 1959 university rugger match. Now the advantage of spending two years hardening the body, if not the mind, in National Service was evident. My seasons for Gloucester were to my credit. In fact, my debut in first-class rugby came in March 1958 when A/C Lewis went home from RAF Innsworth to Neath on a weekend pass. I was listening to music in our sunny front room when it all went dark. A large single-decker bus had pulled up outside. The only buses that ever came into our dead-end were hired to take us on outings to Mumbles.

A very short man, Theo Davies, was at the front door. It was the Neath first-team bus and he bore the news that Bill Young had cried off. Would I play? Within minutes I was on board with jockstrap, boots and towel.

'Who are we playing?' I asked.

'Gloucester,' he said. 'Away.'

Back where I started, but never mind. I ran out on Kingsholm in the black jersey with the white Maltese cross behind the captain, Wales and British Lions prop-forward Courtenay Meredith. The *Sunday Times* writer L.J. Corbett observed, 'T. Lewis, making his first appearance at full-back, came through a trying ordeal with credit.'

The truth is that I cannot remember anything about the game save one scrum five yards from our own line. It erupted and as they all stood up to re-form, I saw George Hastings, the Gloucester and England international prop, move over from loose head to tight head. He had had enough of Courtenay. Our leader moved across the front row to follow him, grabbed the shirt of John Dodd, our loose head, and swung him across to the tight side before turning to Hastings and announcing in cut-glass English, 'Oh no, George, you can't get away from me as easily as that.' Wham! The scrum engaged and another Meredith victim buckled and groaned. Courtenay was part of a famous Lions front row with Bryn Meredith and Billy Williams; now it is impossible to convey to members of the Royal Porthcawl Golf Club that the slim, gentle fellow in spectacles, sipping a small whisky across the room, is the same man who ground down Springbok prop-forwards. The body weight has gone. I tell them to look into the eyes.

I had played most of my first-class rugby for Gloucester, where I won a regular place at full-back. On Tuesdays and Thursdays we trained at Kingsholm. On Tuesdays it was a few kicks and passes, ten laps and five pints in the Spread Eagle. On Thursdays it was five laps and three pints, in readiness for the match on Saturday. There was terrific spirit in the club and lots of superb players. Micky Booth was the scrum-half, a clever player with a natural sense of what to do next and of what to tell everyone in any position on the field to do next as well. That included the referee, two touch judges and any England selectors at the game. They were tough nuts in the pack, led by the gritty hooker Cyril Thomas. We had Brian Green, Alan Hudson, Roy Long, George Hastings, Brian Ibbotson and the international wing-forward who it was safer to have on your side than against you, Peter Ford. I floated behind good players such as the England and British Lion centre Bill Patterson, Dave Phelps, Alan Holder and Dick Smith.

In theory, there was no place available for a full-back at Cambridge because the highly talented Scottish international Ken Scotland was still up. However, here the storyline takes a twist or two. Our Scottish international outside-half, Gordon Waddell, had undergone knee surgery and was unable to play and so Kenny moved to outside-half. That left open the full-back place but only until Gordon was back. Other contestants in the field were Chris Howland, the Sixty Club full-back, and Ian Balding who had played for Bath, Dorset and Wiltshire.

Ian was also a freshman at Christ's and we eyed each other with grim recognition at breakfast every morning as this Michaelmas term hurtled forward. I was in the side and then got injured. Ian stepped in and played a couple of blinders. I was back in but there was news that Gordon would be fit after all. That would mean that Balding and Lewis were wasting their nervous energies. After matches on Wednesdays and Saturdays, we would sneak round to the window of the tailor, Ryder and Amies, where a long row of boards displayed the many university teams chosen for next matches. Was I in? Or was it Balding? The skill was to disguise the anxiety. I would hurtle up Petty Curie, charge through the market square and, in front of King's College, slow to a crawl, sinking hands in pockets in an act of insouciance signalling that I just happened to be passing and thought I would do a slow check on the rugby team for the next match. If it had not yet been posted I would walk on, staring blindly into shop windows, even threatening academic bookshops with a browse, before rounding once more on the Ryder and Amies window.

I am happy to report that in the midst of this fratricidal contest for a rugby Blue, Ian and I became lifelong friends, to the extent that he later became godfather to my daughter Joanna and I am godfather to his son Andrew. This union was sealed in the bar of the Red Lion Hotel in Petty Curie. We decided to have a drink together, brave of Ian because he had no history of beer drinking whereas I had been brought up in Neath with the taste of Evans Bevan bitter on my lips.

Ian asked for a half-pint of beer. I had never ordered a half before. He sipped, I swilled. We knew we could get on, whoever won the Blue. He blanched a little after several glasses and we left. So often is it possible to write in sport that serious opponents become the closest friends. I am thankful that games were an integral part of daily life at Neath Grammar School. I could win; I could lose. I could shake hands and share a beer. He could say the same of Marlborough and Millfield.

Grange Road, the university rugby club's home ground, was an elegant setting for such a physical game. We changed in a pavilion rather than a clubhouse, on top of which members sat in neat rows – vicars, dons, dames wrapped in plaid rugs, the university's loyal supporters. The central and most important person was the president, Dr Windsor Lewis, a former Blue and Welsh outside-half. After the match, we ate thinly sliced cucumber sandwiches and the best of sponges before moving off to the Hawk's Club, the university's sporting club, for beer and maybe snooker with any of our opponents who cared to follow.

I had still not been selected to play against Oxford when we went to Twickenham for our final game, against Harlequins. Their side was studded with former Oxford Blues and it is fair to say that they kicked us off the park. I left the field just before half-time for five stitches above my eye. I returned groggy and was advised to retire by Ken Scotland. That, I thought, was that. I would not make the side.

By ten o'clock that night I was back in my bed in Christ's with a crashing headache, feeling depressed. There was a knock on the door and I opened it to the captain, Steve Smith. He handed me an envelope containing a card bearing an Emmanuel crest. The message read, if I was not doing anything a week on Tuesday, would I turn out for a match against Oxford at Twickenham? S.R. Smith, an England international scrum-half, had the sensitivity of a fine leader although he suffered the unluckiest term. He struggled to recover from a nasty leg injury and could not lead from the front of the field for much of the time. He had also lost Gordon Waddell, but here was a true sportsman, a cussed, competitive opponent but a gentleman at the final whistle. That he should have made that visit to Christ's on the night that I was at my lowest was a mercy I will not forget. Outsiders might say that it was only a rugby match – what's the fuss? All I can say is that it was different on the inside, a frantic, feverish lust to be chosen, and as long as I have breath to describe the events of that term, I will remember it that way.

Port and nuts at Pembroke College were accompanied by a toast, GDBO – God Damn Bloody Oxford. It was hotting up. I sipped the port and savoured the astonishing turn of events – 'You have come to Christ's to give, not to take.'

The actual game, they say, was a poor spectacle in front of 57,000 spectators. We lost by three penalties to one, 9–3, and in a kicking match, I dropped the odd one and caught the rest. Richard Sharp, also a freshman, kept lofting the ball higher and higher and an American, Pete Dawkins, launched left-handed missiles right across the field from his throw-ins to the lineout. I do remember feeling suddenly relaxed. Now is the time, I thought, to race up with the backs and produce the side-steps I had learned on the road at home. Then I looked at the big clock at the north-end stand – ten to four. Hell. It was over.

Into the silent dungeon of a dressing room I retreated where the only sound at the burial of our hopes was the creaking of the hot water through the pipes. Hours later, after a bread-throwing dinner in the East India Club, we paraded at the Grosvenor House Hotel in our finery, I with Joan Pritchard who was soon to become my fiancée.

University rugby in those days was outstanding because the undergraduates at both Oxford and Cambridge were fitter than the club sides. During the last ten minutes' play, the students were more often than not on top. Tutors for Admission cannily found props and big second-row men. Lucan Pratt, of course, assisted in this. Already in Christ's he had Hugh Thomas, the speedy Aberavon prop, as well as Vic Harding, the mighty England second-row forward. I recall Vic wearing a navy blazer, stretched a bit across the chest, that sported a 1958 Middlesex RFU badge. He could be persuaded, for a laugh, to undo the poppers that held it to the breast pocket, revealing a similar badge underneath, which read Middlesex 1951! Estimating Vic Harding's true age was a good pub question. Brian Thomas, an equal, physically, to any current international, was soon to play a massive part in a run of Cambridge success, as was Roger Michaelson. In 1959, only one other freshman made the side, again from Christ's. He was John Brash, later to be capped by Scotland and part of an unstoppable Cambridge future.

The unique talent in the 1959 side was K.J.F. Scotland, full-back for Scotland and the British Lions. Kenny, quiet and thoughtful, had the instinct of evasion running through his body. He ghosted into the movements of his three-quarters, weaving his way into overlap situations. He could run long distances on his own, beating defenders not by the sharp, aggressive side-step but by willowy swerves. It was done by timing, not strength. Having caught a ball deep in his half, he would set off up the touchline and in the split-second that the covering tackler was about to thump him up into the stands, he would grub the ball forward with his boot, collect it a few yards later and continue on his way. He could kick long distances to touch with both feet. After weekday practices at Grange Road, we would stay for a while attempting to perform longer and more accurate screw kicks than each other. It was fun. If I was good at anything, it was catching a rugby ball and screw-kicking a long way with both feet. It was exhilarating to see the ball swerve late in its flight over the touchline. You got the full distance.

In those first two terms I was awash with new experiences, sucked in to some, propelled towards others. I had never drunk sherry before; certainly I had not attended a sherry party at which no other drink was served. The only question asked was 'Sweet, medium or dry?' Unimaginable these days. I had not eaten meals, waiter-served, with so many courses and surrounded by such a military formation of cutlery, wine glasses gleaming alongside, centurions of pleasure; nor had any meal in my life been preceded by a bang on the gong and a recital in Latin. Unforgettable. I had never had a bank manager before but I joined the overdraft squadron with equanimity. Life had never afforded me such personal choices about the next minute, the next hour. I had a kettle and crockery, a toasting fork and a steady hand for toasting crumpets; all-comers were welcome.

Seeds for the future were sown in that Michaelmas term. Fifteen years later I would be appointed rugby correspondent to the *Sunday Telegraph*. In fact, while still an undergraduate, I wrote to the *Observer* to ask if I might contribute the occasional rugby report. They sent me off to Bedford to cover a trial match. Sports Editor Clifford Makins, whom I later found to be a delightful companion, especially at lunch with his correspondent Clem Thomas, gave my copy the blue-pencil treatment and returned it with a mass of corrections, suggesting that this was a byway closed to me.

As for history studies, I had begun a skimpy performance at Christ's attempting to balance work and what turned out to be a freshman double Blue. (Nowadays I am surrounded by history books – the instinct to inquire developed late.) The light blue scarf was a passport for party crashing and that is why the first term of the academic year is also a graveyard littered with broken hopes. Take my good friend Roger Dalzell, a fine scrum-half at Bedford School and a superb gymnast. Roger dreamed of Twickenham but his time coincided with three outstanding performers. In his first year, he was up against the university captain Steve Smith; next came Trevor Wintle and, in his third year, Simon Clarke, all three England scrum-halves. Gymnastics rated a half-Blue and Roger easily achieved that, becoming secretary of the club, but he wanted the blue scarf and so our gang of seven close friends in Christ's worked out that his route to the top would be by boxing. He was a good thumper and began promisingly, haymaking a few opponents to an early canvas. The competition hotted up as the term went on and he ran into trouble when opponents started to turn out in shiny dressing gowns with hoods, shorts with a stripe, and wearing soft leather boxing boots. Roger was still in the Bedford School gym kit. One evening at the Corn Exchange the towel fluttered into the ring. Our man retreated mumbling 'double vision'. This happened on a second occasion and we realised that he was making sure he did not get on the wrong end of a hammering that might put him out of contention for the big fight against Oxford, towards Christmas, and the blue scarf.

Alas, the boxing captain did not choose him but gave him a place on tour to Gibraltar as compensation. Thus the Bedford School shorts next appeared in a bullring off the Spanish coast. As our hero sat on his stool in his corner, the huge crowd roared at the entry of his opponent and fanfares were played. 'Why my fight?' he was entitled to ask because others had been unheralded. His second dashed round the ring to deliver the poor news that Roger was about to fight the champion of Gibraltar at his weight. It is disputed to this day whether the Gibraltarian champion had actually left his stool when Dalzell's right hand arrived at the side of his chin, putting out all his lights. Olé! Olé! The locals hailed him. Dalzell, I am told, retreated from the arc lights, shunning the shoddy triumphalism of modern high-fives, simply humming to himself the Bedford School song, 'By North and South and East and West...' *Floreat schola Bedfordiensis*. Job well done.

During the Christmas vacation, after that first term in Cambridge, I was walking down Orchard Street in Neath when I was stopped by

Neath rugby club's premier barracker, the man with the flat hat and no teeth, Meg Downey.

'Hello, Tone. I hear you got your rugby Blue.'

I fingered the light blue scarf. 'Yes, Meg, but I was very lucky.'

'Aye. Bloody funny. I never saw you in the boat.'

Feet rarely left the ground in Neath.

CHAPTER 6

BATH INCIDENT

It was hot, sunny weather in July 1962. Glamorgan were in the field at bath. Ossie Wheatley, the captain, with a grin, sent me down to third man with the instruction, 'Take a look at that while you're down there, A.R.' He pointed to a young lady dressed attractively under a black, wide-brimmed straw hat that completely shielded her face. Nice shape, I thought, good legs. I had got within twenty yards when the brim of the hat lifted, like a visor. It was Joan, my very own fiancée.

'Hi,' I said. 'Thought you were at home. Great to see you.'

I should have detected by the firm-footed stance and the folded arms that she was in fact at battle stations. She marched a dozen yards or so over the boundary line, infield – embarrassing, in front of hundreds of Somerset spectators perched on temporary stands in that quarter of the ground who had begun to whistle and cheer. She then made her prepared speech.

'If it is your wish to take the Bishop of Portsmouth's daughter to the Christ's College Marguerites cocktail party and not me, then you can jolly well marry her.'

Next, in a move loudly acclaimed by the Somerset crowd, she extended her left hand, removed her engagement ring and threw it at me. All Somerset was now on its feet, clapping every twist of her high heels as she left the field.

First-class cricket is best played with a clear mind and I admit I found it impossible to concentrate from then on. Ossie could not stop laughing; he thought he had simply spotted a decent bird on the boundary. Fielding with your fiancée's engagement ring in your back pocket is not to be recommended; indeed, the Somerset supporters advised me to stick it in several interesting places. Across the field behind the temporary stands I saw the lady go, driving away in a brand new Mini. I had lost a fiancée and all of her bank savings at the same time.

Grovelling worked over the next few days and the ring was back on her hand. We were married three weeks later on 22 August. Wilfred Wooller, by now the Glamorgan secretary, could not comprehend how anyone in his right mind could agree to marry in the middle of the cricket season.

'The committee,' he announced, 'will give you one game off.'

'But I'm an amateur,' I responded. 'I'm not on the payroll. I get no match fee.' I had two games off.

'Well, we'll pay for you and your wife to stay in the team hotel in the next matches. They're at Hastings and Blackpool.'

No one, except the Glamorgan team, knew how well I had chosen the wedding date. Glamorgan were to play Gloucestershire on a new ground. Sponsorship had come in from the Steel Company of Wales, so we were to play at Margam, alongside one of the main steelworks. I had tried to bat there before on a mixture of new turf and marshland. It was a good game to miss. No innings managed 100. A whole second day was rained off. Glamorgan were left chasing 119 for victory with most of the third day available and did not go for them! Twenty wickets fell on both first and third days. The game's top scorer was Martin Young with 24 in the second innings. Gloucestershire scored 88 and 92 and won by 69 runs. Even *Wisden*, that remote authority, had the good sense to announce that 'the ball turned liked a spinning top and rose at varying heights and pace'.

I had drifted into first-class cricket on a golden wave. It had mostly gone right. I was cosseted by predictions of playing for England, even captaining, yet I see now how I failed to ask myself the important questions. How badly did I want to succeed? How single-minded could I be? After all, the securing of a winter job was more vital than playing cricket for four months every summer. Cricket was not the full-time profession it might have been later.

Each season for the next ten years I would wonder whether to continue playing or not. I enjoyed the game and the camaraderie of the Glamorgan team, and it is only when I look back I see that I could be an outstanding professional for a couple of days a week and a good one for another two but I lacked the focus to succeed all of the time. If I had been a racehorse, I could have won a lot of races, even a big one, but the trainer would have fitted me early on with blinkers – not that I could have escaped the demon ring-thrower on the Bath boundary.

CHAPTER 7

ARLOTT

I was like every other young cricket fan in the 1940s and 1950s. We were cradled in the silken hammock of Neville Cardus's writing, and the golden voice of John Arlott lulled us. We were captives of these two liberal minds that not only constructed cricket reports but also presented them as vivid tales of humanity. Cricket was more than a game. Where Cardus found performance and style, Arlott lovingly exposed the sweat and craftsmanship of a batsman who could produce maybe twenty priceless runs on a broken pitch, or of a bowler who took two thoughtful wickets in a Test match. I believe they communicated cricket with dramatic imagination because they were both cricketers manqués and prolific readers; they wrote and spoke what they saw, and a good deal more. Cricket was one lust of their lives but not life itself, and even as they sat poised in front of notebook and microphone, they knew they were watching the game of cricket weave itself into the wider pattern of social life.

John Arlott was a good friend. He could switch his thoughtful scowl to a twinkling smile in a second. I see him hunched over a typewriter in the cricket press box, lower lip in the shape of a strong downward bow and a frown scored in deep valleys on his brow as he completed line after line, slamming the return carriage back to the start with metronomic regularity. He liked to have a glass of wine at his sleeve or sometimes, later in his working life when the chest wheezed and blew, a vulgar brandy with a modicum of water. 'I need my phlegm-cutter these days,' he'd say. Then the eyebrows would rise, the eyes sparkle and the lips would shape the most mischievous smile; he could feel a story coming on. 'Just been thinking about Jack's last century. Jack used to motor on a Wednesday, d'you know, to Kimbolton School, to coach the boys . . . close friend of the headmaster . . . got talked into a father's match in June 1941 . . . got what Jack told me was his last century.' A sip, deep breath, a cough and, 'Hobbs, of course. Jack wrote to me in September 1962.' Jack Hobbs! My cigarette-card cover fielder! You were drawn in so close to the body of cricket, you became part of it. As you listened, you shared the intimacy of John's own experiences. How did he come to know Jack? Ask a question and the tumblers rolled to unlock a fresh story. Did Hobbs play much after retirement from Surrey? Where did his cricket equipment shops fit in? There was no stopping him once he sensed your antennae twitching. 'Jack was a Cambridge boy. Made 197 first-class centuries. He was as modest, honest and kind as he seemed. He virtually had not an enemy.' This was delivered with biblical certainty, another piece of cricket history handed down. That is the lesson for today. Then, on reading a stanza of Arlott poetry on Hobbs, it was possible to understand that it was the craftsman, even more than the stylist, whom he admired:

> No yeoman ever walked his household land
> More sure of step or more secure of lease
> Than you, accustomed and unhurried, trod
> Your small, yet mighty, manor of the crease.

On the flat roof of the high, white pavilion at the St Helens ground in Swansea was a small radio commentary box made for two, often occupied by the talented Welsh outside-broadcaster Alun Williams and his scorer. Occasionally, it became the centre of all interest, even for the players down on the pitch way below, because we knew that John Arlott was in town. In sunshine, Arlott and Williams would erect their worktable and microphone in the open air, keeping the network informed and charmed with the benefit of freshly cut sandwiches and a bottle of Burgundy. When Glamorgan were batting, there might be a chance to wander on to the roof to pass the time of day. That is how I met John Arlott for the first time. The moment he said, 'How do you do?' the southern voice embraced me like an old friend; it was the voice that had whisked me off to the great Test grounds to hear if Hutton was still facing up to Lindwall or Bedser bowling to Bradman.

It was the same when Glamorgan were at Cardiff Arms Park. On top of the Athletic Club the broadcasters took wine with the most magnificent prawn sandwiches prepared by the stewardess, Babs, who put an appearance by Mr Arlott above all visits outside royalty. In the 1950s and 1960s, the BBC transmitted commentary not only on Test matches but also on games in the county championship, the premier league of the day, and if John Arlott loved his native Hampshire most, we were honoured that he nominated Glamorgan second. When in Cardiff, he stayed overnight at the home of Wilfred Wooller, in Cyncoed. Enid, Wilf's wife, would hope that these two heavyweight debaters would not alight on the subject of South Africa yet again – whether apartheid was best fought by playing sports with South Africa or not. Enid admits, 'Wilf never thought he was wrong on any subject. When he had come to bed after arguing with John about South Africa, I often said to him, "But what if John's right?" and Wilf would be speechless with disbelief.' Arlott defeated Wooller and Ted Dexter in the Cambridge Union debate on that same subject but Wilf could never change his conviction that black and coloured Africans would be better served if sporting links with white South Africa were maintained.

I played full-time cricket for Glamorgan from the summer of 1963. It was the first year without amateur status but there was little money to be earned. In order to stay in the game, I tried to become a freelance writer and broadcaster during the winter months. I wanted to be Cardus and Arlott rolled into one. They were the role models.

I was commissioned to write odd articles for the *Cricketer* magazine and in 1964 I was invited to provide a chapter for a large reference book, *Barclay's World of Cricket*. 'The History of Cricket in Wales' by Tony Lewis hit the bell. Michael Melford of the *Sunday Telegraph* had commissioned it, E.W. Swanton, the editor, nodded at it and soon, thanks to Michael, I found proper work as a rugby reporter on the Welsh edition of the *Sunday Telegraph*. BBC Radio Wales used me for rugby reports on a Saturday evening.

It was slow progress but I felt my work drawing closer to John Arlott's and he guessed that. He loved talking cricket and about my cricket, but he sensed that I was longing to be let loose in his world. When we met on the cricket circuit, we talked antiques, books and so much more. Here was a man with serious intelligence in so many directions, massively self-taught. He spotted me as a young man who played good cricket but whose life was not consumed by it. Far from recommending blinkers for me, as so many tutors had before, John Arlott opened up a wider, more fascinating world of association football, wine and cheese, antiques and books, snuff, glass, churches, Sunderland lustre, and a lot more. We would meet in spare time at Bowns of Pontypridd to discuss the high quality of oak furniture, which was becoming more available than before as South Wales valley chapels closed. He helped me buy my first oak chair. It was important to check the time before he launched into a thesis on Stevengraphs – small pictures woven in silk after the work of Thomas Stevens, the nineteenth-century American weaver – or lectured with a tear of appreciation in his eye on the craftsman who had created the two-piece wine glass with conical bowl. 'D'you know,' he would scowl and smile at the same time, 'the bowl and stem were drawn out in one piece . . . and look at this fluted trumpet bowl, with the six-ribbed pedestal stem . . .' and he would nod with an air of huge understanding at the seller as if the truth of this particular craft could only possibly be known to the both of them. 'Know your stems, Tony,' he'd say, the head nodding seriously, eyes with the glint of a cognoscente.

I well remember John's giant sentence of caution, too – 'Don't work too hard; don't want too much.' He was coming to the end of his working days and I am left, even ten years after his death, with this lugubrious warning. It was a comment on his own working life which was far too short to satisfy his intellectual or material needs – another Chippendale table maybe, or a set of letters by Macaulay or Dylan Thomas and is there a manuscript for sale? I remember the dinner at my home in Groesfaen, Glamorgan, when he told us the book that had always rested most heavily on his mind was Thomas Hardy's *Jude the Obscure*. Hardy described the tale as a deadly war between the flesh and the spirit. Jude Fawley, a Wessex villager of considerable intellectual promise, longs to study at Oxford University, but his life is a gloomy switchback and, despite his learning, he dies unfulfilled. He drinks heavily, marries disastrously and scratches at the walls of Christminster College as a stonemason, not an undergraduate, always on the outside. There were occasions, I feel sure, when John Arlott identified with Jude, by his wish to pour more and more learning into his life, to catch up with what he had missed as a youngster and to drive his body and his brain with a grinding purpose. He would have adored and adorned an Oxford college.

John, however, did have the healthy balance that came from real devotion to his family and from his genuine pleasure in sharing his gathered information with others. His eye would sparkle as he told tales of Silver Billy Beldham or of John Nyren, as if he knew them both well. The truth is John Arlott was a wonderful communicator of the game but he was not well travelled; the modern broadcaster would wonder what all the fuss was about a commentator who did almost all his work in England and Wales. The answer, of course, lies in the power of the radio waves that took his voice into homes all over the world.

One night we had dinner together in Manchester and he said in frowning mode, 'I'm giving up soon. D'you know . . .' and then the shining smile, '. . . I've got nothing left to say.' He could have broadcast on cricket forever but I do believe that John did not fight his age and growing tiredness. I argued that his talent and command of the English language, his perception and his humanity would broadcast all new-comers off the air for as long as he chose to continue. 'Naw! Naw! Naw!' was all I got back.

If you knew John Arlott well, you lived with the tragedy of the death of his son Jimmy on the last day of 1964. It was concluded that Jimmy hit the back of a lorry in his sportscar at almost four o'clock in the morning. He died of multiple head injuries. John found himself in a deep, black maze without sunshine, as most would. Many, however, would find a way out in the fullness of time, but John never did, nor did he try. The only tie he ever wore was black and he would revisit that maze daily, perspiring in his anger. He was a man of questions. He wanted to know why. In the cricket season of 1965, he had not been back on the road many days when Glamorgan were playing in Northampton. We learned that John was staying in our hotel and Ossie Wheatley, the captain, invited him to have dinner on the Saturday evening with Glamorgan's senior players. We sat down at eight and were still there when the birds cleared their throats, the sun came up and the first heavy vehicle bumped its way down the hill past The Angel. There was no play on Sundays in those days. Glamorgan's finest were present – Ossie Wheatley, Don Shepherd, Bernard Hedges, Jim Pressdee, Peter Walker, David Evans. There was laughter from John and uncontrollable tears. This was not to be a sorrow put to sleep by friendship but the feeding of a genuine and furious mourning. 'Why had the lorry no light or marker at the end of its extended load? Why was the lorry moving so slowly? I shall campaign for signs on long loads. Poor Jimmy, with his life ahead of him.'

I made notes that weekend. John had been hard on himself and I thought he would soften. He never did. He never closed the door on the black maze; it was open and inviting and he could drift in there in the middle of a friendly conversation, especially at dinner. You could eat good cheese and drink excellent claret in a mist of moroseness. Then it was gone, but not for long.

We collected antiques for each other. John asked me to report any sightings of Sunderland lustre or good quality oak whereas my own pursuit was silver. I had made the novice mistake at the start when I bought silver according to its hallmarks, without knowing that it had been tampered with. A Peter and Anne Bateman silver teapot, for example, had been severely devalued by scrolls and birds and all manner of Victoriana hammered into its once flat surface. I lost money.

This called for several Arlott book recommendations. He gave me a book on silver by Gerald Taylor. I then bought in the unfashionable towns and sold in smart Cheltenham or Brighton. John would ask if I had been lately to Alice's in Llanelli or Bowns in Pontypridd or to the jolly fat man in Cowbridge Road, Cardiff.

When he was in his pomp, The Old Sun at Alresford was his home and his playground. Joanie and I called one day after a match at Southampton for a glass of wine, and found ourselves in the company of a visiting vintner who tempted us with this and that. It was the first time we had ever drunk wine and spat it out into a plastic bucket. There were Sunday lunches, one with an Australian touring side. Ross Edwards, the Australian batsman, whom I met in Singapore recently, will never forget the deep value of the cricket conversation, the flow broken only when the host retreated to the cellar for further supplies, accompanied by sightseeing Australian Test cricketers.

One sunny morning in Brighton, 1973, I was due to play in a Test trial. I had just taken the England side through India, Ceylon and Pakistan, and my touring side was up against a team led by Ray Illingworth. At eight o'clock on the first morning of the match I took a telephone call from John. 'Meet me in Turnbull's, the wine merchant, at 8.45,' he said. 'I will be waiting for you with Mr Turnbull in the cellar.' With me was Ossie Wheatley, my old Glamorgan captain, who was by now a Test selector. We walked into the shop and were directed through a trapdoor in the floor to the cellar. Arlott was beaming. 'Sparkling Vouvray, gentlemen, the only time in the day to drink it, nine o'clock, so as to approach the day with equanimity.' That is the note in my diary, which I had begun to keep daily. Mindful of the cricket, I sipped just half a glass. Two and a half hours later, the second ball I faced pitched on the seam and left me off the pitch. Bob Woolmer bowled it and Alan Knott caught it, standing up, off the faintest flick from the thumb of my right glove. Back in the dressing room, nursing my nought, the attendant announced that Mr John Arlott was at the door in the hope of seeing Mr Lewis. I went down the steps to the concrete concourse at the back of the pavilion where John was distraught. Mopping his forehead with a red handkerchief, he shook his head with apologies. 'No! No! It was my fault, all my fault. Taking you to Mr Turnbull before a Test trial. Gawd, I'm sorry. I've cost you your England place.' Nothing I said in favour of the Woolmer delivery could console him. Not even a telephone call some days later when I had been selected for the first Test at Trent Bridge could persuade him that he was not a crucial part of my potential downfall at Hove. Every inch of cricket was for John a heart-wringing drama.

In all our dinners after games, John realised one huge truth about me. I was the only person in cricket who thought that I could not play the game well. Perhaps my self-confidence had been destroyed by rough, turning Welsh pitches and I never really got back to the young man who believed in slow but certain progress at the crease. He told me how Phil Mead batted, and Jack Hobbs and Emrys Davies and Len Hutton, passing kind messages as he spun the tales. As everyone who has played would say – if only I knew then what I know now. John Arlott more than anyone understood the fights the performer has with himself.

From 1975 my broadcasting on cricket was a mix of close-of-play summaries on 'Test Match Special' and expert comment on television, and my first attempt at ball-by-ball commentary was at Edgbaston in 1979, at a Prudential World Cup match. West Indies were bowling to India and John Arlott left his commentary position with the words, 'After a word from Fred Trueman, it will be Tony Lewis. Twenty tense minutes later I was at the back of the box, asking him, 'How was I?'

'You were not good,' he growled. 'Buy me a glass and I'll tell you.'

He continued over red wine, 'You have never called the bat "the willow" in your life. Your language is so artificial. You are commentating as you think commentators ought to, and the verbs you used were so long . . . Look, don't broadcast, just talk to people.'

Suitably chastened, I moved on to Headingley where the penny dropped, helped by Brian Johnston's ability to prevent anyone from taking themselves too seriously. I sat with John at Brent's fish and chip café that evening – he took his own chilled white wine – and he just nodded across the table. 'It was good. You'll be fine.' The last words on the subject.

John Arlott was like a computer full of recollections and reminiscences. With a double click on the memory box he could download yet another portrait of yet another cricketer or an anecdote crafted carefully and delivered in inimitable tones. He never dealt in second-hand phrases or lazy clichés. The tale he was telling appeared to come from his heart and soul and he made contact with the listener through expressive eyes, gesturing hands, by the dramatic intake of breath and by seconds of silence. Cardus said of Arlott: 'Hazlitt on his much loved jugglers was not more vividly graphic in words than this.' Arlott, of course, had confessed that William Hazlitt was his own role model – a poor man, a prolific professional writer, a journalist, drama reviewer and art critic, essayist and champion of the radical cause in politics. John was not far from that. Hazlitt championed the self-taught. He wrote: 'You will hear more good things on the outside of a stagecoach from London to Oxford than if you were to pass a twelvemonth with the undergraduates, or heads of colleges of that famous university.' That may sit only a yard away from John's *Jude the Obscure*. And note a line from Hazlitt's essay on prejudice: 'We never do anything well till we cease to think about the manner of doing it.' Don't commentate, just talk to them.

John painted pictures in words. He had worked on the images before he got to the game, but he never forced them on the listener; it was as if he had deep storage for descriptions until the moment was right. Even if the phrase was unoriginal it would still carry the felicitous image of the moment. For example, commentating on India at The Oval in 1979: '. . . in comes Kapil Dev, bowls to Butcher outside the off stump, beats the outside edge . . . Butcher head down, bat and hands behind his back . . . now looks slowly up the pitch at Kapil Dev, like a small boy caught stealing jam.'

John in his pomp was an inspiration to others. Towards the end of his career he needed more wine, had less breath and perspired his way through a day during which he had to find time for sleep. His commentary stints were reduced to the first half of the day, his writing for the *Guardian* stimulated by wine or a late afternoon brandy and water. At Trent Bridge one day we decided to go wine tasting in the evening at friends of his, Vintage Wines of Nottingham, and after our work was done we retreated to the old Bridgford Hotel. I was not staying there so I went to John's room and used his telephone to call Joan at home while John took a bath. I was astonished to see him fill the bath entirely with cold water. Then, stripped off, he got in and lay down with a mighty bellow. I could see into the bathroom and saw a white pot belly above the bath line, smooth and round as a chef's tureen. With more bellowing, he hauled the body, now seriously below room temperature, into a bathrobe. Soon we were off to the cellars to swill and sniff the Rioja. Food and drink were important to him and Trent Bridge was his favourite Test ground; the cold water bath was his daily ritual when travelling.

John Arlott was talented but the spread of his compulsions – to stand three times as a Liberal candidate, to write books on Hampshire churches and one on Burgundy wine, to chair the Professional Cricketers' Association – reduced the potency of each ability. He could not improve on his generosity, or his radio commentaries on cricket, but he might have been a great writer if he had not, as he had warned, worked so hard and wanted so much.

He was a romantic in that he always saw the heroic in another's creative work, whether it be the 1,000 net practices that went into the making of Henry Horton's forward defensive stroke or the street skills dubbined into the boots of Tommy Harmer, his favourite footballer. After his final cricket commentary at Lord's he announced to a listening public: 'After a word from Trevor Bailey it will be Christopher Martin-Jenkins.' Nothing more than that. No goodbye.

I went to meet him as he came down the few wooden steps at the back of the commentary box, mopping his brow with the familiar red and white spotted handkerchief, the black tie loose round his neck. I said, 'I thought you would have reflected for a moment and said something more romantic than that.'

The loving scowl was followed by the raised eyebrows and the illuminating smile. 'What's more romantic than the clean break?' he said.

The MCC Committee had invited him to lunch on that final day but he declined. 'Why now?' he wanted to know. 'They never asked me before.' And then he went on to confess, 'Never much liked Lord's.'

After his departure from cricket employment, he returned just once to a Test match and that was to open the Neville Cardus stand at Old Trafford. By this time, he had left The Old Sun and was living in The Vines in Alderney. He had truly left us.

In 1984 I was asked by BBC producer David Rayvern Allen to travel to John Arlott's home in Alderney to interview him for radio on his seventieth birthday. The small aircraft wobbled from Eastleigh to Alderney in driving rain. I walked towards the windowed hut, which was the terminal building. Leaning forward, hands on a shelf, peering through the rain, John smiled, then waved. David Rayvern Allen was already there with him. We shook hands and laughed before John hoisted his faithful brown leather bag on to a flat counter where incoming travellers were handing over their tickets. Out came the bottle of white Burgundy, followed by three glasses and a corkscrew. An hour later we were on the second bottle and in the middle of travellers seeking to check out of Alderney for the mainland. Next we were in John's small car, which complained loudly as he fiddled with gears up hills and round tight corners. It stopped. It took some time to get to The Vines where we failed to complete the forty-five-minute radio recording until the third day. Lunch was good, dinner was brilliant; work, however, was confined to short bursts. To find a voice in the morning, John had to begin with his phlegm-cutter.

'Read us this poem?' David asked at the start of the second day.

John began: 'Beyond the score-box, through the trees, Gleamed Severn, blue and wide, Where oarsmen "feathered" with polished . . .' he fluffed the line. Take two. 'Beyond the score-box . . .'

On the fifth take he exploded. 'Gawd. Who wrote this unrhythmical, non-scanning tripe?'

'Er, you did, John.'

He produced a glorious grin and proceeded to read it perfectly, commenting afterwards, 'When you know it's tripe it's easier to deliver.'

John was modest and rather shy. At the very end of his life, in *Who's Who* his entry did not mention cricket at all. It read: ARLOTT John, OBE – wine and general writer, the *Guardian*: topographer and former broadcaster.

I was honoured to be asked by his son Tim and third wife, Pat, to deliver the address at his memorial service at the Parish Church of John the Baptist in Alresford.

I am not going to take you on a trip through John's life because I will get lost in the police force where he spent some formative years or in the BBC poetry department or in his books on snuff, on cheese, on champagne, on churches on the Scilly Isles or on many other subjects as well as cricket. If I tried to applaud the complete Arlott today, I would fail.

So I must talk about the John Arlott I know. It is my pleasure and honour to begin a trickle of reminiscence, which I hope will become a flood after the service when you are outside in the high street telling each other your own tales. I think if John could see Alresford this afternoon, full of good friends, possibly with a glass of wine in their hands, then he might forgive us for turning up and making such a fuss about him on a Monday morning.

John never believed in privilege, or ease. We often discussed our similar backgrounds – cricket played on the road as boys, little money, the local primary school, fights in the yard and pink custard. And then the grammar school and advancement by further education, which may or may not be available. John's was not: he was self-taught and found his heroes in craftsmen – they had blown glass or turned the leg of a chair or beat a piece of silver or, in cricket, worked out the angles to play the forward defensive stroke without risk on a turner.

Always I shall remember his departures from cricket grounds around the country, maybe with Johnny Woodcock or Clive Taylor . . . a telephone call home. 'On the way' was the message, and off the Wessex boys would go. The Old Sun would soon provide the balm for the furrowed brow.

He certainly loved cricketers and he grew to understand the finer technicalities of the game. As a commentator, by placing himself inside the cricketer's head, he could hear the heart beat, understand the hopes and fears and the financial frailties of the average county professional, the worries and the hard-learned skills. He rightly observed, 'They call it a team game, but it is in fact the loneliest game of them all.' He looked for expressions of pleasure and pain and he would not have enjoyed so much the faceless game played inside helmets.

He especially loved his native Hampshire, the county itself but also its county cricketers. By the time I had read Arlott, I almost knew the pulse rate of every Hampshire player from 'the deeply considered, rationalised technique' of Phil Mead to the mind of the man he called Anderson Roberts 'which works coolly and clearly behind his rather brooding, veiled look'.

There was Ingleby and Marsh and Butch and Henry and Danny and there was Sains, Peter Sainsbury, 'whose hair always looks as if it was cut yesterday'. John could write about the truly great player, like Barry Richards appealing 'both to the savage and the artist in us', but somehow he felt more for the loyal professional like Mervyn Burden, whose humour was never extinguished by failure and whom John simply called 'salt of the cricketing earth'.

Perhaps of all, it was Leo he talked of mostly . . . his friend Leo Harrison. At the dinner table at Nottingham or Manchester or wherever, John would stretch, interlock both hands to describe Leo's leg-side stumping off Derek Shackleton, collector's pieces, or the one-handed spectacular ones off Jimmy Gray's inswing. Of course, it was only when I played against them that I realised Leo did well to get a hand on Jimmy Gray's inswing let alone perform a stumping. John was proud when the professional players of the country made him their president.

John did love radio commentary. I watched at close quarters and agree with Alan Gibson, his talented colleague, that the poet's gifts helped make him a perfect commentator because a sequence of actions he could reduce to a sentence, and emotions to a word. But if you ask me, it was John's judgement that made him a great commentator. For such a prolific reader, collector, talker and listener it would have been easy to overload his commentaries with outside information, with cleverness. Never. A high point of his brilliance was silence. Each word was important, but nothing more important than silence. It was said that he just chipped away at the English language in public. This was his commentary at Headingley in 1957, England playing the West Indies:

'Loader to Johnny Goddard, yet again with an innings collaps-ing around his ears. He settles, the close field fit themselves round, Loader comes in, bowls [great roar from the crowd as the effects microphone takes over] . . . moving down the line of what to him was an outswinger . . . the stump leaning drunkenly back.' But you see, he is not deflected by the one *mot juste* . . . he keeps the cricket balance. He smoothly continued: '. . . 142 for 8 and the possibility, I think, is now not to be precluded that England may bat tonight and sample themselves the effect of a new ball in this light and in this atmosphere.'

I should end with accolades, celebrate 'The Voice of Cricket' and begrudge its passing. I should say how giants like John Arlott built a profession for those who follow. But he would deflect the personal praise, I know, and would prefer simply to be recalled today and always as the loving father of his children and husband of his wife, and true friend of cricketers and craftsmen the world over.

TOWARDS A PROPER JOB

Married on 22 August 1962 in Neath, Joan and I set off to make a new life together in the big city, Cardiff! In South Wales there is east and west; we were west and still shaking our heads about the country's decision to make Cardiff, not Swansea, the capital of Wales. As Joan's smart new Mini eased away from the wedding reception, I fell asleep in the passenger seat. We were on a journey of forty miles up the A48 to a rented house in Heathwood Road. Local newspapermen had wanted a few quotes on cricket for the *Neath Guardian* and *South Wales Evening Post*, mainly from Wilf Wooller who was at the wedding with Enid. From me, they wanted to hear honeymoon plans. Were we flying to the Canary Islands or somewhere exotic? I did not want to admit that we were going to hide away in Cardiff for a few days before I went back to the Glamorgan team, so I told them we were off to the West Country. To complete the fraud, I explained that my wife was driving because I was tired. How does a twenty-four-year-old county cricketer admit that he can't drive? Age grows wisdom and eliminates pride, so I can now, at the age of sixty-five, confess that our wedding night was spent in the company of close friends in Cardiff, David and Sandra Herbert, sipping Brains beer at the Llanishen Indoor Bowls Club. On our fortieth anniversary, David and Sandra joined us for supper at El Porto in Cardiff Bay.

Wilf Wooller, not a man who understood why soppy domestic considerations such as births, deaths, weddings or funerals should ever keep a Glamorgan player off the field, stood by his promise that the county would pay for Joan to be with me during the next two away matches at Hastings and Blackpool. At Hastings I scored 151 runs in two hours and fifty-five minutes in the first innings against Sussex, and 75 in the second. Joan drove all the way from Hastings to Blackpool but when we arrived at the Imperial Hotel we learned that the Glamorgan office had failed to book us in. I am not sure if we slept inside the service lift or alongside it in a broom cupboard, but I know we heard the comings and goings of everybody, including the pop star Chubby Checker and his entourage. Batting was less successful.

One thing was certain, it was time to go out into the world and find work. To buy time, I accepted the job of Assistant Secretary of Glamorgan County Cricket Club, helping to run a national membership campaign with a professional agency. It was during that first winter that Joan and I had our first discussion about county cricket. How long should I play? The conclusion reached then, and each year for the following decade, was 'Well, if you enjoy it, give it one more summer.' This is not to imply a reluctance to play but, in the 1960s, a proper job was more important to me than cricket. Joan was the one who brought in regular money by her school teaching but here was I with a degree, shuffling paper in the Glamorgan cricket office.

At the cricket itself I was naturally competitive and I enjoyed shaping innings for the benefit of the side, but I had no interest at all in the accumulation of runs for their own sake. Averages were fine but not for me. I still believe that averages logged in one-day matches ought to be burned. Batsmen in Glamorgan were unlikely to break run-scoring records because the pitches on which we played were prepared by roller and rake in that order for the benefit of spinners, many on public parks and all uncovered. If you were setting out to make a grand career as a batsman in the 1960s, you would not have

Where it all began – playing cricket on Bracken Road, Neath: (back row) Graham Bird, me with bat in hand, Micky Williams, Clive Harris, Tudor Thomas, Alan Jordan; (front row) Robert Stevens, Peter Jenkins, Cyril Griffiths, Waverley Doughty

Because of the war, my father, Wilfrid Lewis, was almost a stranger to me till I was eight

Opening the batting for Wales v England Secondary Schools with Alan Rees, a future Glamorgan batsman and Welsh outside half

This picture of me with my mother, Marjorie, and baby sister, Heather, was taken in 1942 and sent as a keepsake to my father

5051643 A/C Lewis, A.R. perfecting the skill of spit and polish at RAF West Kirby in the Wirral

Lining up (back, left) for the Royal Air Force v Army match in 1958. Barry Knight (front, left) and Peter Parfitt (front, third from right) would also go on to play for England – but more than my cricket career was nearly ended in Air Force cricket that Summer

Batting during the University match at Lord's in 1960. Fielding (left to right) are David Green (mid on), Javed Burki (third man), Dan Piachaud, Alan Duff, A.C. Smith, Charles Fry and Abbas Ali Baig – members of a most talented team. I also found time to collect a Special Award for my academic work (or lack of it) that year

Clearing my lines in a game for Cambridge against Newport in 1959 – the battle was on for a coveted Blue

Wilf Wooller, the Skipper, batting for Glamorgan against Essex. He was to have an enormous influence on the course of my life

The last-ever Gentlemen's XI lines up at Scarborough in 1962 – it was the end of the amateur era. Left to right: Messrs Hutton, Kirby, Richardson, me, A.C. Smith, Wheatley, M.J.K. Smith, Prideaux, Jefferson, White, Drybrough

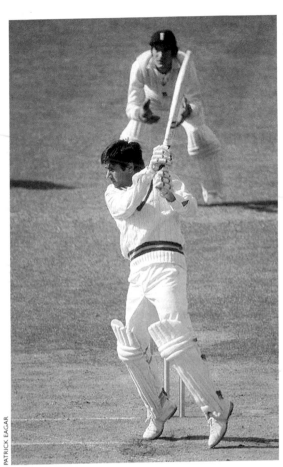

Majid Khan, the brilliant Pakistani Test batsman who helped lift all around him in the Glamorgan side

PATRICK EAGAR

Don Shepherd, a key figure for Glamorgan for many years, begins his classic follow-through

PATRICK EAGAR

In action against
Middlesex

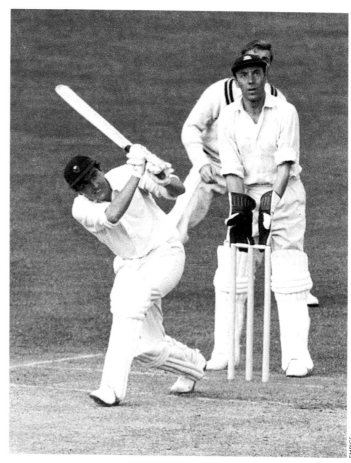

Famous last words:
'I can handle it,
skipper.' Garry Sobers
and Malcolm Nash
meet up at the Sandy
Lane Golf Club in
Barbados,
approximately twenty-
five years after the six
sixes at Swansea

EMPICS

JOAN LEWIS

POPPERFOTO

Captaining
England on my
debut, against India
at Delhi. After a
duck in my first
innings, I scored
70* to help us to a
six-wicket victory

I left my bat in
San Francisco…
The final innings –
opening for MCC
against San
Francisco with
John Jameson
of Warwickshire
and England
in 1980

chosen to play at Cardiff, Swansea, Llanelli, Neath, Margam, Pontypridd, Ebbw Vale or Newport. No Abergavenny in those days! Cricket, however, was fun. I loved it, enjoyed the life, was devoted to the daffodil, but in the back of my mind was the understanding that this was not the profession of a lifetime.

Now that I was married, I realised that my work record to date was unimpressive. My first dash at employment, I guess, was in the sorting room of the Neath General Post Office during a Christmas school holiday. I also picked up the occasional fee for playing the violin in concerts, £1 a Messiah, an Elijah or whatever oratorio was being performed in the vicinity of Neath. Then there was National Service and the weekly queue for payment by the Royal Air Force – salute; '5051643 Aircraftman Lewis A.R. twenty-four shillings'; take the money; 'Sir'; salute and retreat.

I remember those who helped me and how they helped. I had the one failed attempt to report rugby behind me, but in 1963 I tried again with help. Wilf Wooller had become the *Sunday Telegraph*'s Welsh rugby correspondent and his sports editor, Roger Fowler-Wright, gave me a Welsh edition reporter's job, fourth in line after W.E.N. Davies, the former international player, G.V. Wynne Jones, the commentator, and E.R.K. Glover, a Glamorgan cricketer of the 1930s. I was not in action every weekend but small cheques fluttered in. More seriously, I enjoyed the work and this was no surprise to Joan. I had thrown love letters at her like confetti for ten years. Not only did I love her but I could not resist a thick, A4, lined pad – an invitation to scribble. She transformed the small second bedroom of our new semi in Heol Lewis into a working study. I returned from an MCC tour of South Africa in 1964–65 to find an antique desk, second-hand Olivetti typewriter and red telephone extension, party line of course. She had always thought I would write about cricket. When we were teenagers in Neath she had given me *Close of Play* by Neville Cardus as a present and had written inside in her fine writing the familiar words:

> Have you not ever felt the urge to write
> Of all the cricket that has blessed your sight?

Is there no inspiration in the names?
Of those who play our best of summer games!

I did win a job as an account executive in an advertising agency but eventually, in 1965, I tiptoed down Fleet Street with an invitation to meet the sports editor of the *Daily Telegraph*. The guiding hand that led me there belonged to the *Sunday Telegraph*'s cricket correspondent, Michael Melford. For two years I had been the worst foot-in-the-door account executive ever employed by an advertising agency and it was no surprise when C.P. Wakefield decided to close the office in Cardiff. I received the message that I was out of work right at the end of the season, during Glamorgan's match against Essex at Leyton. Michael was at my shoulder and he turned to the nearest telephone to fix an interview with his own sports editor. It was good fortune and I was in his debt. We had a friendship that matured while I was playing and ripened further when I became the *Sunday Telegraph*'s cricket correspondent from 1975 and he took over at the *Daily*.

So, not many weeks after the game at Leyton, I opened the door of the Albion in search of Kingsley Wright. Fleet Street looked magnificently worn and torn, the names of great newspapers carved in stone. I persuaded myself, as I walked past the *Telegraph*'s hefty doors at number 143, that under all the plain coats and hats were newspaper geniuses, great writers, inspirational sports editors and mighty proprietors.

'Hello, old boy. I'm Kingsley Wright.' After a minute of pleasantries he continued in a matter-of-fact way, 'I have watched your freelance work on the *Sunday*, old boy. I like your descriptive.' Strange word to use, I thought, 'descriptive'. He knew little of rugby but a lot about horseracing, enjoying numbers, I think, more than words. We lunched on one gin and tonic, pork chops and coffee. Kingsley wrote the terms of my future engagement as the *Daily Telegraph*'s rugby man in Wales – £5 paid by the piece, ring in every day, forty-five words to a paragraph, no copy taken after five to nine in the evening. 'Good luck, old boy,' a handshake and Kingsley Wright was off back to his desk a couple of hundred yards away. I was worried about the brevity of the meeting, especially as I had travelled by train and tube from Wales, but I had got the job, a proper job – nothing permanent, mind, no talk of a contract or pension or anything like that.

I was lucky because South Wales was the centre of early floodlit rugby in Britain. It was freezing work and Dorothy, my mother-in-law, bought me two pairs of long johns. After several seasons of covering Welsh rugby, I could lay a hand on a telephone within a hundred yards of every ground in the Principality. There was too much of a rush for the nearest clubhouse phone or the red box up the street, so I used to smooth the way early in the season by cruising round private houses offering hand-outs – to Mrs Jones of Pontypool, a ten bob (50p) note; to Mrs Evans of the Cross Keys, a big box of Black Magic; to Mrs Davies of Llanelli, a small gift chosen by my wife. I asked Kingsley if I could include these in my expenses. 'Of course, old boy. It's the way we work.' He was no pushover, however. Whenever I rang him to 'sell' him a match, he would always try to knock back the request, but his main concern was the timing of the game, not the quality.

'What have you got for me, old boy?'

'Cardiff are playing Newport. Great game.'

'No good, old boy. Kick-off half past seven. Too late.'

'Look, what about this one? Abertillery against the Metropolitan Police. It starts at seven.'

'We'll have that. Three paras at half-time, top and tail one and one, and come on to copy before the end.' It was money; it was music.

Our family affairs took an upturn when Joan decided to give up school teaching and open one of the fashionable boutiques she had seen spring up when she had been teaching in London before we were married. It appeared there was money to be made in Carnaby Street and her idea was to bring the latest London fashions to Rhiwbina, a gentle suburb of Cardiff. Following the rage for pop music, which now beat its way into everyone's life, had come a revolution in fashion design, especially in clothes for the young. Small designer labels attacked the mass production for large department stores.

So during the winter months, I found myself sitting in trade shows in London, appraising the latest designs of Mary Quant, Jean Varon,

Jean Muir, John Stephen, Gina Fratini, Tuffin and Foale and seeing Joan sell them in Cardiff to ardent customers. The Popsie Boutique was a first in Wales and Joan was the first to persuade Laura Ashley, who made clothes at her home in Carno in mid Wales, to release some individual items for retail. I recall sitting next to the chief buyer for House of Fraser at a Mary Quant Ginger Group show in a basement in South Molton Street.

'I like that,' the lady turned to say before running her pencil down her order form. 'Yes. Nicely waisted, lovely cut without being too severe, don't you think? I think two dozen in a ten and the same in a twelve.'

I whispered to Joan on the other side, 'What do you think?'

She replied, 'I think it will fit Mrs Paine. I'll take one in a ten and one in a twelve as well.'

In this private enterprise, I was mainly the packer and chauffeur – I had learned to drive by then. We boasted 'in London yesterday, in Cardiff today'. I had an occasional role as fashion-show compère, which was fun, and, very rarely, I was left alone in the boutique while Joan went to London on a buying trip. I knew I used to put off potential customers, who would hover and peer in from outside, but I did boast one profitable day at the till when a gent, with loud confidence, came in to insist that the four suspender belts of assorted colours on display all suited him and he would take the lot.

The Popsie Boutique was by far our best earner. I have to report, however, that the moment we turned the key in the door to open the business, Joanie was pregnant. Within three years, our two daughters, Joanna and Anabel, were in action. Joanna was born in 1967 when I had just succeeded Ossie Wheatley as captain of Glamorgan, and Anabel arrived in 1969 when we won the county championship. We clinched it in our last home match at Sophia Gardens and, in a twinkling, Sophia became Anabel's middle name. She has never complained but is thankful we were not still playing at Cardiff Arms Park.

Joan allowed the lease of the boutique to run out without renewal, closed the door on Carnaby Street and settled for family life. I enjoyed the freelance life but, in retrospect, should have made success at cricket more the daily target of my life. On reflection, 1966 was important when I scored more runs, than anyone in the country, and was twelfth man in the fifth Test against West Indies, but there was no Test tour by England that winter. A few months spent experiencing the game at the top might have removed the fixation on finding a secure job.

No journal or magazine paid too little for me to refuse the invitation to contribute. I wrote 3,000 words a month for *Welsh Rugby* magazine for three guineas. Stuart Weaving was the owner and there was a little extra to be gained by turning out for his weekly 'Sports Forum'. Wills were the sponsors and Stuart, who became a millionaire by running charter flights to South Africa for relatives cut off from members of their families by the discontinuation of scheduled flights to the apartheid republic, gave us £3 an appearance. Sportsmen who would be wealthy in this century were comparatively poor in the 1960s. My panel mates were John Charles and Derek Tapscott, the Welsh soccer internationals, Howard Winstone, world champion boxer, Joe Erskine, a classy European heavyweight, Ken Jones, the flying Welsh wing-three-quarter, Bryn Meredith, the famous hooker, and Lyn 'the Leap' Davies, who had won the long-jump gold medal at the 1964 Olympics in Tokyo. Otherwise, it was the red phone and me, face-to-face every day alongside the Olivetti with carbon paper neatly boxed.

The break into radio came through rugby writing. Tom Davies, sports producer at BBC Wales, offered me the chance to rush back to the studio in Park Place, Cardiff, on Saturday evenings to deliver a post-match report on whatever game I had seen. It should fill one minute and fifteen seconds of airtime exactly. Like Kingsley Wright, Tom was factual and practical; it mattered not so much what I said as long as I finished on the dot. I owe a lot to both editors because I learned speed and discipline at the same time. Soon, I could ad lib a first-edition report to the *Telegraph* copywriters on a whole rugby international, and on radio, speak 225 words at three words a second for one minute fifteen seconds from brief notes. Safe communication was everything. Neither Tom nor Kingsley were interested in traffic jams, trains not running or telephones missing.

Without doubt my radio skills were further developed by Gareth

Bowen, father of Jeremy Bowen, the BBC News reporter and presenter. Gareth was editor of the BBC Radio Wales current affairs programme 'Good Morning Wales', the opt-out of London's 'Today'. I did a winter's stint as presenter and suddenly my curiosity had to widen beyond sport. Gareth was a trained newspaper journalist and taught me directness in asking questions. I often accused him of being naturally nosey, and I think he was, but soon I could see that he had the most important natural talent in the newsgathering business. He knew I faced the problem of credibility, everyone knowing I was a cricketer and assuming that I had no record of understanding politics and national affairs. Writing informative scripts on the miners' strike, disputes in the steel industry or on human-interest stories was a million miles from the forward defensive stroke. Gareth, however, had faith and pushed me on.

To be honest, I learned a lot on my first day. Dai Francis, secretary of the Mineworkers Union, sat across the green baize of the studio table.

'Now, look yer, brother,' his strong hand stretched out and grabbed my wrist. 'Are you telling me that £8 a week is a fair increase for the hardest working men in the world? Have you been underground?' he splattered me all over Studio 6. I looked for the towel to come fluttering in but my producer, Dewi Smith, with whom many instructive pints would be drunk in the BBC club, talked me through the battle. I read a few news items and cued in a taped interview as the next live studio guest was being guided to the opposite chair. I looked up. 'Live' was hardly the word. A large black woman sat slumped and appeared to have gone to sleep. Her eyes were still closed as I moved to the first question. 'What a pleasure to welcome Winifred Attwell to the studio this morning. Tell me, Winnie – you've just come back from a concert tour in Australia – what was it like?' In fact, I knew she had just come by taxi from Tito's nightclub in Cardiff where she was doing a week's cabaret. Must have been a helluva night!

Suddenly, the eyes opened and the face was alive, telling me about the scenes up in the Blue Mountains, around the bars in Sydney, life on the Gold Coast, all vividly anecdotal until suddenly, silence and slump,

TOWARDS A PROPER JOB

her whole body shut down again. I threw in a question about Cardiff, hoping it would hit her hard and bring her to life again. 'Cardiff, Tony?' Up she popped again, teeth providing the crescent of a wonderful smile, all sincerity and fun. 'Do you know, Tony [she got my name right twice], I have relations in Cardiff. I love that Tiger Bay. What a terrific audience last night. I played "Black Bottom Stomp" and, my God, they listened. You couldn't hear a siphon squirt. Gee! I love Cardiff.' Then the lights went out again. Her eyelashes looked glued together. A couple of quick questions and I quit while I was ahead. Winnie left me with a giant hug. It quickly sunk in that I had seen showbiz professionalism at work for the first time.

After a month of 'Good Morning Wales', Gareth Bowen, with proper timing, began to talk about my voice. 'Free it up. Use the full register. You seem a bit inhibited by your sporting reputation,' I remember him saying. The name Mrs Betty Rolls was mentioned. 'An elocutionist. Yes. Cliff Morgan went to her,' he was sure.

I presented myself to Mrs Betty Rolls, tutor to actors, actresses, after-dinner speakers and novice broadcasters, who was boldly dressed in the colours purple, pink and black. The theatre was open. Her diction was slow and precise, the voice coming from the diaphragm depths, and her movements positive.

'Since you telephoned, Mr Lewis, I have listened to your morning programme on the radio. As you suggested, you do sound stiff and embarrassed. You've got a communication blockage. We must help you forget you ever were the cricket captain of England.' I nodded.

'Right, Mr Lewis, I will sit in my armchair and you will stand on that upright chair in the middle of the room.' She took her regal pew and I hesitated, but seeing in her face no change of plan, I stepped up. Sonorously and precisely, she instructed, 'Tell me that you love me, Mr Lewis.'

'You want me to say out loud that I love you?' I smiled without any confidence.

'Not only tell me that you love me, Mr Lewis. Believe that you love me.'

'I love you, Mrs Rolls,' I croaked.

'I do not believe you, Mr Lewis.'

It crossed my mind that it was about midday in a respectable suburb of Cardiff and here was I, standing on a chair, pledging eternal love to a loudly dressed middle-aged lady, a complete, colourful stranger. I would have promised anything to get down.

'I do. I really, really do love you, Mrs Rolls.' She appeared unconvinced.

'Find some power and sincerity in your voice, Mr Lewis.' After many repetitions, she nodded, congratulated me, crossed her legs and said, 'So now, Mr Lewis. Tell me how much you hate me.'

'God! I hate you, Mrs Rolls.'

'You do not mean that, Mr Lewis. Just a minute ago you were in love with me.'

'I hate you, I hate you, I hate you, Mrs Rolls.'

Some lessons take longer to learn than others, but I hated her more than I loved her and soon it was over. 'Now to your diction, Mr Lewis.'

I returned to Mrs Rolls twice more, and pronounced my love and my hate with equal passion. She was so right. I was never going to be extrovert but I did need to understand the theatre involved in broadcasting. Betty Rolls got my lips moving and never again did I place my own image between the material and the microphone.

Broadcasting and writing in Wales was wholly satisfying. I did eleven years under contract to HTV Wales, presenting their weekly sports programme 'Sports Arena' as well as a winter arts magazine. I was surrounded by consummate professionals, Hugh Johns, the ITV football commentator who lived in Cardiff, Dewi Bebb, the former Welsh wing-three-quarter, a sports editor and performer of sound judgement, wide knowledge and sensitivity, and the most talented producer-directors in Euryn Ogwen Williams and Don Llewellyn. We filmed all over Wales before rushing news items through the cutting rooms on to the screen every Thursday evening of the winter months.

By the time I finished playing cricket, my writing and broadcasting work had touched many aspects of interest and I was well prepared for the step into a full-time media life. It certainly ensured that when serious injury came in the early 1970s, I was out of the game quickly rather than staying to fight back with the physiotherapists.

I limped out of cricket a few games into the 1974 season. In the late summer, Roger Fowler-Wright came to Glamorgan, stayed the night with us and offered me a job on the *Sunday Telegraph*. It was exactly what I wanted. Without discussion I agreed to become the newspaper's rugby and cricket correspondent for £3,500 per annum. I was confident. I had been a sporting writer all through my playing career. Within the month, I was scribbling rugby match reports and rewrites, often with a pint and pasty at the back of the Twickenham press box, or else in the cold darkness of the last car on a muddy field. It was, as my mother would have it, my first 'proper job'.

Sporting writers moved from game to game and in that sense became part of a team. There was a Rugby Writers Club and one for cricket, too. Edinburgh, Dublin, Paris, London and Cardiff, the rugby show was always on the road at weekends. Only one international match was played per weekend in those days so the Five Nations tournament spread over three months after Christmas. Writing is a lonely task: newspaper columnists must be comfortable in their own company. I recall a conversation with Peregrine Worsthorne, of the *Sunday Telegraph*, about the wisdom of calling our cricket writers together for a team lunch before the season started. 'An interesting idea,' he thought, 'but I always believed journalism to be essentially a singular occupation. You lock yourself away and do it yourself.' He was right, of course. Unless you attack the blank sheet daily with your own information, you will not have the sharpness to attract a regular readership. On reflection, working for a newspaper is very like playing in a cricket team – it is your own solo, even selfish, performance that contributes to the corporate end.

Cricket, however, had taught me one mighty lesson: you must recognise your weaknesses and fight them in order to improve, whether they are personal, temperamental or technical. Success, I was beginning to understand, involved slaying the devils within, buttressing personal failings, as much as letting talent fly at the mirage of a profession. I remember sitting next to Mike Brearley on an Indian Airlines flight to Bombay, giggling and admitting that when I finished playing cricket, I sat down and concluded that I knew little at all about anything other than cricket. Not true, we agreed. After cricket, we knew ourselves.

To join the *Telegraph* cricket pages was to start at the top. Michael Melford, who was about to succeed Jim Swanton on the *Daily* as cricket correspondent, had first recommended me to Roger Fowler-Wright. Michael and Jim created my opportunity and I am forever grateful to them.

I recall dinner in a beautiful home beside the beach in Gibbs Bay, Barbados. The evening tide crashed in not far from our feet and American accents dominated. Jim and Ann Swanton were houseguests; John Woodcock, Michael Melford, Joanie and I joined the party for dinner. Our American hostess, wearing a long, simple string of Cabuchon emeralds, suddenly pointed at me as if I had popped out of a palm tree. 'So you are Tony and you are joining the *Telegraph*. Don't tell me. I know. Michael will succeed Jim, but you are the young man who is setting off on the long road the great Jim once walked. Gee! What moccasins to fill!' It was like joining a private club, a profession of diligence and courtesy. Cricket was loved and protected, friendships were made all over the Test-playing world. It was the custom to spin a web of personal, handwritten letters across the globe to and from family or friends. There were readings at dinner if some contained common interest. Replies were cooked in the mind for days before the announcement would come over the mulligatawny soup in the Melbourne club, 'I posted to old Billy Becher today. I must do J.J. Warr tomorrow.' In the imprint of the famous moccasins, I walked down the corridor of the Adelaide club, towel over my shoulder, to the communal bathroom; signed for a gin in the Melbourne club and poured my own measure; accepted membership of the Arabs (founder E.W. Swanton); and listened intently whenever advice was offered. Jim and I once were travelling together in a London taxi to the *Wisden* annual dinner when Jim, *sotto voce* from behind a white silk scarf and beneath a black Homburg hat, looking straight ahead, advised, 'Do not keep all your eggs in one basket. The signs in Fleet Street are worrying.' I could hear Churchill, 1941: 'For the moment there is a lull, but we expect that before long the enemy will renew his attacks upon us.'

Serious and often solemn about his duty to cricket writing, Jim cast himself as *fidei defensor* and arbiter of standards. He often appeared pompous and had his favourites, but he could laugh at himself. His Arabs cricketers loved to prick his pomposity. He was teased, for example, about the index of his autobiography, *Sort of a Cricket Person*, which the boys thought confirmed his reputation as a compulsive name-dropper. The first two names listed are Aarvold, Sir Carl and Abdul Rahman, Tunku – John Woodcock suggested, not a bad pair of openers! E.W. Swanton's life, however, confirmed that cricket could be an all-consuming pursuit, that broadcasting and writing about the game constituted a serious full-time profession. We his successors owed him a debt for that. He had high standards of professional performance that made him almost as prolific a freelance writer after retirement as he was a staff man before. The crucial belief was that cricket, a game to be enjoyed, could only be fun at any level if it was contested in deadly earnest. I agreed completely.

In the early 1960s, I was one of a few Glamorgan players who accepted an invitation to dinner at Delf House, the beautiful Swanton home in Sandwich. Glamorgan were playing at Folkestone, before the advent of Sunday cricket, and so we were able to turn up at the Swantons' dinner-jacketed for a fine Saturday night invitation. We were even more on best behaviour when we arrived to find Gubby Allen present, a Test player from the bodyline series, a former president of MCC, the permanent influence behind the scenes as treasurer, and many times chairman of the England selectors. When you batted at Lord's, you could see Gubby to the left of the committee room window, assessing, you imagined, your technique and your temperament, in short your suitability for the big time. When I got to know the MCC set-up better in later years, I realised that whatever happened on the square did not distract him from the televised racing on his right-hand side.

Jim Swanton offered martinis, Ann Swanton played the piano and by the time we dined, the table was not short of opinions, with Ossie Wheatley, Don Shepherd and Peter Walker giving as good as they got. For some reason, I was driven to blanket silence by a Gubby Allen aside

– 'Don't you have anything to say about cricket?'

I did loosen up after dinner when Gubby quizzed me about the proposed changes to the lbw law. I was a member of MCC's cricket sub-committee and we were both due to attend a meeting in a few weeks' time to discuss changes. He suggested that I should dine at his home next to Lord's on the night before the debate so that he could talk through his views and hear mine.

'Whom shall we invite to join us?' he asked.

'What about Peter Parfitt?' I said. 'He's an old friend of mine from Air Force days, and he is the current captain of Middlesex.'

'Good Lord! I don't want Parfitt,' was the censorious reply. 'What does he know? Think of someone else.'

A couple of days later, Gubby rang me at home. 'Look here, Lewis. I've had second thoughts. We will have Parfitt.' Ah! He had discovered that Parf was a good egg.

'Yes. Parfitt will suit. He's left-handed.'

Jim Swanton came more and more solidly into my working life, for example by the chances of work he chose to send my way. He soon wrote:

I don't know whether word has penetrated yet as far as Cardiff, and it would excite little comment if it had, but I'm having a cut at the MCC c'tee this year, and when you get the candidates' voting form it ought to say 'Upon retirement as cricket correspondent etc.' Proposer Cobham, seconder Warr. Now whether I shall get the star of official approval I don't know – I'd much like to get in without it, but the fact is that no starred candidate has ever missed. Anyway, if by chance I make it, I shan't want to continue to do the page 3 topical 'Off the Cuff' monthly pieces in *The Cricketer*. In that case I hope you will take it on. As you know, we can't compete with big payers, but I expect we could run to, say, £18 if we maintain the present length of 850 words: i.e. £216 p.a.

I was thrilled. What moccasins indeed!

I admired the writer Geoffrey Moorhouse, particularly his book *The Best-Loved Game,* the product of loving eyes cast over the English cricket season of 1978 and a far more perceptive book than could have been written by a regular cricket writer. I wanted to research and write like Moorhouse as I wanted to capture wonderful moments like Cardus, and I pencilled in my diary a paragraph that Geoffrey composed at the Eton versus Harrow match at Lord's:

The two strangers are still rapt, still crooning their allegiance to Winston Churchill's old school. 'Get 'em on the run again, Harr-ohoho! Let's 'ave another wicket, Harr-ohoho!' They are missing nothing out there as Eton go into final collapse. Someone else watches steadily from the crowd in front of the Tavern bar, a tall and heavy man, red-faced these days, with much grey in his thickly swept hair, and fine veins running along a predator's nose. Cardus once wrote of this spectator that 'his attitude to cricket is almost as obsolete as his chivalry': after his last match here, with ten wickets under his belt, he tossed the bails into the MCC members' seats, a gesture as lordly as any man could make. However, that was twenty-two years ago, and I see no hint that anyone by the Tavern has recognised Keith Miller today. There is first-class cricket at The Oval this afternoon but the incomparable Miller, of Melbourne, New South Wales and Australia, has chosen to be at Lord's, to watch a bunch of schoolboys play.

Geoffrey Moorhouse, an author meticulous in all aspects of his labours, soon began work on another cricket book, entitled *Lord's*. He asked if I would meet him to answer some questions and he gave me a fine fish lunch in Soho. After the cricket talk I asked about writing, especially the creation of an individual style. He told me not to strain, that writing is merely the result of answering essential questions and style is merely the way you write those answers down. His words were to help me a lot, especially in the fast work of a Saturday sportswriter scrambling together a rugby match report. As the clock ticked louder in Fleet Street, I reached for the Moorhouse lifeboat instructions – tell the hard news, then decide what the questions are. Now answer them, and the language in which you do it builds your style. I owe Geoffrey Moorhouse lunch.

The business of communicating rugby was natural enough for a South Wales boy: everyone played, and most had strong views and theories to expound. In the winter of 1975, however, I had to make a massive adjustment in lifestyle. My *Sunday Telegraph* duties were to follow England and every weekend I set off to club games as far afield as Truro or Gosforth while the road from Cowbridge to Twickenham was well worn.

Inspecting my diary for 1977, I see that the year began with a report of the England rugby trial at Twickenham, including my opinion that a young second-row forward called W.B. Beaumont of Fylde had merited his promotion from the Rest to the England side at half-time. In the middle of the month, I received a letter from Michael Melford typed on notepaper of the Taj Coromandel Hotel in Madras, where England, under Tony Greig's captaincy, were engaged in a Test against India:

Dear Lewis Sahib, If I tell you that Woodcock and I are counting the days until Feb. 18, it is merely because I for one am too old for the dust, dirt and discomfort and inevitable argument before you get anything done. I don't doubt that the players are enjoying themselves and, of course, on a vastly higher income than us. Test tickets are now being flogged and when I tell you that players are seen in front of the main enclosure flogging miniature cricket bats to small Indian boys at 200 rupees apiece, you will know that business is thriving.

The captain Tony Greig's progress round India is what you would expect, having seen him warming up last time – otherwise beyond belief. He is, of course, idolised by the public, and with press and public he has not put a foot wrong. Press conferences are called by the manager in the manager's room, but the manager does well to get a word in, as the captain answers questions with a charm and diplomacy and articulateness to which ordinary mortals should not be exposed.

I wake up in the morning and take an inventory of my ailments without finding too much wrong so far. But now we have run out of Scotch the future looks grim. Marlar arrived last week and has gone off to see MCC in Bangladesh. He invited me to go with him but it would have meant being robbed of one of my keenest ambitions, which is never to go to Dacca again.

India have batted so badly, but how John Lever came to swing the ball at Delhi when he had never swung it before remains a mystery, most of all, I think, to Lever.

Warm regards from *The Times* correspondent who is struggling with a piece on the Calcutta Derby, which we saw on Saturday. R. Guest, whom Woodcock had interviewed on the previous day for a Sportsview piece and who rides mostly in Denmark, beat J. Lynch a neck. Yrs ever. Michael

Compared with a man who slogged away daily in an office, the colours in my life appeared more varied and richer.

There was detail. Mastering the tiny professional corners of the job would be important. I knew from a decade's experience of rugby writing as a freelance that the best operators were in possession of specific knowledge and a telephone. It now sounds unbelievable that there were no computers and no mobile telephones. There was no job without the lifeline to Fleet Street, to the sports desk and to that delightful colony of cynics, the copy-takers – 'Yeah . . . yeah [yawn] . . . yeah [scoff] . . . yeah . . . yeah [exasperation because they are listening to an idiot] . . . yeah, yeah . . . how much more of this is there? There's more? Wait . . . I'm changing the page . . . yeah . . .' and so on. It was fatal to try to be nice to them. It was far better to assume that you were, in fact, the lowest form of newspaper life and you were jolly privileged to have had your transfer-charge call accepted by them so that you could deliver your considered garbage into their ears. 'Are you going for allegory, mate?' was the biggest put-down of all because it told me that they knew far more than I did about English grammar. They sounded East End market but could give you a burst from H.W. Fowler if they cared. A career in first-class cricket had left me short of literary images. 'Faaack off, mate, you're out' had been the pinnacle of many a bowler's communicative ambitions. A professional batsman regularly met the bowler at the end of his follow-through at which point the expletives might be pouring out. A short burst of blue language from Fred Trueman left you in no doubt that you had just edged the most perfect nip-backing outswinger that ever was brought into the world, but, strangely enough, a stoical stare and turn away by Brian Statham embarrassed me much more.

After five years or so, the copy-takers of the *Telegraph* seemed pleased to deal with me. Certainly in the matter of evening floodlit rugby matches for the *Daily* I kept it simple, but as the *Sunday Telegraph*'s rugby correspondent I felt I could be adventurous. In the end, I won them round to the extent that they would greet news that a Lewis 2,000-word feature was coming their way with, 'Hello, yes, good morning, but I have to tell you my break is in twenty minutes.'

As I think of telephones, I think back to summer days when Joan, Joanna, Anabel and I were staying at Greenway on the River Dart as houseguests of Rosalind and Anthony Hicks. We had the fun of staying there on holiday with Rosalind's son Matthew, Angela his wife, and their children. We were neighbours in Glamorgan. I quickly discovered at Greenway how important it was not to be positioned near the telephone in the large hall if ever it rang. Matthew's grandmother, Rosalind's mother, Dame Agatha Christie, also in residence, had a short, shiny black dog called Bingo, who did not like telephones ringing. At the first brrr he would go 'grrr' . . . and launch himself like a missile into the hall, his jaw lowered like a plane opening its undercarriage to drop the wheels, before skidding along the hallway straight into your leg. Bitten-by-Bingo was the common fate of the uninitiated. A week with Bingo would have cured for life Vivian Jenkins's desire to be near a telephone and in touch with his office.

I frequently worked in the same rugby press box as Vivian Jenkins of the *Sunday Times* and watched how he worked. 'Friday is important,' he would say. 'Your job begins on Friday.' This meant that he travelled early to a home international and visited the press box on the day before the match to ensure that his telephone had been installed and was working. I cannot say that he was the absolute master of planning and organisation but he knew the rules. His faithful friend, Bryn Thomas of the *Western Mail*, was always on hand to tidy up loose ends.

Viv and I were at Morpeth for one of the newfangled John Player Cup knock-out matches, where the home club had generously hired a double-decker bus as a touchline press box, sideways to the play, a bit of a neck-twister. I was by this time the *Sunday Telegraph*'s rugby correspondent and we had hefty reports to transmit. After the final whistle, we sat upstairs for about an hour, knowing that we had booked telephones in the houses adjacent to the small ground, about two hundred yards away. Rain began to lash heavily against the bus windows, which misted over. When the bus started up and began to move off, our concentration was unbroken. Suddenly, Viv jumped up, legs tangled in his famous plaid rug, and shouted, 'Stop the bus! Where's the bell? Stop the damn bus. My phone! My phone!' Our lifeline to Fleet Street, the row of houses with the phones, was not to be seen. We were off to the bus depot.

Our differing temperaments surfaced. I patiently pressed the bell to attract the driver below while Vivian thundered downstairs, scrambled to the partition that separated the driver from the passengers and hammered on the glass, yelling clear threats of dismemberment. Viv's panic worked in one sense – the driver got the message. It misfired in another, however, because the driver was too frightened to leave his cabin. Instead of allowing us to direct him to the road with the telephones, he bumped the bus back to the centre of the rugby pitch, leaving us a long walk through the downpour before contact was made at last with a copy-taker.

It was not a good night for seeking out Vivian's company because after a glass or two, he was capable of grabbing any passerby by the throat, accusing him of being the bus driver.

I learned rugby lessons from Vivian Jenkins, proving that analysis of opponents in the tiniest detail has been with us forever.

While I was a rugby writer, the squad system was introduced to international rugby and Ray Williams wrote his compelling thesis called *Winning Rugby*. Carwyn James advanced team preparation to new heights when in 1971 he coached the Lions to victory in New Zealand. It was easily assumed that the older players and writers had played their rugby by natural talent and a few pints of beer. Wilf Wooller, however, could describe endless practice in passing the ball at full speed a couple of strides ahead of the receiver. The ball transferred at a decent speed, long or short, could beat the opposition if the back division was moving at its fastest. He would draw diagrams on match programmes in the press box when he saw a back sending out a pass without leaning inwards to draw a defender. Another Wooller theme was the value of the short punt ahead when opposition backs lay up too flat, but, essentially, the kicker had to be running from a deep-lying position so that he was moving at top speed when he kicked. He would often point to the Welsh wing, the sprinter J.J. Williams, and sigh, 'Kicking and chasing at speed! Still could be a big part of the modern game.'

Wilf, like Viv, played international rugby in the 1930s when there was no television and it was impossible to make a detailed study of your opponents. Viv once did manage it, when he was selected to play for Wales against England at Swansea in 1936. England fielded the side that had beaten the All Blacks at Twickenham 13–0, a game already famous for the try by the Russian on England's right wing, Prince Alexander Obolensky. How could Wales stop the brilliant Obolensky? Against New Zealand he had cut across the field from the right to the tryline on the left, leaving a prostrate defence behind him. How could the Welsh defence work it out?

A few days before the game, Viv went to the Castle cinema in Swansea because he had heard that Obolensky's try was included in the Pathé Pictorial News. Patiently, he sat through both A and B movies and then in a flickering four seconds Obolensky scored. 'I thought, did he turn out to the right touch before coming in off the right foot?' There was nothing for it, Viv had to see the films again, three hours of them, to wait for a second look at the newsreel. 'Damn! How far was he in from touch when he cut inside?' So he sat through both movies for the third time to accumulate a full twelve seconds of Obolensky side-stepping and sprinting. The tale is as long as he wants to make it.

We shared it last with Sir Tasker Watkins, president of the Welsh Rugby Union, at Cawshays' dinner for Viv's ninetieth birthday at the Cardiff Hilton Hotel in 2002.

The match was a giant clash because Wales, too, had defeated New Zealand, by 13–12 in Cardiff. Viv's meetings with his team-mates Cliff Jones and Wilf Wooller were crucial. They had the speed to suit the plan, which was this – Viv would stay solidly on the inside of Obolensky, Wooller and Jones would race back and across and try to get outside Viv in order to tackle the flying wing-three-quarter on the outside break.

It ended Wales 0 England 0, and the report reads:

Prince Obolensky, on the wing, could not break through an unflinching Welsh defence. Attackers were subdued and eventually obscured by systematic defensive covering and dour tackling. Barney McCall and Viv Jenkins blotted out the threat from Obolensky.

Viv told us, 'Barney McCall, our left-wing, did well but it was our plan, which worked. Obolensky, seeing Wilf and Cliff cutting back and across so quickly, turned inside and woomph! I gave it to him, every time.'

I had another mentor in Alan Gibson, who wrote cricket for *The Times* and broadcast as a commentator on rugby and cricket. On Saturday evenings during the winter, he presented the BBC West of England sports programme and once invited me to contribute with an account of the match just played between Bristol and Cardiff. I sat in front of Alan and unfolded my written report. He wagged a corrective finger at me and when the microphone was off said that he would not allow reading on his programme. 'Write down the scores but otherwise just tell us the story,' he said. I never forgot that. Don't read; tell the story, even if you have to hold a stopwatch in front of you for the producer's sake. It echoed John Arlott urging me not to broadcast but to talk to people, and led to another skill, useful for longer pieces – preparing the written script that could read like a story.

CHAPTER 9

BROADCASTING FOR A LIVING

My broadcasting experience in Wales and the captaincy of England made the next step a logical one, into the BBC cricket commentary boxes. I was fortunate to work with both radio and television as commentator and summariser, and eventually as the BBC cricket presenter on television, which was to give me permanent employment at Test matches. At first, I was mostly in radio, and it was not easy to mix the roles because each has its own disciplines. In radio commentary, you have to be up with the moment, on the front foot playing the shots, appealing for lbw and diving for catches as they happen, and screaming the warning of a run-out. As a summariser, as Fred Trueman and Trevor Bailey were, you sought to be a high-quality, back-foot player, pausing but ready with swift reactions. The television commentator waits a pulse after the action so that, in the main, the pictures lead the way. The summariser works to collect relevant analysis in words and pictures, constantly in communication with the director who is pushing the buttons in the van behind the stands, and making available the illustration of the point you seek to make. On television, viewers could be shown the scoreboard; on radio, the producer, Peter Baxter, used to put a written note in front of us – 'Would the commentator please tell the listeners the score!'

The radio box was warm and inviting. You could not sneak in unnoticed when Brian Johnston, the corporation's cricket correspondent, was at the heart of it. It was as if you were welcome to join his party for a day out at the cricket. You stepped over hampers, fruit cakes and bottles of this and that to take your place among the nicknames – Arlo (John Arlott), the Alderman (Don Mosey), Blowers (Henry Blofeld), the Boil (Trevor Bailey), Fred (Trueman) and CMJ (Christopher Martin-Jenkins). Bill Frindall, the scorer, was the Bearded Wonder. I was Arl, from my initials. Brian simply took it from the commentators' rota pinned up in front of him – 'After a word from Fred Trueman it will be Arl.' Then there was Backers, Peter Baxter, the gallant producer who had to organise, or pretend to control, these flying egos. A cork would pop before lunch – a glass of champagne maybe, or wine. Arlo may well have extracted a bottle from his deep briefcase, but his cork used to plop out quietly; practice made perfect. Arlo never left home in Alresford without typewriter and corkscrew.

Meanwhile, Johnners solicited cakes and confectionery over the air, enough for all, and then distributed them to deserving causes in St John's Wood area where he lived. His was the warm presence and the spark of endless fun. This was not work; it was pleasure: the commentaries bubbled without anyone having to force humour. Johnners always led the way with accurate information, the score, the situation and all that, sounding most official in his Old Etonian way, but in his approach to the full day he behaved like a Butlin's redcoat, making sure that every single broadcaster and listener was happy, part of the fun and enjoying their proxy day out at the game.

For example, one day in the late 1960s, I went to see Bill Jerrett, my doctor, in his Pontyclun surgery. 'Test Match Special' was on full blast and I am not sure to this day if I got round to telling him what was wrong with me. It was wise not to present him with a trifling complaint during the course of a Test match.

Not all the commentators suited every one of the listeners, but the skill was in the producer's mixing of the chemistry of voices and personalities. We all took something different to the microphone. It was possible to be scornful of Brian Johnston's jollity, and indeed, John

Arlott, his constant companion in the box, scowled whenever Johnners failed to treat the endeavours of a professional on the field with the appropriate gravitas. Arlott's wide web of story telling and imagery was always strictly attached to the cricket, but as he got older he became more lugubrious and a jape from Johnners was just what the listener needed. John was not pleased by the attentions that Brian Johnston drew towards the commentators and their lives in the box. It was too 'in' for him. John, however, wholly appreciated the lightness of Johnston, his natural broadcasting talent, and the fun. They both were wise and generous, absolutely professional, and their partnership has never been matched. I am left with the sounds of the rich but contrasting voices, their genuine love of cricket, and the irresistible spice of their different paths through life.

These were the doyens when I arrived in the 1970s, true outside broadcasters with no scripts, but seriously prepared. They were in complete control of what they said. They could be trusted to hit the appropriate mood and the words for any eventuality. And a thought repeated – John Arlott, more than anyone else, could manufacture silence: he would admit into commentaries the applause of the crowd for Peter May walking out to bat and the babble of shock and horror if an England favourite had fallen. John Arlott and Brian Johnston should have been knighted because their work made a national, even international, difference to that particular form of communication.

Commentary boxes were usually wooden sheds or lofts with windows situated at the top of old pavilions. Most of them were in line with the play. Whenever I walked into one I was a disaster waiting to happen. I could drop my notes, nudge a chocolate cake on to Bill Frindall's scoresheets, fall over a cable and unplug the kettle. I was aware, however, that the world championship of commentary-box chaos would never be mine as long as Christopher Martin-Jenkins was in the business. Chris would sprint into this tangled, small world, marginally late, with strong emissions of 'dash', 'shhhhugar' and 'schhhubert', putting a foot in a marzipan cricket bat, a pen in his tea and the back of his chair on Don Mosey's chilblain. 'Sorry . . . er, sorry . . . er . . .'

Trevor Bailey and Fred Trueman were the permanent team of experts. Both had been players in the best of England sides but it would have been impossible to harness two more opposite cricketers. Trevor's hard, rather pukka intonations delivered criticism or compliment in a few easily understood words. That was how he batted, with a few easily recognisable and uncomplicated strokes. That was how he bowled, asking the batsman the nagging truth about his judgement of length and ability to kill the ball that moved off the seam: there were no frills about Trevor's excellent play, or about his broadcasting. His understanding of the game was sound, of course; he enjoyed the banter and the pop of the champagne cork before lunchtime – he was champagne prefect – but he was no spinner of yarns as was Fred Trueman. Fred rarely blunted his Yorkshire accent or watered down the inherited Yorkshire conviction that only they understood the game and were right about everything, without bothering to buy a drink for you while you clung on to the bar listening to them thundering home this eternal message.

How fast was Fred Trueman, I am often asked these days? The answer is very fast indeed. He was one of the outstanding bowlers of his age. His run to the wicket was powerful and rhythmical. He dragged on the toe of his back foot to deliver the ball with front foot well over the popping crease as he was permitted to do under the old no-ball law, and that helped him to hurry the batsman. His delivery action was classical and from a sideways position he could bowl the outswinger whenever he wanted. The inswinging yorker was in his armoury, as well as the bouncer. All this skill was garnished with the ripest language heard in the game. He was such a big wicket-taker that Glamorgan batsmen wanted him to be away at the Tests rather than playing against us for Yorkshire, and yet I was always thrilled when he was in the side.

I first met him when I was about to play my first Glamorgan match in Yorkshire, 1960 at Bradford Park Avenue. In the absence of Wilf Wooller, Gilbert Parkhouse was captain. The pitch looked green and there was a considerable gathering of natives filling the low stands and peering over the wall along the pavilion boundary, as if they had seats round a bullring. As was his habit, Fred Trueman began his day in the visitors' dressing room. Glamorgan had some youngsters in the side apart from me. I was batting at three, Alan Jones at four, Billy Davies at seven, Brian Evans at eight, and David Evans, who had not long before taken over the wicket-keeping from Hadyn Davies, at ten. The experience came from Parkhouse, Hedges, Watkins, Walker, McConnon and Shepherd.

Within half an hour, Fred had told us some hilarious stories but in between them had bowled out three dozen of the finest batsmen in the world. Graeme Pollock can't play that 'un he would say, flipping two fingers downwards to demonstrate the wrist action for the bouncer. 'He gets his bat up here, always on t'front foot. Ooh yes, I can roll over Mister Pollock.' He would act out a batsman in a defensive mess. Then he looked at Alan Jones. 'I hope you can hook, sunshine,' he said. Alan went white. Nervous laughter escaped from taut thoraxes. It was funny but life-threatening! Fred had just removed the middle pole of Peter Burge, the off-bail of Garry Sobers, the right knuckle of Bill Lawry, the jazz hat of Hubert Doggart and hit Jackie McGlew under the heart when our skipper returned from the toss. Gilbert announced that he had won the toss and we would bat. Bat? Bat? Fred got up and was about to leave when he turned back at the door. 'Well, it's grand to meet you young lads, new to the game. I wish you well. I'll be seeing you in t' middle, one by bloody one.'

Fred delighted radio audiences for many years but seemed to lose some of his enthusiasm for the game as he saw standards of play drop so badly that he found himself repeating hour after hour the words, 'I just don't know what is going off out there.' At his best, he was a superb broadcaster. Whatever was thrown his way by Johnners, Arlo, the Alderman or others, he could always come up with a tale to inform or entertain.

When I was young, I listened under the bedclothes to Alan McGilvray, the Australian broadcaster, describing the play from an England tour down under, so it was exciting to be working alongside this faraway hero. Alan turned out to be tetchy, to say the least. In Johnners' language, McGillers, like Arlott, did not believe in any sort of commentary-box banter on the irrelevances of the commentators themselves, their breakfast, and their taxi driver, nothing to make it self-centred. He and I had an acid start at a champagne reception for the Ashes teams.

'How dare you call England "we" on the air?' he chided. 'You're supposed to be impartial. I don't want to work with people like you. I never say "we" when talking about Australia.' Wow! Welcome to 'Test Match Special'.

'Did you ever play for Australia?' I shot back at him. Answer, no. 'Then that's why you've never done it.' Game on. Red and irascible, McGillers snorted. Happily, a waiter arrived with the champagne. 'But you're right. Let's drink and forget it, Alan,' I offered.

A smile from McGilvray lit up the whole room. He had made his point, I had hit back, and he appeared to like that. Suddenly, we were comrades in arms and remained good friends. Cricket to him was far from a trivial picnic. He winced whenever Johnners talked about 'turning the arm over' or standing 'behind the timbers'. To McGillers, the players were going about 'their work' and performances were measured in those terms.

I have always found the presence of Christopher Martin-Jenkins in the radio box assuring, offering the lighter resonance and accurate eye of someone who loves cricket and can play a decent game. His writing for *The Times* requires well thought-out opinion and so he goes to the commentary box with his mind made up about the current issues and that helps him to be positive. He can be dogmatic but has an endearing humour. I have always admired the wide scope of his cricket activity, embracing as it does writing, broadcasting and honorary work for organisations such as the Cricket Society.

Peter Baxter, the long-time producer of 'Test Match Special', works hard to form commentary teams when England are abroad on tour and I was useful to him because I was travelling and writing for the *Sunday Telegraph* and could join in radio as well. Outside broadcasts were always an adventure, all over the world. I remember Peter standing in the open-air stands in Melbourne with head and microphone inside an upturned leather box in order to hear his own voice as Bob Willis's

England got home with the last gasp to beat Australia by three runs.

I once joined Peter and Don Mosey for a one-day international in Ahmedabad in India. It was early in England's tour and they looked fresh and eager in a temporary commentary box, tangled underfoot with cables. Peter told us that he was not sure if there was a line to London, but we commentated for about an hour just in case we could be heard. Then came the confirmation that we had been talking to ourselves. Engineers crawled round our seats plugging and unplugging. Wires were passed over us, cables under us. We heard Chris Martin-Jenkins back in London offering classical music and saying, 'We are doing our best to re-establish contact with Ahmedabad.' Suddenly, we realised we had been lashed to our chairs – terrific for bondage, bad for the loo. Eventually, the well-known Baxter temper ignited, which sometimes worked in India, but not often. 'Whoever you are in Bombay,' he yelled into the microphone, 'stop shouting hello, hello stadium. Get off the line, Bombay, and let me hear London . . . Yes, I am Ahmedabad . . . you are not Ahmedabad, you are Bombay . . . I am Ahmedabad. How can you be Ahmedabad when I am Ahmedabad?' It was deafening stuff until Don Mosey turned to Peter and in that northern grammar school accent, always ladled on to expose Baxter as southern and educated by privilege, said, 'You public school twit. You are both Ahmedabad because you're actually carrying out a conversation with the Sikh engineer in headphones who's standing five yards behind you.'

Blowers had a large slice of theatre in him. It was a steaming, hot Saturday morning in Bombay when we trotted down to the studios of All India Radio in order to send two reports back to the BBC Radio sports room in London. The producer, Andy Smith, was waiting to receive a two-minute piece from Henry for 'Sport on Two' and I was to supply my programme, 'Sport on Four', with a few minutes' travelogue. It should have been the second day of the Test match but, in the expectation of a total eclipse of the sun, a rest day had been called. Night was going to fall in the middle of the day, everyone had to stay indoors or risk going blind and many superstitions were gripping the population. For example, if a pregnant woman snapped the branch off a tree, her baby would be born with a broken arm.

Henry began recording first. The small studio filled up with twenty or more disbelieving spectators. I put on headphones to hear the best of British at work, and watched Henry slipping magnificently into his stride, all pistons and steam, along the Great Western Railway line – 'In four hours' time we expect a total eclipse of the sun over Bombay when the skies will fall dark and birds fly out of trees . . .'

'Henry,' I heard Andy Smith call out from the London end. 'Henry.'

It is not that easy to stop a great locomotive. Henry was already building the urgency and, aware of the admiring spectators, began to inject a slight breathlessness around words, including his own brand of false chuckle, very much part of the much-loved Bloefeld delivery style, as if to say to the listener in Blighty, 'My dear old thing, you're missing one helluva drama out here.'

'Kapil Dev with the new ball would be tricky to play . . .'

'Henry!' He heard Andy this time. It was as if the royal train, surging out of Paddington, had been flagged down at Royal Oak. The brakes went on, Henry's spectacles misted up and I could see that he had heard but could not stop his lips moving. It was Slough before he had stopped. I hoped that Andy had a good reason for pulling the communication cord.

'Henry, this is fine, but you're supposed to be telling the 'Sport on Two' listener what might happen after your total eclipse, not before it. You'll have to do a rewrite as if you've been through the eclipse. Guess it. It doesn't matter. We'll keep an eye on the news. It's the cricket scene you're there to report. We can do it within the next hour, after Tony.'

'My dear old thing,' Henry blustered, 'I can't hang around here for an hour.' The grand old engine was too proud to give way. 'Look, keep recording. From the top. Going ahead in five seconds.' He cleared his throat. I thought I heard a whistle and the capacity crowd in the studio leaned forward again. 'Today in Bombay we have just witnessed a total eclipse of the sun, when the skies fell dark and birds flew out of trees . . . The board of control was right to call a rest day because if Kapil Dev had been at his fastest there is no way the England batsmen could have had a clear sight of the ball . . . and superstition abounds here [toot! toot!] you know. They say that if a pregnant woman breaks a twig or a branch off a tree . . . [toot! toot!] . . . and just before the eclipse, the streets of Bombay were empty and that is because it was wholly believed that anyone who looked at the sun, even for a split-second, would be immediately struck blind . . .' It was a breathtaking, brilliant picture of a scene that was about to happen (toot! toot! Swindon already).

That afternoon I played golf at Chembur with Joanie, Jack Bailey, secretary of MCC, and John Thicknesse of the *Evening Standard*. The eclipse arrived, the skies did fall darkish for a few seconds and birds flew wildly out of trees, crazy with the confusion between night and day. We did not stare at the sun, just kept our focus on the ball and the course ahead of us. As it happened, we would have done better to look a little to left and right because in the semi-darkness our caddies had run for cover, leaving our bags neatly stacked at the foot of a tree. We never saw them again.

Cricket commentators need to develop an inner editorial sense. The balance between reporting and romance must be preserved, between fun and hard fact. From the mid 1970s, former cricketers were taken on as commentators. I believe that the professional broadcaster is always necessary, but if proof is needed that a former Test player can grow into the job with style, Jonathan Agnew, the former Leicestershire and England bowler, has provided it. Professional cricketers in the twenty-first century plan a broadcasting future while they are still engaged in the playing of the game. It will become even more competitive to win a place in the commentary box.

Luck and coincidence sometimes leap out of the shadows to create a new opportunity for the freelance journalist, just when the mind is dull and the eye for the gap in the market has misted over. Luck! I was fortunate to captain England at cricket because Ray Illingworth decided to give the India and Pakistan tours of 1972–73 a miss. Ray was fortunate to get the leadership when Colin Cowdrey, the man in possession, snapped an Achilles tendon, and Cowdrey got his first chance to lead when Peter May was forced to undergo surgery in the summer of 1959.

It was luck and coincidence that landed me at the microphone of a new studio sports programme on Radio Four called 'Sport on Four'. I had made a contribution to the flagship programme 'Sport on Two' on the subject of cricket in India, simply setting the scene for batting at Eden Gardens in Calcutta. I described the pandemonium of over 100,000 people in the ground, and how the cricket intelligence of this vast crowd led them to fall silent to hear one of the great spinners, Chandrasekhar, buzz the ball down the pitch to a 'frozen' England batsman. It worked well as a four-minute straight piece for radio and I was pleased to get a telephone call from the head of Radio Sport, Bob Burrows. But 'thank you' was not all he said. His department was about to launch a sports magazine programme on Saturday mornings. He would like me to present it. This meant interviewing, mainly in London, on the Friday and presenting the show on the Saturday from 8.10 until 9 a.m. I would be supported by the sports room's reporters who would provide relevant features and a wide range of high-quality occasional contributions. There would be room for the offbeat as well as for items that directly reflected the news and current sporting events.

I loved it. It was ten years before I vacated that chair and then only because I was struggling desperately to complete the bi-centenary history of the Marylebone Cricket Club. My copy of 140,000 words was so late in the summer of 1986 that the bi-centenary year of 1987 threatened to pass before the book could be published. I was followed as presenter of 'Sport on Four' by Cliff Morgan who also stayed ten years until the programme was taken off the air. In a dream world, and asked to return to any work station of my life, I would choose to go back to 'Sport on Four' and the creative, argumentative world of the BBC Radio sports room. We tapped away at tank-like typewriters – Peter Jones, Des Lynam, Gerry Williams, Chris Rea, Alan Parry, Bryon Butler, Ian Robertson, Tony Adamson, Mike Ingham, Christopher Martin-Jenkins and so many others. I sat down with my producer to help create fifty minutes of high-quality conversation for radio. Producers were made in the image of Bob Burrows himself who taught them never to be satisfied and always to tug the programme around again and again. Ask yourself the listener's questions and provide the answers.

At this time I had an extremely busy schedule and a lifestyle that my parents would not have recognised. I worked hard. 'Sport on Four' could have been made-to-measure. Mostly it was transmitted from Broadcasting House in Langham Place but also from chosen events, and was full of rich sporting conversation. Johnny Miller, the golf champion, was good enough to sit quietly at the edge of a practice putting green in Turnberry to open his heart about the shocking disappearance of his winning skills. He had been through a period of introspection, settled in the warmth of his family and his strengthening Christianity. I learned more about the acid drops of professional competition in that chat than anywhere else. When repeated failure arrives, self-esteem erodes, the dash and devil quit your play, and you are left contemplating only diagrams in a coaching manual or giving serious consideration to tips from the last bin-collector at the practice ground. Then you are one step from hell. Johnny did win again, but he had read the tea leaves of his declining fortunes in the cup and was the stronger for it.

Arnold Palmer trudged off the course at Royal Troon into the BBC on-course caravan. I said, 'I watched you on the par three seventeenth, 223 yards, and saw you settle on a three iron, and I thought of how many three irons you have hit to par threes in your career. Do you ever stand and think, hell, I've had enough?'

'Nope,' he replied. 'Troon gave me the Open in 1962 – I don't think you were here – and it was a record, something like twelve under after four rounds.' Then his tough skin wrinkled, as it must have done many times, into a big smile. 'You never turn your back on a game or a course, or even the three iron, especially one that has been that good to you.'

'Sport on Four' came from the Spartakiad in Moscow, the New Year's Day Test match in Sydney, the regatta in Cowes, Wimbledon, Ibrox and Murrayfield, Lansdowne Road and Cardiff Arms Park, the Commonwealth Games in Edmonton and the Crucible Theatre in Sheffield as well as the racecourse at Aintree. It came from Melbourne, Perth and Paris. Regular experts were at hand to build the debates and the pictures – John Oaksey, Peter Bromley and Terry Biddlecombe on horse racing and Denis Law on football. Mary Peters offered delightful wisdom and modesty from athletics, as did Anita Lonsborough from the poolside. Ian Wooldridge of the *Daily Mail* contributed pieces that brought sharp perspective while Jilly Cooper wrote brilliant essays of lateral thinking. Angela Rippon joined me at Aintree. I whizzed round Silverstone, microphone in hand, in a souped-up saloon car driven by Stirling Moss. My first question to Prince Philip on the royal yacht, moored just off Cowes, was, 'Can you describe, Sir, the thrill of sailing to someone like me who has never sailed at all?' His reply was unforgettable – 'What a silly question. There is no answer to it.' I had a sneaking feeling he was right, but did not debate it. Fire two. 'When did you first compete at Cowes, Sir?'

Making the first-ever BBC Radio sports broadcast from Russia was an interesting experience. Moving strictly within the limits of an In-Tourist itinerary, we inspected the preparations for the twenty-second Olympiad. We attended a freezing football match and saw the footprints for the five sporting centres situated in the wide curve of the Moscow River. We were led by the minute with much care and translation by Mr Golubovski and my interpreter, the ever-present Valeri.

On the Saturday morning I was able to greet listeners at home with words threaded through the signature tune, 'The Shuffle' – 'A very good morning . . . *dobroye utro* as they say here in the Soviet Union. Tony Lewis saying welcome to Moscow for "Sport on Four".' It was a typical 'Sport on Four', full of nuggets of information and surprise, and above all, excellent conversations spoken in good English and link-ups to other sporting scenes. 'After all,' the introduction ended, 'on 19 July 1980, the twenty-second Olympiad will be here in Moscow, and we are only 625 days away.' I described the green, elegant Lughniki meadowland by the Moscow River, where the footprints of a track and field stadium were drawn. Then it was off to Walton Heath where Jack Nicklaus was playing in the very first European Open Golf Championship – Faldo beat Weiskopf by one stroke. We moved on to Brighton with Gerald Williams for tennis – Chris Evert had pulled out with injury and Virginia Wade had been beaten by Betty Stove. That was our cue to visit the neat Moscow flat of a lady who had played in two Wimbledon singles finals, Olga Morozova. Then Cliff Morgan previewed the rugby at Cardiff Arms Park, Wales against New Zealand, and recalled the famous 1953 victory by Cardiff over the All Blacks, in which he played. I was able to add that I was fifteen at the time and remembered a disappointing day at home in Neath. Chosen for a soccer trial with the West Glamorgan schoolboys, I turned up at Cwrt Herbert Fields for a two o'clock kick-off only to be told that they had started at one o'clock. I trailed back through the town, carrying my small suitcase of kit unopened, and decided to go to the cinema alone. The main feature at the Gnoll Cinema was 'Down Among the Z Men' starring Harry Secombe and Carole Carr. Halfway through the movie I heard the film projector clatter to a halt, the screen sticking on black. Someone was scratching a rough message – Cardiff 8 New Zealand 3. The whole Welsh world stopped for rugby football in those days. Wishing the listeners *do svidania*, I was off to Moscow airport and back to London.

Just to provide the feel of 'Sport on Four', here is a transcript of an interview I did with Fatima Whitbread, the javelin thrower in August 1983. I was commentating at Lord's when, on my television monitor, I saw Fatima so nearly win a gold medal in Helsinki. I arranged to meet her with her mother, Margaret, in a London hotel, and brought up the subject that had been on my mind – can fast bowlers learn anything from javelin techniques?

Margaret Whitbread: On the way home from Helsinki we quickly looked up in the newspaper the result of the Test match between England and New Zealand, but I would like to say that I feel Fatima or myself could help some of the England fast bowlers improve their speed of delivery. Because their technique isn't quite right, and I hope they don't think we are being rude but it's so similar to the javelin throw.

Tony Lewis: What do they do wrong?

Margaret Whitbread: Their last two strides are wrong – mainly their last stride. That is far too long. And they're overstretching which is causing them to fall away to the left-hand side and also putting tremendous stress on the lower-back area.

Lewis: There is a lot of similarity, obviously. The sort of bowler I'm thinking of now is Graham Dilley. Have you seen him bowl?

Margaret Whitbread: Yes. I watched him bowl very recently when Kent were playing in the NatWest, and I felt that day again, after watching him previously in the Test matches, that he's definitely far too long in the last stride and his speed of delivery could be improved enormously. I'd love to coach him for a few days.

Lewis: Well, I hope he's listening. Fatima, have you noticed this about cricketers, too?

Fatima Whitbread: Yes, I have, obviously. It's very similar to the javelin throw, and I like to watch cricket anyway, but we take a special interest in watching their technique. I think they could all do with a bit of coaching.

Lewis: A shortening of the stride?

Fatima Whitbread: Of the last stride, yes. Because it would put an awful lot of speed in the release of the ball from the arm, which would give a tremendous help.

Lewis: The difficulty is that they can't throw the ball, of course. They have to bowl it with a straight arm.

Fatima Whitbread: Oh, that's all right. I understand the difference between throwing and bowling because a lot of novice javelin throwers try to bowl, and I say to them, just try to imagine throwing a cricket or rounders ball, if I have a particular problem in school or if I'm doing a coaching session. Don't worry. I wouldn't encourage them to throw the ball!

Lewis: You've got me worried, you two. You know more about cricket than I do.

This was a fascinating view because fast bowlers who were accused of being occasional chuckers, such as Charlie Griffith, the West Indian, were thought to get themselves into a spear-throwing position at the delivery stride. What Fatima and her mother were saying is that the splayed foot position and the quick falling away of the body through the delivery of the ball were to be recommended. It may be a throwing posture, but there was absolutely no need to bend the arm at the elbow and throw the ball.

I never believed in interviewing experts in one field in order to get their opinions on issues in another, but this interview with Fatima was highly relevant, real 'Sport on Four'. The skill in presenting a magazine programme is in the writing. The script has to be talked not read.

BBC Radio Four has preserved the best. Very few bribes persuade Joan to switch it off in the kitchen. In fact, she tests the cooperation of her family greatly by switching on Radio Four at 8 a.m. and turning it off at 10 p.m. 'My university of the air!' is always her response.

There was always a contradiction at the heart of my thirty years in broadcasting: I loved the job but was uncomfortable with the notoriety that television especially brought with it. By the end of the century, there was a profession that was actually called 'celebrity' and magazines such as *Hello* and *OK!* were crammed with photographs of those whose market value soared according to their walk-past-the-lense appeal. Politicians indulged in spin-doctoring information for public consumption. Television newsreaders who recited a confident autocue became famous, and were even knighted. Television interviewers were celebrated although they lived in the glow of the reputations of those answering the questions, the ones who had put their talent on the line to create something original. I understand, of course, that a fine critic is an important arbiter of taste, and a skilled interviewer who is loaded with presentation skills and the curiosity craft can help put creative work in an appropriate setting, but my sympathies always went out to those who faced the blank page and filled it with brushstrokes or scribbles or dotted the treble clef with a composition all their own.

My lack of any instinct for theatre was plain one Christmas when the family were on holiday up in the tea plantations of Habarana in Sri Lanka. All four of us were there with the Bostock family, Tim Rice and his family plus nanny, and J.J. Evans from Sydney, and we were all enraptured by making our own entertainment in an old Dutch plantation house without the aid of radio or television. Murder in the

Dark was the nightly favourite but my nightmare was Charades. To me, performing a charade was as dreadful as being asked to do the Full Monty. Once, I had to convey to my team the film, 'The Naïve and Sentimental Lover' and after grinning and gesticulating stiffly I ground to a complete halt, slumping in exhaustion on to a glass tabletop, which cracked and splintered under my weight. It did occur to me that I was always too aware of those around me. Had this been a problem when I was batting? When I was High Sheriff of Mid Glamorgan, Joan thought the whole county was in danger as I advanced from one ceremony to the next, sword in my hand and jabot flying.

I took this lack of theatre and confused thinking into the light entertainment side of my broadcasting career. I was part of the 'Animal, Vegetable or Mineral' team that played the game in the Regal Theatre in Lower Regent Street for fourteen World Service radio programmes. I trailed behind the other panellists, Bettine le Beau, Rachael Heyhoe Flint and Ted Moult. Terry Wogan was chairman. I had an agent, the Bagenal Harvey Organisation, that helped me mop up these fringe activities as profitably as possible. I had not been long out of first-class cricket when Geoffrey Irvine rang from Bagenal's offices to ask a favour. Would I stand in for Colin Cowdrey, who had been forced to cry off, at a dinner in a couple of days' time? It was the thirty-fifth annual reunion supper of the Confectionery and Allied Trades Sports Association at the Baronial Hall, Dunster and Colonial House, Mincing Lane, London EC3. It was to be held on 18 February and the very next day I was to report to the BBC in Manchester for the classical music quiz, 'Face the Music'.

At the Baronial Hall, I was immediately aware that no one expected me. The cloakroom lady suggested the VIP bar on the left. It was full of past presidents bearing heavy gold metal blobs on the end of royal blue ribbons that were fixed round their necks. I bought my own drink, sent out unreturned smiles, and leaned on the bar with relaxed terror. One or two I believe were looking out for Cowdrey. When dinner was called I did find a named place on the top table, A. Lewis, ex-Capt. Glamorgan Cricket Club. In front of me was near darkness. Tables were arranged between pillars and extended a long way back under a particularly low ceiling. I did know that there were hundreds there – the liquorice makers of Pontefract, the Quality Streeters of York and the Mellow Minters of Cardiff. I was seated but sniffed icy indifference.

During dinner I asked laser questions such as how do you get toffee clusters to stick together, and how do you get the fruit and nut into the bar of chocolate? No one so much as mentioned the word cricket. I tried rugby football. Nothing.

After coffee, the chairman proposed the toast to the association and the president replied. I was next on the list. The chairman stood up and said, 'Now, gentlemen, the moment you have all been waiting for.' I eased my notes from the inside pocket of my coat. 'Pray silence for . . .' I moved my chair back, '. . . Nadine.' Thunderous cheers. I replaced my notes, fingering my tie, the most expensive of my life that I had bought that afternoon at Turnbull and Asser especially for the next day's recording of 'Face the Music'. Nadine arrived by long strides in time with her taped musical accompaniment. Her extremely high heels wobbled her into a centre spotlight. Her face was deathly white; she wore a short black dress with lots of feathers round her neck and her good legs bore an unfortunate snag in the black stockings. I was on her side; we were both part of 'the entertainment'. She appeared to be without inspiration, but audience participation was definitely her thing. She sat on a table, one leg crossed over the other, as an ancient retainer released a stocking from its suspender and peeled it off her leg. Further on, in half-darkness, she stopped to lift with her fingers the spectacles of a highly inebriate, groping senior sweet-maker. She moved back from him, then grabbed her own naked breasts, swayed into him again and whopped them one in each eye to deafening acclaim! It was while Nadine was rousing the natives in this half-hour frenzy that I began to doubt that my opening story about Alec Bedser would suit. Nadine was a hit. The floor was strewn with her bits and pieces and with flowers and napkins and trousers and menu cards as well as by dutiful assistants on their knees. I walked behind the top table to ask the chairman for a ten-minute break and shamelessly told him who I thought I was and what I had done and why there should be a spot of hush when I spoke. I would not be keeping them long.

'Ah! That's who you are,' he puffed. 'Perfectly all right, old chap.'

I began scrawling a fresh start. What about Nurse Thomson, the Sydney abortionist? Or the one that ends, 'Sorry, Mr Wooller, I should have kept my legs closed,' bringing the answer, 'Not you, son, your mother.'

There was gentle applause as I stood up. I threw out the names of cricketers from many counties, waiting to trap any section of the audience in a geographical cage so that I could find common interest. At last, a voice came out of the darkness, 'What abart Keif Flecha?' In I went with all my Fletcher ammunition, plus Tonker Taylor and all the good men of Essex. I swiftly shifted to Yorkshire and Fred Trueman, thank God for Fred, and then suddenly I was ahead of the game. The audience laughed and warmed whereupon, like a good pro, I said thank you and sat down.

Immediately the chairman leapt to his feet. 'Now then, chaps, settle down.' He extended an arm towards me and I thought he was going to call for a big hand for the guest speaker, but he announced with an evil grin, 'Colette.' The spotlight hit the top table this time. All the other lights were off. Colette was making her high-heeled way along the top of it, stepping carefully between plates, knives, forks, coffee and liqueurs. She was a long, leggy lady, wearing mainly feather boas and a G-string. She arrived in front at me, turned her back on the horde, struck a challenging pose and shouted, 'Give us yer tie, darling.' For some brain-dead reason, I unknotted my fine piece of material and handed it over. She stretched the expensive length of Turnbull and Asser between her fingertips and, in time with her now thundering taped music, she threaded it down through her G-string, under and out behind her. The audience were immediately hers and so was my tie. Colette slipped off the table and went walkabout. *Ave atque vale* Turnbull and Asser. She was already in the half-distance, lifting a pair of spectacles up on to someone's forehead . . . I was out on Mincing Lane before you could say Mint Imperial.

I hardly slept and looked rough on the train to Manchester next day. I recorded two programmes on the panel with Joyce Grenfell, David

Attenborough and Robin Ray. 'Face the Music' was a superb programme and I loved the experience. No sooner had I returned my
borrowed tie to wardrobe, I resumed life as a rugby correspondent,
turning my mind to Twickenham where England were playing France
on Saturday.

It wasn't long before BBC's Light Entertainment department lured
me again. Geoff Irvine telephoned to say that I was wanted as a
chat-show host in Birmingham by the producer and director of a live
programme called 'Saturday Night at the Mill'. I was a rugby and
cricket correspondent. What had they seen or heard to persuade them
that I could perform a million television miles from sport in the tinsel
life? But freelancers do not miss boats or they sail without you. Work
was work and with school fees to pay, it was *la vie en bleus* for me – life
in the boilersuit.

So late on Saturday night, after BBC's popular 'Match of the Day', it
was chat-show time. When Michael Parkinson's show took a rest,
'Saturday Night at the Mill' took over.

BBC Pebble Mill in Birmingham was full of friendly people,
urgently competing with London. I became joint presenter with the
thoroughly professional Bob Langley – and this is how I got to be
there. They had run a series featuring well-known people who could
demonstrate other surprising skills. Richard Baker, the familiar broadcaster, played the piano. Tony Lewis, the former England cricket
captain, played the violin accompanied on the piano by his sister
Heather. I tuned the fiddle and answered questions. Halfway through
the chat I was asked to play. Alas, under the heat of the studio lights,
my A string had gone flat. A professional violinist would have expected
that and re-tuned before playing. Not I. I proceeded to play without
the use of an open A – not impossible for an expert in good nick but
for someone who had not hammered out a Wesseley scale for twenty
years it was like batting in crepe soles on a soaking wet pitch. I did not
get to the pitch of the ball but I did slide into position. In other words,
I got away with it and was asked by Roy Ronnie and Roy Norton,
producer and director, to join the team for a series of sixteen shows. I
entered again the sea of celebrity, egos swimming in all directions.

During two series at Pebble Mill, I interviewed Joan Collins, Britt Ekland, Tim Rice, Sir Bernard Miles, Leslie Phillips, Beryl Reid, James Hunt, Jimmy Young, Sheila Hancock, Ginger Rogers and many others. I arrived once driving a Rolls-Royce bearing Dame Edna Everage and ended up swinging a shoe with her to the music of Kenny Ball and his Jazzmen. And then, one sunny day, along came Mr Oliver Reed!

'Wine?' I offered as we prepared to discuss the forthcoming interview over a light supper.

'Yes, white,' beamed Ollie. I poured him a glass.

He grinned and stretched strong fingers round the bottle, pretending to chide me, 'Not a glass of white, the bottle.'

While he downed the wine, he told me about his train journey to Birmingham from Euston Station in old carriages that wobbled and rocked from side to side. He had settled near the refreshment bar, resolving to drink lager from a can without spilling any. He failed first time, and so he tried a new can and failed again. 'So I decided to keep buying cans of lager until I succeeded,' he went on. It was a game unlikely to bow to the mantra of practice making perfect. My man was many cans of lager ahead of the game.

I suggested a line of questioning but was knocked back with three assurances. 'Just lead me to my Scottish ancestry, my dyslexia and to Glenda Jackson.' That sounded fair to me. There is nothing worse than an interviewer who wants to burn up the conversation before getting on the air, and this was a live show. I made a note as we sat in for a full studio rehearsal that my striped shirt was far too busy and I thought distracting for the viewer. My director confirmed, 'You're strobing.' I would change for the programme.

Ollie decided that he would like to spend the couple of hours between rehearsal and transmission at about 11 p.m. in the BBC club. By the time he had sunk several large gins and tonic and I was swimming in orange juice, we were ready for our face-to-face under the lights. Run autocue. There was no walk-on. Ollie was safely seated alongside me as I informed about 15 million viewers that his latest film with Glenda Jackson had just been released. I turned to put the first question but my man was on the move. He was gesturing to camera one and calling for a close shot of the fly of his trousers. This was not exactly what I had planned. Slowly he lowered the zip and inserted his hand. Very slowly he leered at the camera and appeared to be pulling out something large and almost unmanageable. Inch by inch, it came out – a plain, grey shirt. 'This is for you,' he said to me. 'I didn't like the stripes of your shirt in rehearsal. Did nothing for you. Put this one on.'

'But I've changed my shirt. This is not the one I wore in rehearsal.'

Ollie never let the chance to shock pass him by, and I had thwarted him in the shirt act, but what about his fallen trousers?

I thought about bare legs and blurted, 'Scottish ancestry, Oliver. You must be used to bare legs in a kilt.' He looked round and called out to Kenny Ball and his Jazzmen, our resident musicians, 'Can you play a Scottish reel, Kenny?' Kenny and the boys never needed a repeat request; they were quickly into a Celtic reel and Ollie decided that he and I should whirl together. Unfortunately, the microphone attached to my shirt was connected to a block at the side of my chair and as I rose my shirt was tugged in the opposite direction. It was pantomime, but I knew how to lower the escape chute. I got him trouserless back in his seat, referred to his new role as Chief Inspector Wilson and, allowing for a fifteen-second count, called up the film clip. While it was being transmitted I heard encouragement in my earpiece. 'Don't panic,' my leaders said. 'We'll cut five minutes off it. Just do fifteen minutes. All right?' I gave a thumbs-up to the camera and went in with a serious question. What about his work with Glenda Jackson? Suddenly I had a serious movie actor on my hands. He talked brilliantly about the effect of dyslexia on the work of reading scripts and, once on the subject of Glenda Jackson, he was riveting – the effect her talent had on others, the widening range of emotions, the sharp editorial judgement. The sweat poured from his forehead and yet his opinions were well formed, his rhythm constant and enunciation perfect. He had become that dangerous combination for an interviewer to face: drunk but absolutely articulate. Indeed, the content lurched suddenly to the morose. I could sense the audience's enthusiasm shrinking. Our audiences tended to recoil from hearing their stars discuss uncomfortable subjects. I had been through a harrowing interview some weeks before with Dick Emery who presented the gloomy side of a tough upbringing in the theatre. I wanted more bubble to end on an up note.

I should never have doubted the timing or professionalism of Oliver Reed. He ended, '. . . and there is another superb quality in Glenda Jackson, Tony. [Long pause.] She's got fantastic tits.' There was a football roar from the audience. Applause. Applause. Hand over to Bob Langley. I was home and sort of dry. Monday's newspapers gave the story a big run. Mostly they agreed with the one I kept in my scrapbook – 'Tony keeps his cool as Oliver – minus trousers – bowls him a TV bouncer.' I could live with that.

Why did I move from radio to television cricket? First came the opportunity. Peter West said that he intended to retire from the presenter's job on television. Second came the advice, which I solicited from Richie Benaud, the lead commentator. He believed that I would be able to do the job because I could stand in front of camera without script and talk expert cricket in reliable English. In this world, you could not put your head down and read prepared words, however well written. There would be sudden calls to camera in the event of rain stopping play, the collapse of an innings, a switch away from play to an interview, or a couple of minutes spent recording a link to camera for the evening's highlights programme. Outside broadcasting was bur-dened with the possibilities of technical breakdown; you had to be able to fly solo.

The very words 'outside broadcast' suggested an exhilarating inter-face with the listener, whatever and wherever the hazards of the moment. So clearly can I hear the words of one of the memorable outside broadcasters, Wynford Vaughan Thomas, pausing only to wait for the aftertaste of what he called 'my favourite gargle', a large vintage port, at the bar of the Cardiff and County Club – 'Ah dear boy! Sitting with my microphone alongside the rear-gunner on a night-time bombing run over Germany . . . have I told you? Well now, Edna, I think a large one for Mr Lewis as well.'

Wynford had no need to bait the trap. I was a willing captive of his stories that told of the romance of broadcasting away from studios. He climbed the mighty mountain Cadair Idris, the Chair of Idris, with microphone in hand to describe the steep slopes where, in 1283, Dafydd was slain, trying to escape the English who had broken the last stronghold, Castell y Bere, the Welsh fortress that lay below. He told tales of cock-fighting in the grass hollow, still visible on the outfield of the cricket field in Dolgellau. It was Wynford who added a touch of shocking colour to the Lewis family's most important sepia-tinted hero, the Reverend Lewis OBE. Known throughout Wales by his bardic name, Elfed, the great preacher, poet and hymn-writer continued his ministry in the Welsh language at King's Cross in London for over forty years. 'Wonderful man,' Wynford often repeated. 'He was blind for the last fifteen years of his life. Used to move quietly among the lady altos, moving his hands slowly over them saying, "Now, I don't know who you are, but let me guess." The ladies called him "Elvet the velvet".' A puckish spinner of tales, that Wynford.

By the time BBC Television asked me to front the cricket, I had many years of experience with HTV, not to mention 'Saturday Night at the Mill', behind me. Peter West was a hard act to follow. He was popular, with an excellent timbre of voice and massively professional – the television director's dream. On top of that, Peter loved cricket and respected the best players without being afraid to ask the pointed question. I brought to the job a slow pulse. If there was a crisis, I was not the man to rush around the commentary box. Think clearly, move slowly was, I thought, the best way out of trouble. It is fair, however, to mention that Joanie has always worried about us being caught in a hotel fire; she believes that every one of the residents and staff would be well clear before I had thoughtfully accepted the fact that the flames were real. In the end, I was honoured by Richie Benaud's description: 'Tony Lewis, one of the best, most knowledgeable and unflappable presenters in the game of television.' If anyone inspired and encouraged me to think that it was, in fact, a team game and a privilege to be selected, it was Richie. He suggested that a day's commentary was like a day playing Test cricket – you needed energy, a clear mind, a solid performance, but not missing the chance to be adventurous, with concentration and quality through all three sessions of a day's play.

I first played a match against Richie and his Australian tourists in 1961 at Fenner's. I learned a great deal more about him when I was included in a Commonwealth side he led to Pakistan in 1968. He never fussed over players; either they did well or they did not. He would advise, but only when asked. He would not waste words. It was as if he saw random thinking and spoken words as energy leaving the body. On or off the field, he thought everything through and, once prepared, was positive and bold. In response to an habitual flicker of runs to the on side, Aftab Gul, later to open the batting in Tests, he positioned a semi-circle of nine fielders on the leg side, all fifteen yards from the bat. Mr Gul was rendered runless.

Richie was not always prepared to give advice. On one occasion, when Pakistan were on tour in England, their coach Mushtaq Moham-med, who was also a member of the Commonwealth side in 1968, came to the commentary box to ask if Richie would take a look at Mushtaq Ahmed in a net and give some technical advice because he had 'lost it'. Richie decided that he did not want to be seen to help one side rather than the other in the middle of a Test series.

At the end of the 1996 season, Robert Croft, the Glamorgan off-spinner, played his first Test and came up to the television com-mentary box to seek a chat with Richie. Robert had bowled with superb control, drifting the 'arm' ball from leg to off and turning the odd one enough to prompt hesitancy, and finding the breezy Oval perfect for his looping flight. He had picked up a couple of Pakistan wickets, too.

'Change nothing,' Richie said.

Robert went on, 'But did you think that . . .'

'Change nothing, Robert.'

'But what next? What do I work on?'

'Change nothing, Robert.'

'I've been holding the ball like this, Richie . . .'

'Don't change anything, Robert.'

It was not in Robert Croft's nature to proceed without many

consultations about his bowling but he has played out a career full of earnest experiment and success. I do remember that first advice for its minimal debate because there was nothing to discuss. For that match, Robert held the fluttering bird of off-spin in the palm of his right hand and Richie, not wanting to frighten it away, and understanding that good form often vanishes on the wind, urged him to be silent and preserve it.

In order to balance the picture, I should record how Richie, back on that Commonwealth tour in 1968, helped two young fast bowlers make the final stride to Test selection. Keith Boyce of Essex and Ken Shuttleworth of Lancashire were both being no-balled about three times an over. On rest days, he was on the outfield with them, making them think about their stride to the popping crease, pressing them to hit targets along the way from the start of their lengthy runs. By the end of the tour, they were foot perfect. Preparation and practice – exactly the way he had persevered with his own most difficult art of wrist-spin.

Richie Benaud is a model of professionalism. He is a man who prepares his appearance for camera, his throat for talking, his cases for carrying and his equipment for transferring the brainwork to the written media all over the world. This is not to say that he gets it all right. He usually does, but the pinnacle of his fury is reserved for planning that has gone wrong. He was ahead of the field with computers but was never at his most calm and controlled when on his knees under a commentary-box desk, listening to the butterflies in his modem, searching for contact with ethereal transmitters beyond his comprehension.

Back in Pakistan, he did not forgive himself for a lack of foresight. We were travelling by bus across the Thal desert by a narrow, twisting ribbon of road across burned-out terrain and a million miles of sandy dust. Our bus had been described to us as 'first-class air-conditioned', which turned out to mean that it had a luggage rack on the roof and the door was missing. A casual diagnosis would have declared the bus infirm; the gear lever had the shakes. The driver rammed it easily enough from first to second to third, but when it got to fourth it shook so violently he had to have a small boy sitting on the floor behind it to hang on to it and keep it engaged. The lad shuddered across the desert. Then, in the far distance, there was a movement on the horizon; another motor was on the move. It was a small distraction from card games, chatter and of no disturbance to the readers and sleepers. Someone mentioned the other vehicle about ten minutes later. Two minutes after that there was agitation at the front. It was a trans-state carrier that was thundering our way and holding the centre of the road, which appeared wide enough for one only. Asian drivers love playing chicken. We were fifty yards apart when everyone looked up, except the captain. Richie was deeply into his book and chewing gum slowly. In any case, it was not his nature to flap around; he was much more comfortable in the pre-selected temperature of ice-cool.

We hurtled at the carrier. The giant wagon, affronted by the nerve of a mere bus, never wavered. We swerved at the last moment but not in time to escape contact. The right sides of the vehicles scraped together, causing barely a dent on the carrier but smashing windows on our off side. Richie was on that off side and I was a couple of seats behind him. Members of the Commonwealth touring team jumped down from the vehicle to review the damage and witness the squabble between drivers. Our captain, at this time, had not looked up from his book. Then, very slowly, and still reading and chewing, he unhooked his suit holder from the luggage rail above and, without taking his eye off the text, crossed slowly to a seat on the opposite side of the bus. He said nothing, but I knew he was cursing himself. What the hell had persuaded him to sit on the off side of the bus? If there was trouble it was bound to be there. What had gone wrong with the Benaud planning? 'Be two overs ahead of the play' was his life's mantra. 'And be lucky.' I have no doubt that he would never again take a seat on a bus without forethought. It was a rewarding experience to play under his captaincy, no detail too small for his attention, and all directed at attack. The Benaud coat of arms might bear the motto 'domination by preparation'.

So that is why, in later days, when we were to play golf in Perth, Western Australia, I learned from the professional that 'Mr Benaud is out on the course with his yardage wheel. He's got a guy to beat this afternoon.' I was that guy, and he beat me.

Television commentary boxes provide privileged viewing, allowing the commentators to sit in line with the bowling. When I began, television coverage was from one end only, but there was a spirit of innovation rushing from Channel Nine in Australia that led the world. The BBC were smeared with the old reputation of being unadventurous or, at best, slow to change. We now live in days of hawkeye, spin vision, speedometer, a host of slow-motion replays, split screens and modern graphics and the presentation of cricket is all the more important because it is linked to the game's commercial attraction. Sponsors and advertisers are the wellspring of funding for professional clubs and players. The more television the better, but along the way, the beautiful game has needed protecting.

Nothing makes me switch off the television quicker than over-hype from the commentary box, or a commercial plug for the local hotel in which the commentator is staying on favourable terms. When commentators talk up some of the play to make the ordinary sound outstanding, they are dumbing down the game itself.

With the reservation of over-hype, cricket on television has developed into a high-class production. In Britain, the crucial moment came when the BBC lost the contract and the game was taken on by Channel 4. There were some very talented contributors to the BBC's coverage, not least the producer-director Alan Griffiths, who loves his cricket. Highlight packages were sensitively edited and the whole unit was prepared to listen to ideas or criticisms. Richie Benaud, of course, always came fresh from Channel Nine work and would discuss possible innovations in the technical coverage, but the BBC never pushed to take a lead in the televising of the game. It was tugged along by the popular experiments of others.

It was possible to criticise the BBC for not being in the van of technical experiment and improvement, but more fatal to their cause was the failure to demonstrate commitment to the game itself. Certainly, the presenter's job had shrunk as the coverage was squeezed into smaller spaces. Once, there was the chance to create a magazine feel in the twenty minutes before the first ball. Eventually, it was 'Good morning, welcome to Trent Bridge, here's Moira Stuart with the News.' When they came back to Trent Bridge it was just in time for the first ball. On weekends, 'Grandstand' took over, making my job redundant and, to my mind, relegating the occasion. An increasing number of visits to horse racing and other sports interrupted the once continuous coverage. Channel 4 hit the screens and won Bafta awards for its creative coverage. Right at the centre of their success is a director with whom I had worked and talked for many years, Gary Franses. He was another who adored cricket, and it showed. They were able to extend coverage to include magazine work with news gatherings, and apart from a deafening concert by the talented Jools Holland in the lunch interval at Lord's, I never found a flaw. Mark Nicholas is a natural presenter, knowledgeable and theatrical up front.

My own television career stretches back to a well-remembered semi-final match in the Gillette Cup on 28 July 1971, Lancashire versus Gloucestershire, sixty overs a side starting at 11 a.m. Lancashire, chasing 229 to win, stumbled at 163–6 in the face of John Mortimore's off-spin. Mortimore bowled the fifty-sixth over, already having figures of 3 for 57 in 10 overs, but ran into the flashing blade of a young man called David Hughes who struck 24 runs off the six balls. It was 9 p.m., dark, and 23,000 people inside the ground feasted on this wonderful climax to a great one-day game. The lights shone brightly from the pavilion and train lights twinkled through the gloom from the railway station beside the ground. I was a summariser alongside Jim Laker: Richie was at the other semi-final with Peter West. The producer of the nine o'clock news came through. Would Jim do a minute's résumé live? Jim dropped in his minute as the fielders arranged themselves for the final over. 'That was a first,' he said, 'a report to the nine o'clock news in almost total darkness.' So saying, he sucked on his peppermint and smiled slowly. Nothing persuaded Jim to move in any direction without thinking.

I saw then, as I confirmed when I became his stablemate in the late 1970s, a cricketer through and through, who did not wish to waste time with chatterboxes or indeed any variety of broadcaster unless he knew what he was talking about. The game of cricket was fascinating and merited every bit of a commentator's concentration and considered thought before the mouth was opened. Richie was a perfect working companion and they had huge respect for each other. No one could claim that Jim had the liveliest of broadcasting voices, but his clipped Yorkshire accent delivered pearls of cricket intelligence in the fewest possible words. Towards the end of his BBC career he had health problems and slowed down. 'I always used to dash home after a game, wherever I was in the country,' he told me. 'Now I stay overnight rather than get very tired. On motorways, I never push my car above sixty miles an hour. Get the tempo right if you can.'

Commentary boxes, or garden sheds as we called them, provided frugal accommodation for the commentary teams. In my early days with BBC Television, I never saw Peter West, Jim Laker, Mike Smith, Tom Graveney or Ted Dexter sitting earnestly behind the commentators tapping out articles for newspapers and magazines on typewriters. They all had columns from time to time, but few got round to scribbling during match transmissions. Richie Benaud, particularly, broke that mould and many joined in, including Jack Bannister and me. Typewriters, however, were noisy, so either we scrawled with pen on paper or removed ourselves to the press box to hammer out the words. Then came computers and infra-red telephones that coped with e-mails and the despatch of articles to any part of the world. Richie again set the standard by sheer guts and stickability. I would not describe him as an IT wizard, but with handbooks, help calls to his suppliers, assistance from Steve Pierson and Dave Bowden, our floor managers, who would produce all sorts of adaptor plugs and extension cables from the engineering vans, he managed to transform windy, dirty huts into high-powered offices. He ensured that two collapsible tables became part of the BBC's travelling kit.

Richie could not have been content to broadcast and then spend the rest time snoozing or wandering round the ground. His morning chore was a detailed study of *Timeform* before he nominated the horses that would win on the day although he very rarely placed a bet. Jack Bannister added to the industry of the box because he was a bookmaker as well as a cricket correspondent. Gone was the odd glass of wine; now it was mineral water and a measured output of work by the end of the day. David Gower joined us and was soon rattling the keys of his computer too.

Geoffrey Boycott was scribbling, but with a difference. Geoffrey had set about his broadcasting career as he had his cricket with Yorkshire, determined to succeed whatever the obstacles. As a commentator he was first class. The notes he was making at the back of the box were always preparation for his next stint in front of the microphone. He was not a former player who believed he could busk through broadcasting for the rest of his life any more than he could have succeeded as a batsman without net practice. He thought the game through and delivered his comments in a positive way.

I enjoyed commentary round the world. Sharjah in the United Arab Emirates became a cricket centre and it was fun doing the television commentary there, even though it soon became the gambling centre of the cricket world. I sat with Tiger Pataudi, Iftikar Ahmed, Chisty Mujaheed and other commentators in an open commentary box. Asif Iqbal was the cricket organiser for the local businessman Abdulraman Bukhatir. Spectators besieged us with requests for predictions about the next ball, the next over, the next hour's play, anything to place bets on the outcome of the match at many stages. Huge cell phones were used to be in touch with the Bombay bookmakers and in the evenings the bookies' runners were on the hotel corridors with parcels of money for the winners, thousands of dollars in brown envelopes. When Javed Miandad hit Chetan Sharma for six off the last ball for Pakistan to beat India in 1986, I watched spectators mob Miandad. He was presented with a gold and diamond bracelet that we were told was worth $45,000 and many other gifts.

In Bloemfontein in the late eighties the Lewis family were met at the airport by Ewie Cronje in his combie – lovely man, delightful family. That his son Hansie should betray the whole fraternity of cricket by taking bribes to fix matches was unthinkable. Hansie had led South

Africa with much style and when I was president of MCC he spoke brilliantly on the spirit of the game at a dinner given by the club at Lord's. He wondered if I could make him an honorary member of MCC. I responded that we only gave honorary playing memberships to those who had played forty-five Tests or more and had retired. He would surely qualify, but not yet. What a wise rule!

The market for betting on world cricket was made by television. In 1985 I was approached by an Indian from Bombay who said that all he did was to sit in front of several television sets and place bets through the play. Would I be his adviser on the road as I attended some of the big matches round the world? The offer was £45,000 per annum and a fair percentage of winnings: huge amounts in those days. I never imagined how many telephone calls I would have to take in any twenty-four hours to perform my duty and happily never knew because I turned it down. I was perfectly entitled to be a batting consultant as a non-player, but it did not feel right.

Television cricket led to the escalation of monies paid for commercial rights. There was a huge upside in that money flowed into the game, especially into the International Cricket Council, which could, at last, perform with authority. The downside was the creation of swamplands of shady bidding, accompanied by brown envelopes and presents waiting in distant lands. It made it absolutely vital that those who handled the bids and made the decisions on behalf of their countries were honest and true to the game, to their boards of control and to themselves. Money can create power and we know what absolute power does.

If I look back for one last smile, I think of the work Geoff Boycott and I were doing just before handing back from Edgbaston to Broadcasting House in London one sunny lunchtime. We were on a couple of chairs on the roof of the pavilion. Prompted by the director, Keith Mackenzie, we broadcast the current viewers' quiz and answers. Mackenzie was getting agitated, as often happened when London popped up, and we were brisk but we did have the problem of the brightest sunshine completely masking the picture on the monitor. We were pushed on faster and faster but, as it happened, there were twenty seconds to fill at the end, a lifetime. I was not pleased. As soon as our picture faded and Keith instructed London to take over, I exploded with, 'For fuck's sake.' Moira Stuart, the newsreader in London, did well to continue unmoved because my expletives went out live over the whole country.

After lunch I read out a prepared apology and also apologised on the telephone to the managing director of BBC Television, but I was feeling disappointed and a bit down overnight until I received a message from Ian Chappell in Australia – 'Congratulations, AR mate, one-all.' Ian was soon to take an unassailable 2–1 lead, not because I was in absolute control of emotions and language, but because I retired.

Now I sit in my armchair at home on a green hillside near Llantrisant, South Wales, admiring the superb coverage of cricket and all the excellent commentators, without ever wishing to be back among them. I loved my job and my working colleagues. Just before I retired, Joanie and I stayed with Richie Benaud and Daph in their apartment in Beaulieu in the south of France and then travelled with them to Tuscany. There we stayed with our mutual friends the Chidgeys in their old farmhouse, standing at the top of a slope of olive trees in Cettinale. Graham Chidgey was once the proprietor of Laytons, the London vintner; Angela, his wife, is an artist of real talent. In Cettinale, Richie and I walked the country roads, maintaining 4.3 miles per hour according to our stopwatches. It was our target because Ian Botham's walks were done at that intimidating tempo. Then we sat and read, pausing only to sip wine and eat delicious food. Chateau Montrachet 1983 was served, as the Benaud choice. We sipped into the clear nights and the word cricket never touched our lips. Richie's outstanding work in television cricket would continue. As for me, my feet were moving inexorably along diversions new.

CHAPTER 10

AFTERTHOUGHTS

My own playing days began in 1953 when I played for the Glamorgan Second XI and shared a small double bed with three other players in a bed-and-breakfast house on the Taff Embankment where long-distance lorry drivers slept and prostitutes stalked. We ate steak each evening at the Model Inn opposite the cricket ground at Cardiff Arms Park, with plenty of chips and the new, crispy onion rings. If bedsits were available, we preferred Richmond Road where Glamorgan had a special arrangement to rent by the week for regular players. It did not matter to us where we slept; we were getting close to first-class cricket, and we felt good. One of the four-in-a-bed, Alan Jones, proceeded to score 36,049 first-class runs; another, Gilbert Dauncey, played twice in the county championship – highest score 34 against Gloucestershire at Swansea in 1957; the fourth, Hywel Lewis, was one of the South Wales and Monmouthshire League's leading run-getters of the day. Four young batsmen, two heads at the top and two at the bottom, all hoping one day to walk out on to the field on the opposite bank of the Taff in the daffodil sweater and cap.

All our brief memories were the same, of Glamorgan winning the county championship in 1948, and Wilfred Wooller, the captain, striding out in front of his team, followed by the tall and distinguished fifty-year-old amateur off-spinner Johnnie Clay. Mr Clay got rather fed up with being chosen as twelfth man for England when South Africa were on tour in 1935 and so he informed the selectors that either he played or he stayed home to work at his business. He won his Test cap in the last game of that series at The Oval.

Johnnie Clay's name triggers thoughts of what you might call Glamorgan's 'speciality of the house' in those days, off-spin bowling. I saw the last overs of Johnnie Clay, but in 1951, when Glamorgan beat South Africa in Swansea, his successors Len Muncer and Jim McConnon were almost impossible to play on a real Swansea turner. The Springboks played forward and popped the ball into the well-known leg-trap of Allan Watkins (leg slip), Phil Clift (short square) and Wilf Wooller (short mid-on). Len Muncer pushed the ball through at Swansea, but Jim McConnon aimed to beat the batsman frequently with high, looping flight and spin. He took a hat-trick in that match against South Africa, went on to play for England in 1954 and won a place in the MCC touring team to Australia in 1954–55 ahead of Jim Laker.

There is one more name to add from that era, Don Shepherd, undoubtedly the finest Glamorgan bowler I ever played with, taker of 2,218 wickets at 21.32. Don imparted finger-spin but was much more the off-cutter. He, too, benefited from the attentions of new generations of wonderful close catchers such as Jim Pressdee, Gilbert Parkhouse, Majid Khan, Roger Davis, Bryan Davis and the finest of the lot, the best I ever saw, Peter Walker.

What did these four bowlers have in common? The answer is that none of them began as an off-spinner. Johnnie Clay was a fast bowler, Jim McConnon fast medium, Don Shepherd had been trained on the Lord's groundstaff as an opening bowler, skilled at the outswinger, and Len Muncer, first with Middlesex, was a leg-spinner. There is a lesson to be learned from these careers – it is worth experimenting with different bowling styles. Never believe you are a born spinner or seamer. Dennis Lillee has argued convincingly that young bowlers should run as quickly as they can across an open field and bowl the fastest ball of their lives into space, at no one, and if they are really quick and comfortable then they are indeed fast bowlers. If this is so, there must also be certainty about the reverse – if you manage just ten yards and cannot find the speed, you can relax in the knowledge that you are not going to part the hair of the world's best batsmen with your bouncer. Wilf Wooller proved with McConnon and Shepherd that it is possible to reinvent cricketers of talent and improve them. He believed that everyone on the staff should try to become a bowler of sorts and that practice made perfect. Think of Alec and Eric Bedser on trial with Surrey as young lads. Eric was a seam bowler but applied as a batsman and off-spinner because they thought that the club would not take on two seamers at the same time, and a fine off-spinner he became. It is true today that cricketers should avoid casual bowling in nets, and use the time and the opportunity to improve their bowling skill. Johnnie Clay had a net in the garden of his home in St Hilary and was often seen walking along Cowbridge High Street gripping and spinning a rubber ball. Don Shepherd turned his arm over every playing day of his life in order to look after his action, which was classical sideways, as high as he could make it, and full of strong pivot on a straight left leg.

We are left with one question in this new century. Are potential spinners failing to serve the long and necessary apprenticeship because they have been turned into useful defensive bowlers for the games of limited overs?

In the mid 1960s during a Glamorgan match at Neath, I was looking for a net bowler because I was out early and wanted to work on my foot movements. It was sixty-five-year-old Johnnie Clay who took off his jacket and bowled for an hour. His length was too short at first, but once he had dropped into the old rhythm, flight and spin that had got him 1,317 first-class wickets at 19.76, I could see what all the fuss had been about when he was in his prime – the action sideways and high, the sharp twist of the fingers on the ball, the high loop in flight from a quick arm speed and the sudden dip at the batsman's end.

Come my championship debut, I was lbw to Jack Walsh of Leicestershire first ball. To be honest, I thought he had bowled the ball wide by mistake. It was left arm over-the-wicket wrist-spin, heading straight for second or even third slip. I did a guardsman's step across to the off stump as I heard it buzz in the air, sensed the bite on the turf and lifted my bat high – the perfect pad up. Bomp went the ball on my right pad. Debut over, done and dusted.

Jack Walsh, an Australian from Sydney, was forty-three at the time. The war took the finest years of his career, but he did play 279 matches for Leicestershire during which he took 1,190 wickets at 24.55 runs each. He was a prodigious spinner of the ball with what was then considered to be the full range – the legger, the googly and the chinaman. Wrist-spin was an important element in English county cricket. As a batsman, there was no career for you if you could not play it. Where did it go after the 1950s? After all, it is often said that wrist-spinners must have hard pitches with bounce but there were more of them in the British game before the covering of pitches in first-class cricket than there were afterwards. Still, at that early age, my problem was not to trace the global strengths of wrist-spinning, but to find out how to survive. There was help at hand.

'Has anyone told you what to do next time, Tony?' The slightly apologetic Carmarthen voice to my left belonged to Willie Jones. 'Push out, Tony bach. If it turns in you're covered; if it doesn't, well, you never know, God might be on your side.' Not the worst advice by a long way. It was during the second day's play of my debut match that one of our Test cricketers, Allan Watkins, stood in front of me with a bat in his hand. This was no Tortelier masterclass, nor was it yelled instruction from the orderly sergeant; it was delivered with sensitivity but with the confidence of a left-handed batsman who almost raced out to bat every time Jack Walsh was bowling. Left-arm wrist-spinners? He loved them. It was as if Allan was saying, 'Now, I'm going to tell you this only once . . .' He told me, first, try to read the wrist-spinner from the hand; secondly, watch the ball revolve in the air and pick up the spin at that stage; thirdly, if you are still uncertain, settle for playing the spin off the pitch, having first expected every ball to turn into the stumps. 'You may look a fool,' he concluded, 'but you're still there next ball.'

Could I get off the mark in first-class cricket? Walsh bowled; forward I plunged. The ball struck the solid bat full toss I was so far down, and went past Maurice Tompkin who appeared to let it go. I amassed 9 edgy runs. In my second match, against Warwickshire at Neath, I was c Spooner b Hollies 19. Another wrist-spinner, the very one who had bowled Bradman for a duck at The Oval in 1948. Eric Hollies did not appear to be working hard with his fingers but bowled an immaculate length and got plenty of drift into the right-handed batsman. His googly was obvious. I went home to study *Wisden*. How many more wrist-spinners were to come? Could I survive? There was John Wardle of Yorkshire, Doug Wright of Kent, at Lancashire Tommy Greenhough was just starting and Roley Jenkins was with Worcester-shire as Roley gave the ball a real flip from low down, sending it humming high towards the batsman. Bill Greensmith was taking wickets in Essex. From overseas, George Tribe came to Northants, Colin McCool was at Somerset, Gamini Goonesena and Bruce Dooland were at Notts – all high-quality wrist-spinners. It was essential to learn and I did it by trying my own hand at leg-spinning. I was very much a net bowler, but I got to know a great deal about the skills involved. My six first-class wickets are often scorned, and rightly, but I did learn a lot about batting against wrist-spin by trying to bowl it in practice.

When I played a few Tests in 1972–73, I came up against world-class wrist-spin. Pakistan had both Intikhab Alam and Mushtaq Mohammed in the side. Intikhab was a superb practitioner with plenty of over-spin and therefore lots of high bounce on hard surfaces. He bowled a readable googly and a cleverly disguised flipper that hurried straight on. Mushtaq could bowl gently floating spinners until it became absolutely necessary to spin the ball hard, and then he would build speed into his whole action – the pivot, shoulder turn, arm and wrist and fingers. Both got the fast loop from an attacking action. From the batting end, they were different; Mushtaq being shorter got the steeper loop and was slightly more of a finger spinner. Intikhab had strong and rhythmical shoulder movement. They were both aggressive.

Chandrasekhar of India was different again. Chandra's withered arm was a whip under the buttoned shirtsleeve. He was little short of medium-pace. His flight did not come from a high looping trajectory. When he bowled the googly, the ball stayed in the air a fraction longer, drawing the batsman forward. He was not a big spinner of the leg-break, and so most batsmen played him as a top-spinner and googly bowler who very occasionally turned the ball away from the right-hander. When the leg-spinner did bite and turn, however, it took everyone by surprise, perhaps even Chandra, and he got important wickets that way. Whatever he was bowling, the ball fizzed with the quick arm, the fast loop, the big bounce. In modern parlance, Chandra really put some work on the ball.

Wrist-spin has been renamed over-the-wrist-spin by Richie Benaud. His own bowling was further proof that the variations of over-the-wrist-spin may be known by the batsman, but all bowlers are different. Richie had wonderful rhythm and power running through his legs, his shoulders and arms down to his fingertips. He possessed athleticism that some of the other outstanding exponents did not. Abdul Qadir, Mushtaq Ahmed and Shane Warne are differently made but they have something important in common. Each was a master of the plain well-spun leg-break. Over and over, they could drop it on a length. The googly, persistently bowled by Chandra, was a variation on that. Richie used to talk about keeping the teaching of leg-spin simple before launching into a thesis about 'the slider' and, for the initiate, the 'sliding top-spinner'. I overheard a conversation between Richie and Shane Warne one day on 'the spinning axis of the flipper', and was reminded of a highly specialised chat I once heard between two tight-head props on the most efficient handholds to use on an opposing loose-head who is less than five feet ten inches tall.

I have no problem with complicated skills. It means that when the complicated becomes natural, you are succeeding. When kids on the street are referring to 'sliders' and trying to produce them with tennis balls, then we are winning.

The distribution of kit for youngsters and itinerant tutors of cricket can never replace the influence of the schoolteacher, parent or uncle, drawing in the very young to take part in informal play. In 1994, in Perth, Western Australia, I stayed at the home of Roddy Kinkead-Weekes, the former Oxford University and Middlesex wicket-keeper and batsman, and was asked by Matt, the nine-year-old boy next door, to play a game on the street. His mum had told him that there was a Pommie cricket captain around for a few days. 'You bat, Mr Lewis,' he said. His mum had tuned up his good manners, I thought.

Young Matt bowled brilliant wrist-spin, the googly too, then the quicker one although not yet performing the Shane Warne slide. I found myself concentrating hard. Being castled by a Matt bosie was not the sort of news that would stay a secret between him and me. He came out with a 'Well played, mate,' and tossed the ball to some friends who had become spectators. They all bowled with actions like Warnie with every one of his post-delivery gesticulations acted to the full. When they applied wrist-spin to a heavier rubber ball, they produced far more turn and bounce.

It was impossible to imagine this sight in Britain. I am pleased to report that at the age of fifty-six, I survived the examination and obviously won enough marks for Matt to invite me to inspect his bedroom. There, on one wall, was a full-length picture of Shane Warne and, on another, Allan Border. I was working on the *MCC Masterclass* book at the time and one day Dennis Lillee drove up bearing his long-awaited contribution. I asked Matt if he would like to meet the great fast bowler. 'Aw look, all right mate, as long as he knows I like Border better than him.'

Where have all the leg-spinners gone in England? What did happen after the 1950s? Pitches continued to be uncovered and were sometimes damp and slow, but there were quick ones, too, because there was no gospel of top-dressing with the Surrey loam that eventually anaesthetised many of our natural surfaces. By the 1960s we had only Bob Barber, tricky but not practised enough, and Robin Hobbs whose looping flight was indispensable for England on overseas tours. He was not an automatic choice for the Tests but it was felt that he would get the bounce abroad that he missed at home. Robin was a very good bowler and there should have been more like him. The craft of leg-spinning requires half a lifetime of hard work and it will never revisit Britain until we see the kids roll 'em down the garden path for fun and start flipping a hard rubber ball while waiting for the bus, and we hear them shout, 'Come and see. I've got the googly.' Wrist-spinning is not just to be learned from a textbook or video and an esteemed teacher; it is a way of life. But then the young Don Bradman, who stroked a golf ball on a string with a cricket stump round the back of his home in Bowral, would have told you that batting is the same. England has made serious ground towards being the best prepared of all Test teams, but we must send out evangelists among the young, show them the role models, and plant the early skills. We have cricket-speak to describe what was once ordinary, and fitness and preparation are kings. The unspoken words are 'talent' and 'practice' without which . . .

One day in the summer of 1960, one year at Christ's completed, I opened the *Daily Telegraph* at home to find that, after the Firsts, Seconds and Thirds in the History Tripos (Preliminary Examination) there were listed three specials – those who had not failed completely but who had scraped an offer of continued residence. The Freshman Blues were history; I was on a last chance. My mother read out loud – 'Special Awards to Princess Elizabeth of Toro, Roedean and Girton; Lord Eliot, Eton and Kings; A.R. Lewis, Neath Grammar School and Christ's. Well-done darling! In such company, too.'

It was believed by senior dons that Christ's was acquiring too strong a reputation as a rugby and football college. Certainly in my first year we had nineteen Blues in all sports but there is no natural law to say that sportsmen cannot have first-class brains. Soon I was to play cricket alongside two of them, Edward Craig, a superb batsman who became warden of Churchill College, and Mike Brearley, who taught at Newcastle University and in America and is now, after being an England cricket captain, a psychologist.

The skill of a Tutor for Admissions, of course, was to select those who could work as well as play. My own small group of freshman friends in Christ's attacked career possibilities with a determination based on sporting competition. Welsh rugby international and university captain at Twickenham, Roger Michaelson was the first graduate ever to enter the London Fruit Exchange. A wonder at languages, including all the Spanish and French market-dialect required to purchase satsumas at the right price, he created Migrant Fruit, a highly successful business based in Canterbury. Dr Trevor Wintle, a general practitioner, played scrum-half for England. Ian Balding, a Blue at full-back, trained that great Derby and Arc winner Mill Reef, and became one of Her Majesty's racing trainers. Sir Michael Lord, a Blue in the centre, continues a distinguished parliamentary career as I write. Brian Thomas, the big Welsh international second-row forward, got a 2.1 in metallurgy and pounded the beat between work in that area and rugby club management. John Brash, a Scottish international wing-forward, has pursued his own independent path in commerce and club golf, while Roger Dalzell, secretary of university gymnastics, scrum-half and boxer, runs his own company, Bulldog Publishing. I was one of a competitive and successful lot.

In 1997 I was back in Christ's to celebrate the 550th anniversary of God's House, to which the origins of the college can be traced. The sight of old portraits of John Milton, Jan Smuts' among them, and the gong announcing the recital of the college grace above flickering candles brought a tear of appreciation to my eye – *EXHILARARTOR omnium CHRISTE, sine quo nihil suave, nihil jucundum est* . . . Christ the gladdener of all, without whom nothing is sweet, nothing is joyful . . .

After a speech or two, I looked across to the high table where Sir Jack Plumb, now in his eighties, was seated. He nodded my way and afterwards called me across the hall.

'Lewis, I must tell you that I have much admired the civilised style of your sports writing,' he began. I could not believe it. My God! Approval from the great man! Write one paragraph for J.H. Plumb and you could be in his rooms all day while he demonstrated how errors of syntax had distorted the historical meaning. Here I was, making the grammatical grade almost forty years later. He went on, '. . . which persuades me, Lewis, that I was once perfectly correct to keep you afloat in the face of the examiners.'

I was greatly helped as an undergraduate in my attempts to balance work and play by another historian, my supervisor, J.P. Kenyon, who had published works on the Stuarts. John Kenyon understood that university cricket in those days was truly first class and required my attendance six summer term days of the week, right up to examination day. In my first year, under the captaincy of Chris Howland, we beat three counties. John Kenyon, with huge sighs and large coffees, took my supervisions soon after 7.30 a.m. so that I could dash up to Fenner's. In my second year, there was another key to my ultimate survival – I had given up rugby football, the violin and snooker in the Hawks Club.

The Hawks was one of the more civilising institutions in my sporting life, matched in Oxford by Vincents. Membership was restricted to university full Blues although undergraduates in their third year could be accepted if they had represented the university against Oxford in the second team of two different sports. I was a member after my first-term rugby Blue. The President was another Christ's man, Donald Steel, captain of golf. Conversations flowed between the sports at the luncheon tables, leading to mutual respect, before golfers disappeared to Royal Worlington, rowers to the river, rugger men to Grange Road and, in summer, cricketers to Fenner's. Most days a large number of sportsmen could be found attacking the huge omelettes cooked by Edna, the long-serving Hawks Club cook. And did the Steward, Harry Lambert, actually eat his dead comrade's shoes to stay alive at Gallipoli? If you believed it, Harry's twin deaf-aids always worked in your favour. 'Half a bitter, Sir? Certainly, Sir.' To be a doubter, however, was to risk severe thirst because Harry was too deaf to hear some orders even if they were delivered very loudly in front of his face. There was a president and a committee but Harry and Edna were the pillars of the Hawks Club in St John's Passage.

After the morning dash to the books, I would walk up Regent Street, cut in behind the University Arms and cross Parker's Piece, the wide-open acreage where all sorts of cricket could go on at the same time. Fenner's was often icy and windy at the start of the cricket season. Yorkshire were always there in May and Fred Trueman used to hold court in the old pavilion next to the big, open fire – 'I come to Cambridge, sunshine, for 6 for 26 and some undergraduate crumpet that'll keep me warm.' Young victims laughed nervously at the inevitability of the joke becoming fact.

Fenner's was gorgeous on the balmy days after the examinations when the lads drank ale from the Tolly tent and picnicked with pretty girls on the boundary's edge. Fenner's was trim, firm, green and airy. It was exhilarating to trust the turf and swing the bat into your smartest cover drive. Bowling, they say, was more difficult, especially when the eastern winds had whipped the moisture from the pitch and absolute skill and concentration were required to keep a faultless line and length. Stoicism was a major requirement. Of all the bowlers with whom I played at Fenner's, the most accurate was Alan Hurd who played for Essex. He was an off-spinner who varied his flight, spun the odd ball, and was rarely dominated. Add the flatness of the surface with the vulnerability of undergraduate hands and you must marvel at Ossie Wheatley's record of 80 wickets in a Cambridge term in 1958. It says much for the good, old-fashioned away-swinger, too.

The Fenner's groundsman for more than forty years was Cyril Coote. He was father-confessor and adviser, blunt but never uncharitable. He knew his cricket and in spite of the deformity of a leg, was one of the finest minor county players. He would watch the play, and help when asked. When he was not working on the ground he held court in a corner of the old pavilion Long Room, the big clock made by Munsey of Cambridge ticking away beside the large fireplace. Each panel on the wall bore the gold-leafed names of a glorious past. Cyril would turn and point and say, 'There he is, Sir, Mr May. Y'know that shot you played to get out? Mr May would never 'ave played one like that, Sir. He'd have had his head down. Past 40 for Mr May was 100, y'know, Sir. Those professionals would have had to bowl at him all day, Sir. You just chucked it away.'

Sometimes he would wander further back to his beloved Jehangir Khan, from the thirties. 'If you'd been up then, Sir, you'd have seen an international cricketer. He'd bowl all day, bat all day. There wasn't anything he couldn't do, Sir, that Jehangir.' There was always Mr Doggart or Mr Sheppard, Sir, or Mr Dexter, but always it came back to Mr May. 'Y'see, Sir, them county bowlers dreaded coming 'ere.'

The pavilion was built in 1877 from money raised by the Reverend A.R. Ward. He was a former Cambridge captain who became president and treasurer in 1873. He raised money by personal appeal and among the contributors was the Prince of Wales, later to become Edward VII, who had a special pitch reserved for him at Fenner's while he was up at Trinity. In my day, the handsome Victorian pavilion was a happy and friendly place. There were a couple of white seats on the roof, and a wide canopy over the ground-floor verandah, which was supported by delicate, wrought-iron filigree. A gentle incline of half a dozen steps led down from the verandah through the small members' enclosure to the field.

During my three years playing in the university match, both Oxford and Cambridge had talented players, none more so than Oxford in my first year. Their captain was Alan Smith whose shambles of a walk belied a seriously athletic presence. He was rather like a rag doll, arms and legs flapping independently, until someone behind his back electrified the wires and made them all work together. He opened the batting and was the wicket-keeper. In later days, he was wicket-keeper and captain of a Warwickshire team that won the county championship. He played in Test matches for England and served the game further as chief executive of the Test and County Cricket Board. In the 1960 match he definitely had the ammunition to win and was probably frustrated by a burst of rain. His opening partner was the talented Lancastrian David Green, a most dangerous stroke-maker. Then came three Asian jewels, Abbas Ali Baig, who had already scored a century for India in a Test match at Manchester, Javed Burki, soon to captain Pakistan, and the Nawab of Pataudi, a future captain of India. Add to those the capable off-spin of Dan Piachaud, left-arm spin of Colin Drybrough and the leg-spin of Alan Duff, and the extra batting of Charles Fry, and they simply needed the genuine fast bowling of David Sayer and Andrew Corran to complete the perfect side. Every one of them played county cricket. It was the best university side of my era.

In 1962, when I was captain, I found it difficult to select a young player of considerable achievement at Repton, Richard Hutton, son of Sir Leonard. His bowling was lively, delivered with a gangling action, and his batting was mainly a lunge on to the front foot. Mike Brearley, the secretary, and I watched and waited. Maybe he was not a good net player. Perhaps he was shy. We could not see automatic selection staring us in the face. Then, after we had played a couple of matches, I received a letter from Richard's father. He would like to take me to dinner. A few days later I went with the great Sir Leonard to a small basement restaurant in the Market Square. Sir Len straightaway assured me, 'He can play, y'know.' I did not believe that he was there to exaggerate his son's claims and a plain statement from such a man was really what I needed. Richard had mislaid his talents. It did not take me long to discover that father and son both hid the most bewitching dry humour behind clear blue eyes and slow conversational style. 'Yes, Richard can play. He can bat and bowl and catch.' It would have taken some fathers five courses and coffee to embellish those abilities in a son, but Sir Leonard moved quickly on to inquire, I thought, about team selection. 'What are you going to do then?'

'I am not sure,' I said.

'Have you considered stockbroking?'

History shows that Sir Leonard was right about Richard, an England Test player in the end, if not about my future as a stockbroker.

Mike Brearley went on to be a fine England captain. He never adopted a stylised Oxbridge posture, it was not in him; he was a clever, determined and stimulating friend. Much reference has been made to his academic record as if it was the essence of his captaincies of Middlesex and England. There was certainly a mental ability to analyse players and situations and also, when I was a correspondent on tours he led, I could sense his directness with players that let everyone of them know what was expected of them within the effort of the whole team. He was not the only cricket captain to have these qualities and it is important to remember that he was not some egghead hauled from university cloisters into the Test matches. Mike was in the England side for his durable and often stylish batting before he took over the captaincy from Tony Greig. He was a battler at the top of the innings and a fine slip fielder. If ever I was disappointed by his play, it was with the bat. I knew him from Fenner's as an excellent player but saw at the higher level one technical flaw that denied him many big innings – he did not naturally maintain a wholly sideways posture through a stroke. His right shoulder came round strongly and opened him up to the bowler. This allied to the pressure he was under to prove his batting class persuades me that we rarely saw the best of Mike Brearley in Test matches.

I particularly like his contribution to one of the Geoffrey Boycott debates. In Australia, when Boycott was being bowled out regularly by Rodney Hogg and at the same time was in public dispute with Yorkshire, everyone was using up millions of words on a character assessment of Boycott. Mike Brearley killed it by informing the press that 'We haven't come all this way to Australia to understand Geoffrey Boycott.' End of story; back to the cricket.

The first-class status of Oxford and Cambridge university cricket clubs was extended beyond their own benefit because they no longer served the British game and were scorned for it. Derek Pringle chose to play for England rather than captain Cambridge in the varsity match. I did not agree with him at the time and when we chatted I suggested he might regret not leading out his side at Lord's. What we both considered to be most indicative of the demise, however, was the very fact that the University Match, one of the historic, great matches alongside Gents versus Players, now clashed with a Test. That would have been unthinkable only twenty years earlier. The side I led at Cambridge included Edward Craig, who had scored more runs at Charterhouse than Peter May; Mike Brearley; Raymond White, who played for the Transvaal; Tony Windows, soon to brighten Gloucestershire supporters with his clever swing bowling and his personal collection of hard-scoring strokes; and Tony Pearson, a Somerset opening bowler who in 1961 had taken all ten Leicestershire wickets in an innings and who would have done well if medical studies had not taken most of his attention. Roy Kerslake later captained Somerset, Graham Pritchard played for Essex and Mike Edwards had a lengthy and distinguished career with Surrey. Richard Hutton, the late developer, Mike Brearley and I, all played for England. At Oxford, Abbas Ali Baig and David Pithey were the Test players present and future, and the captain, Colin Drybrough, became captain of Middlesex. Duncan Worsley had raised Lancashire's hopes as an opening batsman.

Derek Pringle was right because he had spent four years at Cambridge and knew the strengths of the game there. I was reaching for the vanishing past. Maybe it was because he wore an earring that I found it difficult to embrace his new cricket world. Eventually, it took a bold move by the England and Wales Cricket Board to spread the university experience to include provincial universities. They set up regional centres with the aim of providing high-quality cricket for those students who could work and play, linking them with the club and the county game. Oxford and Cambridge no longer merited priority positions in the first-class game. Clocks do not go back. In fact, the old Fenner's pavilion clock ticks solidly onwards in a cricket backwater – my hall at home!

Right from the start of my cricket career, Wilf Wooller had told me that he wanted me to captain Glamorgan one day, and that it would mean remaining an amateur. That meant no fees for playing but all expenses paid.

'Stay close to me, I'll show you the ropes,' I recall him saying. I was just seventeen, I had scored 28 runs in three first-class innings and, blushingly at first, I found I could not be one of the boys. At lunchtimes, dutifully blazered and often with a tie, I sat with committeemen, either in their private dining room if they had one, or on a table away from the professional players; not at every ground but enough to make me sensitive about this strange social arrangement. I heard stories of how amateurs at some of the great old grounds had separate dressing rooms and some did not even stay in the same hotel as the players. Allan Watkins was especially vivid on the subject. He told the tale of touring India in 1951 under the captaincy of Nigel Howard. After yet another endless train journey across the subcontinent, the professionals would alight on the platform from their third-class carriages that had metal grille windows open to the air on each side, with their faces, hair and clothes covered in the red dust of the countryside, while further up the platform, the amateurs – the skipper, Donald Carr, Don Brennan and the manager Geoffrey Howard – coolly ambled out of their first-class air-conditioned coaches surrounded by porters and bearers. 'Cattle trucks. Cattle trucks,' Allan used to repeat for the sake of the story.

In 1806, a match was played for the first time between the Gentlemen, the amateurs, and the Players, the professionals. It was the start of a series of what were called great matches. By the time I was playing, amateurism did not suit my family background or my father's bank account but I was privileged to play for the Gents against the Players in the final contest at Lord's in midsummer 1962, and at the close of the season at Scarborough.

After the Second World War, the social wall between amateurs and professionals began to crumble. Fewer and fewer people could afford the time to play without payment. Warwickshire, in 1951, appointed their club captain from the ranks of the professionals, Tom Dollery, and he led them immediately to the county championship. In 1952, England followed the example when Len Hutton, the Yorkshire professional, became the England Test captain. He was never Yorkshire's captain, however.

The old social order was changing and most of the post-war amateurs received generous expenses, were made secretaries of the county club or held a sinecure on the payroll of a benefactor who loved his cricket. Glamorgan was one of several counties that could not imagine the day when the captain was not an amateur. From our debut in the English County Championship in 1921, amateur leadership was unbroken until MCC abolished the status and called everyone 'cricketer' in time for the start of the 1963 season. My own life as an amateur lasted from 1955 to 1962, under Messrs Wooller and Wheatley. It was not a world of privilege or stigma; it was simply an order accepted by cricketers so that they could do what they did best, play cricket at county level. Change was left to the governing body of the game, the Marylebone Cricket Club.

Lancashire had a small dressing room reserved for the captains and their amateurs. It was offered to Richie Benaud when his Australian team played there in 1962 but he turned it down. At Old Trafford, Ossie Wheatley and I had to pass through the players' dining room in order to join the Lancashire committee who always lunched with some formality. Impeccably uniformed waitresses offered sherry and handed out menus. As I saw it, this special treatment was the only advantage to being bowled out by Brian Statham in the first session of play. By teatime you could still be on the Stilton and port.

There was a particularly spacious dressing room for amateurs at The Oval. In 1960, it accommodated just Wilf Wooller and me. We had a wall of coat pegs each, wicker armchairs for viewing the game, a dressing table with clothes brushes and a basket for used hand towels. At 11.25 our personal attendant announced, 'The umpires are out and your team is ready, Skipper' and along the corridor we walked. The rest of the team tagged along behind. It was Alec Bedser's last match as well as Wilf's, twenty-two years after his debut.

The Oval pitch was green and lively and we batted badly in the first innings. The Skipper stormed into the professionals' room, cursing them, and when he returned to our dressing room, he shouted across at me, 'And in case you don't know it, it's the duty of the bloody amateurs to lead from the front.' He had been top scorer with 32 out of 101. I had got 5.

We followed on. The pitch was still seaming wickedly and I was in the process of scoring the longest 10 in the history of cricket, trying like a man blindfolded to lay a bat on the bowling of Alec Bedser, Peter Loader and David Gibson. It was 85 for 5. In came the Skipper. As he took guard, Peter Loader, Surrey's quick bowler, announced that he was going around the wicket. He raced in and let go a very fast bouncer. The Skipper, six foot six, 16 stone and no hooker, turned his back on the ball, ducking his head out of the way. It hit him a thumping blow on the shoulder. Next ball, Loader did the same. The Skipper took it on the shoulders again and it ricocheted high in the air to Arthur McIntyre, the wicket-keeper. Loader swaggered down the pitch after this one and stared. He waited until the Skipper looked up and said,

'I've waited a long time to pin you, Wooller. You won't retire; they'll be carrying you off.'

He snatched the ball and hurried back to his mark. I was witnessing war. Bouncer after bouncer sunk into the Skipper's back and side. The repartee was hot. Wooller, the Test selector, shouted at Loader, 'God. I thought you were quick. How the hell did I ever pick you for England? And you've just proved that you're a coward, Scrubs, hitting the guy who can't hit back, eh!'

'I haven't finished with you yet, you big . . .'

I shrank beside the umpire, Eddie Phillipson. I expected the double-decker buses to stop outside The Oval and workmen to down tools on the gasometers. Loader was on his way again. Whack! Another bouncer. Thump! The ball hit the Skipper's turned back. A few balls later I was out, caught by Micky Stewart off Dave Gibson, and I left like a lad removed from a horror movie halfway through to save me from a harrowing experience.

The records have it that we were out for 137 and lost by an innings. The Skipper saw off Loader. He got 30. In our amateurs' dressing room, John Evans, the physiotherapist, began to treat the scarlet blotches on the big man's body with swabs of lead and opium mixture. So this is first-class cricket, I thought. The Skipper eased over on his side.

'Well tried, Tony,' he said. 'You didn't get many, but you stuck it out. That's what you've got to do when you're captain, when you see great pros like Hedgy and Watty playing for their lives at the other end.' Bernard Hedges had got a tremendous 57, and Allan Watkins 23.

It was the first time I learned how deeply Wilf Wooller had set himself to follow the example of Glamorgan's outstanding pre-war leader, Maurice Turnbull. 'He was an autocrat,' the Skipper recalled. 'Maurice brooked no nonsense but he drove himself hard. He led. He took full decisions. He took full responsibility.' John Evans continued bathing the bruised body. 'That's why I'm glad you got that rugby Blue, Tony. There's got to be toughness down there inside – take the knocks. Maurice Turnbull took all the responsibility and the raps. The players just got on with their jobs. I learned some valuable lessons from him.'

No one called the Skipper Wilf until long after he had retired from the game in 1962. From my first matches with the Glamorgan Seconds in 1952, I had never thought of addressing him by his name. He was called the Skipper, even by non-cricketers. Basically, he barged around believing that everyone should be as combative as he was. He could never understand why I did not defend apartheid in South Africa as the best order of society for the advance of coloured and black people. The quality of their material lives was rising all the time, he would argue. Incomprehensible to Wilf was my belief in odd days of rest for the team during a season to break down the feeling of county cricket being a daily chore. His was the real work ethic, every minute of the day, and mind focused on players peaking at the appropriate moments. We did more or less agree, however, that in a short season of four months, the more you bat, bowl and field, the better you will perform.

He was always keen to discover his own rumbustious, sledging qualities in his players. One Saturday evening, in the Flying Horse Hotel in Nottingham, the team partied in an open lounge area opposite reception and between two Georgian fireplaces. We were drinking champagne won by Peter Walker for taking the most first-class catches. Guinness was being applied to the bubbles to make more of a man's drink, Black Velvet. I stood in front of one fireplace, Wilf was opposite, in front of the other. Suddenly, he reached for the large onyx clock that ticked loudly on the mantelpiece behind him and swung it, like a pass from Hadyn Tanner, the great Welsh scrum-half, across the space of a dozen yards, straight at me. I took it into my chest as if it was a rugby ball but the weight of it and its force knocked me backwards. I heard laughter as I disappeared halfway up the chimney of a mock Adam fireplace. It gave me quite a crack. Immediately, I got to my feet, wound up an equally ferocious pass and winged the heavy clock back to the Skipper. He plucked it out of the air as if he had been tossed a tennis ball by one of his five kids in the garden. A sip or two later, I went off to the lavatory, but suddenly I was not alone. A large shadow fell across the porcelain. The Skipper. He slapped me on the shoulder, almost knocking me straight down the urinal.

'Bloody great,' he said. 'You got up and threw it back. Now they know what you're made of.' There was a pause for nature and he added, 'Call me Wilf.'

'Yes, Skipper,' I replied.

There was no perk for amateurs or professionals at Glamorgan's many grounds. Cricket clubs did not own the grounds and at the far end of almost every one of them were rugby posts. Our changing room in Swansea was a room underneath the main bar of the sports club. Beer used to drip down the walls of the dark concrete cell. At Cardiff Arms Park, we were the summer lodgers in the rugby dressing rooms. We changed among the touchline flags and took the field smelling of dubbined rugger balls. Sometimes, when rain stopped play, Wilf Wooller used to challenge Willie Jones to a goal-kicking contest, out the back of the north stand on the famous rugby pitch. Wilf's reputation as a Welsh international was well known but Willie's 'Victory' caps for Wales and his outside-half wizardry for Gloucester were not so well known. They would tuck their whites into their socks and it was worth watching. They placed the ball on the corner-flag spot so that only one goalpost was visible. The test was to hook the ball between the posts. Willie took all the goal-kicks for Gloucester in the round-the-corner kicking style that is the accepted method these days. Wilf was a soccer player and was well able to compete. Willie was left-footed, Wilf right. Willie always scored more hits than Wilf, which is not to say that Wilf accepted defeat – Wilf was never wrong, never on the losing side.

If the Gents v. Players match at Lord's was virtually a Test trial, the end-of-season contest at Scarborough fitted the Festival's requirements of being hard-fought cricket played in the true spirit of the game by the seaside. I played in several Scarborough Festivals, often being included for all three of the three-day matches. The professionals stayed at The Balmoral, which we called The Immoral, while the Gents stayed at The Grand, high above the beach, and each evening dined in the Cricketers' Room, black tie only. We used to make our way down the central stairs after drinks with Tom and Stella Pearce in their first-floor suite. Tom, a former Essex captain, was the organiser of the cricket at the Festival, and Stella made sure that ladies were properly escorted down the stairs as the Palm Court orchestra played and ruddy-faced spectators from the cricket sat sipping their drinks and spotting who was who. On the fine wooden panels of the Cricketers' Room were photographs of every amateur who had ever played at the Festival, some offering superior stares over the upturned collar of an I Zingari blazer, others waving from the saddle of a north-beach donkey. These were moments when, by instinct and instruction, our fingertips grasped at the past.

Play was from 11 o'clock until 6 o'clock and the Scarborough brass band played off and on in their little bandstand all through the day. There was often some casual cricket, but you could not fool a Yorkshire crowd for long; also first-class runs and wickets were at stake, which guaranteed that players tried. The Scarborough ground is open, fresh with sea air, and yet intimate. On one side, a spectator bank is built into a natural slope, and along the path at the top there was a small line of bars. In the days when the taste was for a lager or two, we called it Denmark.

For lunch, we would walk across the field to small marquees draped in bright colours and prettied with potted plants and flowers. There was no rush. It was a social, even sartorial, perambulation. No autograph request was turned down because of haste. In the marquee it was a dry sherry or two, a gin maybe, before luncheon, earnest conversation with guests of the Festival, civic dignitaries, workers for cricket, representatives of the splendid Scarborough Cricket Club, the aroma of sweet-scented stock and colourful geraniums, ladies in wide-brimmed hats, Stilton cheese, a glass of vintage port and back to the game. Just outside the marquee you could give a sympathetic nod to the third cornet player whose valves had been full of spittle throughout the lunchtime recital.

Always there was Major Leveson Gower, nephew of the famous Shrimp Leveson Gower. The Major was diminutive, balding and bespectacled and was famed for his faultless remembering of Bradshaw, the railway timetable – he was what was called a movement officer in wartime – and also for standing on tiptoe and peering down the fronts of ladies' evening dresses. Greta Bailey, Trevor's wife, as mischievous as any, would fabricate some journey of extreme complexity, which she was due to make on a Sunday of course. 'Tell me, Major,' she would say, 'I would like to be at a meeting of the Lowestoft Women's Circle, a week on Sunday, at half-past two in the afternoon.'

'Ah!' the little Major would exclaim loudly, moving in close for a peep. 'Now then! You would need the 06.13 from Scarborough, changing at Malton, for the 07.00 for York. There's a Sunday goods train with two carriages for passenger accommodation from York to Scunthorpe . . . then Scunthorpe to Grimsby, down to Boston for the 11.04 . . .'

'But why can't I go straight to London and out to Lowestoft from there, Major?' Greta would ask, moving even closer.

'Ah, but you see, you'd arrive cross-country in Lowestoft at 14.07, eight changes, and from London not until 14.24. Cutting it a bit fine for your meeting, don't you think?' Besides which, it was much more fun for the Major.

As Colin Ingleby-Mackenzie prompted the ladies to wear ever more revealing dresses as the Festival went on, the Major's train routes got even more amazingly complex. Great fun!

Eventually, the cricket at Scarborough became irrelevant. It lacked seriousness and cricket looks a poor game when it is frivolous. It did take on fresh importance from 1971 to 1981 because a devoted patron emerged who believed in the old Leveson Gower maxim, 'sportsmanship and fun at the seaside'. This was Sydney Hainsworth, chairman and managing director of Fenner and Company of Hull, who put up the Fenner Trophy for competition over three days in limited-over matches, much more in the vogue of the day.

Unfortunately, the first-class season, with its spreading competitions, elbowed into the Scarborough time of the year. Sydney reluctantly heeded the changing times. He ended his patronage of the Festival with a story by Lord Willis. Lord Willis sent a script to J.B. Priestley and asked, 'Should I put more fire into this play?' Priestley answered, 'No. I should put the play into the fire.' That is what Sydney did to the Fenner Trophy.

Indeed, the official abolition of amateurism meant that amateurs like me were at last paid for playing. Sir Jack Hobbs made a most understanding comment. He said, 'It is sad to see the passing of the amateur. They were a great asset to the game, much appreciated by all of us, because they were able to come in and play freely, whereas many professionals did not feel they could take the chances. Now, times are different and I can understand the position of the amateur who has to make his living. You cannot expect him to refuse good offers outside cricket.'

Thus amateurism melted into changing times, and cricket lost a lot that it has never replaced. It lost the man who was not dependent on the whim of a committee for his livelihood, who had style and presence and who was not easily deflected from the purpose of nurturing good cricket. Most importantly, I think, he was the man who could afford time to attend to the aspirations of the professionals without envy, without putting himself in a position of professional competition with them.

It can be argued that my own amateur life had been contrived and therefore artificial – false. However, I must tell you that I have been forever grateful to Wilfred Wooller for imposing it on me. It was no more artificial than assuming military rank, but you had to be worth it.

At the end of August 1968, Garfield Sobers, then captain of Nottinghamshire, hit six sixes in an over, the first ever to achieve that feat in first-class cricket. I was the fielding captain; it had nothing to do with field placing.

In fact, Glamorgan were waiting for a declaration as Notts moved on untroubled to 308–5 – when Garry came down the steps at the St Helens ground in Swansea. This was the moment for me to give Malcolm Nash, our excellent left-arm swing bowler, the chance to prove that he could bowl cutters. By the late 1960s, Derek Underwood was confirmed as the outstanding slow bowler in England although not in the style of Tony Lock. He was quicker through the air, but that is not to say that his flight lacked deception. He could wrap his fingers round the ball and turn it on the more helpful surfaces, but day by day his superb accuracy came from rolling the ball or cutting it; some turned, some did not. Batsmen often got in a terrible tangle as close fielders preyed and Alan Knott, the finest wicket-keeper I have ever seen, demonstrated his wonderful skills. Underwood and Knott were a magical duet to watch but not so much fun to play against. I have watched a ball pitch on middle and off and turn past the outside edge of my bat, followed by a ball looking the same but going straight on to shave the inside edge of my bat and landing in Knotty's gloves down the leg side. Malcolm Nash believed that if he tried the Underwood style, he too could top the national averages. This was the day of his promised opportunity.

At first, he was treated with caution by the Notts batsmen, who we could see had their eyes on being not out when the innings was closed. Garry Sobers was different of course. He lost patience with his men and after playing sweetly but safely he decided to get on with it. There was a cracking shot to square-leg that sent the ball screaming into the concrete terrace at the Civic Centre end and bouncing back on the first bounce to the square-leg umpire. A second six followed, swung to leg towards the Cricketers Hotel. Then Malcolm shifted his line to outside off stump. This third ball was lofted on to the straight terraces, just wide of mid-on. It was then that I went to talk to him. The match situation did not matter all that much but I wanted to give him the chance to end the experiment and get back to the seam and swing bowling that would get him 991 first-class wickets in his career. He was a good performer, capable of ruining a whole innings if there was a hint of swing in the air.

'If you want to go back to your usual stuff, Malcolm, and whack it in the block hole, that's fine by me,' I told him. 'Look after yourself now.' But Malcolm had entered the dangerous area where pride moves in, but on rubber legs.

'I can handle it, Captain. Leave him to me.' It was as if he was fighting Mohammad Ali and refusing a stool after being knocked down three times in the last round.

Alas for Malcolm, the next ball, still delivered à la Underwood from round the wicket, disappeared over his head on to the pavilion terraces.

The fifth ball was wide and Garry failed to middle it. St Helens, however, had a short straight boundary and although Roger Davis held a brilliant catch at long off, he carried the ball over the line for a fifth six. The towel should have gone in then, but like the rest of the team, I was stationed far away on a boundary. The ball was pulled down short and the rest is history, the only dispute still open being how far the ball was hit over straight midwicket down King Edward Road. Malcolm was only twenty-three and had a longer career ahead than he could have imagined – in the record books.

There was huge excitement in the pavilion and in the dressing room, and leg-pulling for Malcolm Nash.

'Don't worry,' he responded. 'I'll make a fortune out of it. They'll make a movie.'

'What will they call it, Mal, "Gone with the Wind"?'

Wilf Wooller's television commentary for BBC Wales was so emotional he had lost his way during the over, and it took days of editing and re-editing to fix it for posterity. Garry Sobers was a great sportsman on the day, embracing Malcolm, buying him a drink, saying how it nearly happened to him one day, well, for a few balls anyway.

Of course, Garry Sobers could bowl, too. He had massive talent and a huge desire to succeed. His new-ball bowling was genuinely fast with late swing if he wanted it, or rearing bounce. His orthodox left-arm spin was respectable and his wrist-spin was perhaps most useful at the highest level in the breaking of partnerships; lithe and loose, he could flip down all the variations. All of his instincts were sporting and he never flirted outside the true spirit of the game.

After his retirement, Garry preferred competing at golf to watching cricket and he took some hauling off the Sandy Lane course. We did link up when India toured the West Indies in 1988–89 under Dilip Vengsarkar. We followed the whole tour from the commentary box together, with lots of opportunities to talk sport.

Garry came to English county cricket with a large group of overseas players, who were first permitted to join counties in 1967. To add to the entertainment value of cricket, the one-day game was introduced and took hold. My generation, that is those who played their best cricket in the 1960s, was part of a cheated age. We had been brought up when large crowds followed the county game and, as we played, the turnstiles creaked slower and slower. The counties were so insolvent that when the Gillette Cup was started in 1963, the counties asked the home club committee members if they would provide accommodation for the visiting team in order to save money on hotels. I recall staying at the generous home of Lancashire committeeman Charlie Hull, in Oldham.

I remember, too, the Bass Charrington Single Wicket tournament at Lord's and representing Glamorgan because I won a casual day's knock-out with my team-mates at the Barry Cricket Club ground. Brian Close became the self-appointed leader and immediately proposed that the prize money be shared equally between all the players. It was a two-day event and so we accepted £30 each at the start. Billy Griffith, secretary of MCC, arrived in the dressing room to make the draw. A.R. Lewis of Glamorgan will play . . . G.S. Sobers of Notts! I scored 52 runs from the statutory 5 overs. Garry passed my total in 3.4 overs and I was let loose in London for two days with £30 in my pocket.

There we were in 1989 commentating for audiences across the world on one-day international matches. 'I have no objection to limited-over cricket,' Garry said. 'All I wish is that I could have played a lot more of it. I don't believe in countries choosing a one-day team and a Test team. In a perfect world, every Test cricketer is good enough to bat a bit faster, bowl a bit meaner and throw himself around. We pigeonhole youngsters too soon in their careers.'

The pinnacle of ambition everywhere is to captain one's country, however briefly. It is so easy to look back and get it right – well, at least to see clearly where you once got it wrong and, if we are talking England captaincy, it will always hurt. Bob Willis still has to trample the hot coals of his decision to put Australia in to bat on the shiny flats of Adelaide in 1982, and losing by eight wickets. No one would ever throw it at him but Bob is the sort to confront his demons. Nasser

Hussein, another sensitive soldier, has a long life ahead of revisiting Brisbane 2002 and spinning the coin with Steve Waugh. He may even dream he chooses to bat but he will still see baggy green helmets batting first on a plumb track in sunny weather and then see his men stumble from pavilion to crease and back, collecting a death-rattling 79 in England's second innings. With England captaincy, there is nowhere to hide.

Each captain takes his own strengths and weaknesses into the job. For example, David Gower appeared to float on a cloud of insouciance, but appearances were not the truth. Captains, in orchestral terms, have had to be soloist-conductors; they must take their individual playing skills to the concert and conduct the whole show. Gower would be Barenboim, playing a lyrical Mozart piano concerto and conducting mainly by the nod of the head. Ian Botham was not in charge for long but he would have matured to be a soloist-conductor of a concerto for trumpet and orchestra. I allude to confidence not conceit.

These, however, were established Test players. A.R. Lewis was less well known because I became an England captain in my very first Test match, in New Delhi, at the age of thirty-four. Just to make sure the news has arrived home thirty years later, I can report that England won and I was man of the match, but instead of the cash prize that is handed out these days, I was presented with a roll of sari material.

I look back as solemnly as Bob Willis to wonder how my team could have lost the second Test, when, on an easy surface in Calcutta, we failed to score 192 to win. Amiss, Wood, Fletcher, Denness, Lewis, Greig, Knott, Old, Pocock, Underwood, Cottam – 163 all out (Tony Greig 63). I went in at 11–3 and left at 17–4. All the work was done superbly in the field and I still try to dream the happy conclusion – if only I had tried to hit Bishen straight! I draw no consolation from the fact that the batting was not so straightforward as I choose to remember. The totals were declining . . . India 210, England 174, India 155 and England 163. Enough! The more I peer backwards into the mists of the River Hugli, the greater the horror story. Fifteen years later, another England captain was destroyed there. Mike Gatting, an

Ashes-winning captain in Australia, may still wake up at night replaying the reverse sweep at Calcutta that helped to lose the World Cup final to Australia. The ball from Allan Border was slow and looped, without the speed to come on to the bat and . . . It is true that most captains try to play the innings appropriate to the side, or perform the bowling feat to order, but a sporting life is not like that.

At that time, my cricket had been geared to three-day matches not five. I learned quickly, especially on Christmas Day 1972 when some of my successful England team were sitting on the roof of the bus about to be driven back to the hotel in Delhi. The crowds of old Delhi waved and cheered. I was about to climb up to join them when Alan Knott caught my sleeve and asked me to sit with him inside the bus, unseen.

'You've won a great Test match,' he said, 'but I've been one up before. There are four Tests to come and that's a lot of cricket.' I nodded. A Test series is more Ring Cycle than Butterfly.

Cricket captaincy appears more of a cerebral exercise than it truly is and that is because you can look back on a successful campaign and be calm and talk structurally with hindsight. Cricket writers fill their ever-waiting columns with criticism, theory and possibility. So much writing over the last decade has been about upgrading the preparation of the England team to match the Australians. It is stimulating to come up with talk of academies, the Aussies' toughness of character, bowlers 'getting the ball in the right place', batsmen needing 'soft hands' and the rest of the microscopic inspection of England's failing game. I guess it would be a lot duller to conclude the obvious, that not enough of the very young play cricket, playing fields are being sold weekly, and England are not skilled enough, even when translated into 'England do not bowl enough dot balls'. My point is this. Nasser Hussain, whom I believe to be a very good man and an inventive captain, would often be more convincing if he said, 'Look mate, I've got this gut feeling,' rather than trot out the cricket-speak. On the field, a cricket captain should go with his instinct, however sudden and shocking. It is a big moment in a Test match when a captain bins the formula hatched with his coach and goes with the moment, but those are the decisions that release a cricket brain. Richie Benaud suddenly decided to bowl round the wicket into the rough at Old Trafford and won an Ashes series. Mike Brearley made it clear that he did not want a coach-mentor at all.

There are, of course, long-term strategic considerations that can be established in conversation off the field. You want your best side on the field at any one time for the conditions of the moment. You must consider the strengths and weaknesses of the opposition, and you will need a deep understanding of tactical needs when it comes to changing the field and the bowling or making declarations and so on.

Cricket matches, especially Tests, are played over a long time, and this creates the opportunity and the need for thought. Thinking and theorising are essential, but gut feeling and instinct are the special qualities of the outstanding captain in the field, born out of a deep understanding of the game, and the instinct for getting your retaliation in first, as the British Lions coach Carwyn James used to say.

Ray Illingworth was a good example of cricket intelligence and the instinct for knowing how to win. He came to captaincy when he moved from Yorkshire to Leicestershire, and to the England job when Colin Cowdrey snapped an Achilles tendon. It was no surprise at all that he was a successful England captain because he was always the man behind Brian Close at Yorkshire. Something happened to Ray the moment he walked on to a ground. His nose twitched, he could smell the wind – 'too cold to swing, tha' knows' – and that was only in the car park. Before he had reached the middle, he could sense that 'it were damp two yards in from far end' or that the ball will be 'moving off them tufts'. He could spot an uneven cut of annual meadow grass from a hundred yards.

Mike Smith (MJK) was an outstanding reader of opposition techniques both in batting and bowling, and a shrewd reader of temperaments. It came naturally to him. Mike Brearley was a natural inquirer. Cricket captaincy was the perfect role for him, planning the development of the individuals within the team game. It was like solving a giant puzzle with hundreds of variables leading to a maze of possibilities and an ultimate certainty.

A captain needs a confidant, at least I did, and leading England against India and Pakistan, with a friendly but highly competitive ten days in Ceylon, I turned to Keith Fletcher. He was the man behind Brian Taylor in Essex and they did a fine job, so I asked Keith to field at first slip, where he was very accomplished, and to chip in with his opinions whenever he felt the need. There were plenty of opinions flying around apart from his. No captain goes without information from his wicket-keeper and I was lucky to share Alan Knott's view of the play, and Tony Greig's, too. With a bank of information and opinion, we were able to get ourselves into winning situations in the field that, over the Indian series, we did not quite convert with the bat. If Geoff Boycott had come with us – and I asked him to be vice-captain – I believe we would have won the series. It was that close.

There was the pressure, too, as every captain knows, of trying to demonstrate your specialist skills with maximum success while getting the best from everyone else at the same time. A Test series is a major campaign and the form of everyone in the team is the captain's concern. Mike Brearley admitted that he found captaining England difficult at times when he clearly would not have been worth his place as a batsman. 'I wondered if I had the right to be playing. Then I started to wish that I did not have to be active and energetic, or be seen in public; sometimes I just wanted to crawl away, as in one Test in Melbourne.' Mike demonstrated the virtue of persevering. It is not something you can get on prescription in the chemist's; it must be inside you, more heart than brain. I have admired many England captains for the way they have managed to separate their own performance from the team's; they have not allowed their own talent to be weighed down by concerns for the overall performance. Graham Gooch and Michael Atherton are two who led England with skill but who were ready to face the new ball after a ten-minute turnaround. Bob Willis managed to build up a steam of hostility and yet at the same time was calm and detached enough to captain the team. Ian Chappell, another captain I have admired, took on the extra burden of fielding at first slip. It is fine to argue that he was in a good position from which to see the game at close quarters, but it piled up the requirement of concentration needed.

My affection for India and its cricketers was born on that tour and has remained with me to this day, for Pakistan, too, where I was lucky to find myself creating an interesting piece of Glamorgan history. The captains in the three-match series were both Glamorgan players, Majid Khan and A.R. Lewis. In Karachi, the third Test was ended by riots and a dust storm; it was the only pitch that offered a result. Wonderful for England, in that second series we saw the rehabilitation of Dennis Amiss who had run up a few failures in India. I was delighted because I had made a mistake in the first place in leaving him out after three Tests. That sort of talent does not disappear so quickly and in a series played, as I have said, close to the bat against world-class spinners, you can pop a few early balls into eager hands before you have settled at the crease. I returned from the subcontinent convinced that whereas team spirit was always good because it felt like England against the world, the most important personal quality required is self-determination. I wonder if that is now the quality most under threat from coaches, tutors, counsellors and the tribe in attendance to lessen the pain of Test match failure. India and Pakistan taught me that the strength has to be inside. My friendships with those I played against have lasted. It was a privilege to be in their countries and always is to return there.

If leading Glamorgan between 1967 and 1972 was more difficult, it was only because the players were at different stages of development. They were not all so assured or as secure in their methods as Test players were. The second team were part of the effort and there was more to think about and do. It was a consuming job and I felt that six years was about the right length of stay in it. You can develop your team, aim for the top, and then allow another captain to rebuild. Matthew Maynard did just that in the 1990s.

Once you are a Glamorgan man, you tend to stay that way forever, especially if you are brought up in Wales and have learned your game here. Glamorgan's Ailing and Failing Club, that is Peter Walker (conquering cancer), Ossie Wheatley (new hip) and me (replacement knee) still have lunches together every couple of months – pasta and too much red wine. The Glamorgan club lays on a superb old players' day during a home match in the summer. The turnout is excellent. Vivian Jenkins, who played in the 1930s, is the president and as he slips into his nineties, he is brought by his son and close family; he never misses. Jim Pressdee marches in from South Africa where he has lived since his playing days. Admission to the ranks of the former players is by the playing of one first-class match. Trevor Arnott, a romancer of a county captain, used to spin a yarn about the team setting off by bus for Nottingham in the 1930s with only ten players. When they stopped at the town cross in Ebbw Vale, they persuaded a total stranger to jump on board to make a first-class debut at Trent Bridge. They dropped him off on the way back and never saw him again. I am sure that can be proved or disproved, but, by the numbers attending the old players' day, perhaps it happened more often to more strangers.

It was difficult to be a regular attendee at Glamorgan matches because my work was always outside Wales, either on the international cricket-writing and broadcasting circuit or working with the Wales Tourist Board, presiding over MCC for a couple of years and chairing the Wales Ryder Cup bid. Now, however, I look forward to spending more time at the matches.

What do I still carry with me from my Glamorgan playing days? Above all, reaching the pinnacle, the county championship title. When you win, you have what is called good team spirit; when you lose, and do so continually, you have a fractious group of players all believing that they have had a bad deal. The answer is, therefore, do not worry or fret or turn on your own colleagues, but work harder. Ultimately, team games can be broken down into individual efforts, and selfishness can begin to mix the glue that will hold the pieces together again and lead to a winning run.

Glamorgan finished third in 1968, first in 1969 and second in 1970. Each season provided its lesson. The big leap from the bottom of the table to the top came in 1968, by which time I had seen proof that one brilliant individual can lift the play of others. Majid Khan, twenty years old when he joined us in 1967, showed us how talented he was against any opposition and how unselfish a great cricketer can be. Even so, come the championship year he was prepared to bowl with the new ball. Our first match was against Yorkshire at Swansea. Majid was a proclaimer of intentions such as 'I will get a hundred today' or 'I can play you with both legs together', as he once challenged Don Shepherd in Derby. They went to the nets and Majid proved that he could truly do it on a wet practice pitch. On that early May day at Swansea, he said to the players in the dressing room, 'What is all this talk about Boycott? Give me the new ball. I will get him out for you.' In the first innings, he opened the bowling and sent down 19 overs for 31 runs but took no wickets. Nash took four and Shepherd four, but Boycott was out to Lawrence Williams for 68. Majid himself scored 65 before taking the new ball again, removing Boycott for 5 and Hampshire for 23. He took only 8 first-class wickets in the year but promised to return from Pakistan as an off-spinner. He had seen that Malcolm Nash, Lawrence Williams and Tony Cordle were developing quickly into regular wicket-takers; Nash ended with 75 wickets at 18.98 runs apiece, Cordle 52 at 20.32 and Williams 52 at 21.36.

No one before Majid had been so positive about the possibilities of success. Having explained the bonus points system to him, he declared, 'We will win the title with batting bonus points.' Points were without limit, 1 for every 25 runs scored over 150 within 85 overs. Majid studded our innings with punishing stroke play. He never looked towards the personal targets of century or half-century; he simply stroked his way onwards as quickly as possible. When I was chairman of Glamorgan, I signed Viv Richards as a catalyst. They are rare and talented cricketers who can step into a dressing room and turn losing to winning because by their example, more than by what they say, they switch on the optimism of the other players. It used to be so easy to tramp round the first-class circuit in comfortable mediocrity. Glamorgan found inspiration and courage in Majid Khan. He transformed the county in his day because everyone else played to the limits of their talent, too.

Now, in the following century, England needs a Majid Khan, and if there is one clue I would point to, it is his youthfulness. Majid was eighteen years and twenty-six days old when he played his first Test, against Australia in Karachi. England amazingly believes that polishing the talent of twenty-five year olds will shape the players they need. Michael Vaughan became an accepted class batsman at twenty-seven. Until the drive for excellence begins the moment the boy leaves the cradle and progress thereafter is by competition, and until more of the very young play the game in Britain, England will never produce a Majid Khan, someone who can look the greatest of bowlers in the eye and announce, 'I will beat you today.'

When you look back, you can spot the moments when you were handed golden nuggets of sound advice. No dreamy reminiscences these, but simply what the old history lecturers used to value as the thinking of the past by which the present may be better understood and on which the future should be constructed. What were the batting tips and who offered them?

'Go right back, go right forward if you want to survive as a batsman in county cricket,' said Cyril Michael, a Neath headmaster who was a fine club cricketer and a Glamorgan selector. It is obvious advice, but how many betray their early teachers? I have watched Steve Waugh for his whole career and find that, although not possessing the languid skills of, say, Greg Chappell, he has made himself a human machine, sliding right back or right forward, staying sideways, left shoulder pointing to the opposite end. This accepted technique married to his self-determination would have delighted Cyril Michael.

Imperishable was the advice from Garry Sobers. In 1963 at Cardiff Arms Park I was at the crease to face the third ball of the morning, to be bowled by Wesley Hall. There was only one fielder in front of my popping crease, Conrad Hunte at short-leg. Wes retreated to the start of his run, just a handful of yards from the small stand and white fence at the North Stand end. I made the confident gesture of looking round the field before taking strike. Apart from Conrad, there was no one within fifty yards! Deryck Murray was the young wicket-keeper and alongside him was an umbrella of catchers. I think the three balls were identical – lightning fast, red blurs, pitched well up. They prompted stabs from me that made no contact with the bat. All three swung away. At the end of the over, I was still there. As I had walked out of the dressing room to bat, I had seen Bernard Hedges, due in after me, remove his false teeth, wrap them in his handkerchief and store them in his blazer pocket. Jim Pressdee, across behind the door, had been stuffing cottonwool in his cap, and he was going in at number seven! I was not frightened of being hit but by the realisation that for the first time in my life I had not truly seen the ball – three times. Had my eyesight gone in front of that full house on a sunny day? The West Indies slip fielders ambled past me to the other end. One stopped to say, 'This is where you learn, son. Speed is only relative. If you are still here in five minutes, he won't be so quick an' you'll be hitting the ball with the bat for a change.' He cracked into laughter and, with a wide smile, patted me on the back. Garry Sobers then sloped off to join the others and I hung in for a half-century . . . before holing out to Sobers' wrist-spin. Over a drink at the end of play he was laughs and smiles again. 'Oh!' he grinned. 'I forgot to tell you. When you've seen the quicks off, watch out for the joker with the chinaman.'

I could pass on many of Ted Dexter's theories on batting, but that is a book of its own. The important Dexter message to me was also about facing fast bowling. Ted stood behind the net at Fenner's where I was making heavy work of the batting practice. I was in the Glamorgan side playing a match against Cambridge University and, before play on day one, had persuaded Jeff Jones, our England fast bowler, to send down a couple of fast overs. My feet were all over the place and the ball kept fizzing past the outside edge of the bat or off the edge. I had been in poor form for a week or more.

'Can I tell you something?' asked Ted. I was delighted to listen. 'You're making too many positive moves before the ball is released. Stand still and keep your head still until the ball is in the air. You'll have to move quickly but it's strange, the longer you wait and the later you move, the more time you have because you will only move once.' Jeff continued to send the ball hissing past my bat into the back of the net. 'Keep going, it will happen,' encouraged Ted. At last, I got the bat on a ball from Jeff, who was a truly fast bowler, and suddenly everything was synchronised. I began to get runs after that and I reckoned it had been like a clockmaker adjusting the balance and the timing. It is difficult to stand still in the face of fast bowling, but you must.

This is not to say that you must stand still as a rock. There are tiny foot movements that simply get you poised and ready for the move. Brian Close moved well back on his stumps and across; Tom Graveney was on the front foot but tall enough to meet the rising ball standing up. Especially against fast bowling, some of the finest players have moved back and across their stumps. It does not matter which way they go as long as they are not committed to the ultimate stroke, backwards or forwards. Sachin Tendulkar moves his front foot a little bit forward and across, say two inches, and the back one moves in line with it, but they are small movements and always on the balls of his feet. These movements are to get ready. You have to start somewhere. He can move backwards or forwards. 'Head still,' said Ted Dexter, 'be poised and light on the feet but wait to make the decisive movement.'

When Tony Greig was leading England against the West Indies at home in 1976, we discussed the barrage of short-pitched balls sent down by the West Indians. Tony thought he would make his team practise indoors against bowling with bouncy, hard, rubber balls. He wanted to impress the lesson of the still head, dropping the gloves under the bounce and swaying or ducking a bouncer that was just about to remove your cap. What a test, putting this theory into practice against Andy Roberts, Michael Holding, Wayne Daniel and Vanburn Holder, with Joel Garner, Colin Croft and Malcolm Marshall queuing to get at you!

I also remember Majid Khan's advice. Majid and I were sitting with pads on one day, waiting to bat at Edgbaston, when one of the Glamorgan boys asked why he was so silent. There are always players in a county dressing room joshing, maybe to counteract the tension of the contest and their role in it. In his dark brown voice, Majid slowly explained, 'People who talk a lot allow the power to leave their bodies. Gossip weakens you. I say nothing in order to keep my strength inside me for the fight in the middle.' Pure de Vigny, I thought, *La Mort du Loup* – '*seul le silence est grand: tout le reste est faiblesse.*' Majid might have written it. He was a noble cricketer full of natural talent and innate good sportsmanship and with the essential personal qualities to refuse to be dominated by an opponent. That turned his play into something very special. Talent alone does not work.

In many ways he was young and boyish with the warrior instincts of the Patan country. 'Get me some runs today,' I once said as we met midwicket in a vital county match in the championship of 1969. We were at Cheltenham College playing against the leaders of the table, Gloucestershire.

'Only if you buy me an ice cream for a 50, and two ice creams if I go further,' he replied. So it was a two ice-cream afternoon, double cones, and I was happy with that. Majid was proud and brave and the more dangerous the bowling, the more his batting was packed with watchfulness and long bravura passages.

No one questioned his silence. It was considered an absolute strength and some tried to emulate his approach. He was so quiet and intent on the most important day of our county championship win in 1969. He walked solemnly to the wicket at Sophia Gardens to face a strong Worcestershire attack on a difficult pitch, the ball bouncing high and low and turning square from the start. After an amazing display of stroke-making, he had scored 156 out of 214 in 180 minutes. We scrambled to 265 but his innings virtually won the match and brought us the title. Silence and inward strength, I am sure, still work.

Geoffrey Boycott was a consummate opening batsman, always worth listening to on the subject. I remember playing a Test trial with him at Worcester in 1974. I was fielding in the gully when John Snow took the new ball against him. Snowy was a superb bowler, controlled and intelligent, and fast when he wanted to be. The bouncers came skimming over Geoffrey's cap – no helmets in those days – and after one particularly torrid over, Boycott walked in my direction to say, as if he was using the chat to steel himself, 'It's my job, y'see. I am an opening batsman and if I want to be the best in Test cricket, this is what I have to do every day. It's part of the beauty of the game is playing fast bowling.' Geoffrey was unequalled in preparing the mind for batting. On the other hand, he was not too good at working from the other end to help his partner's play. Running his own runs often seemed quite a different exercise from running his partner's. I have admired his play as well as been infuriated by it.

When David Gower came back into the England side to play against Pakistan at Old Trafford in 1992, he needed just 34 runs to overtake Geoffrey Boycott's record aggregate of 8,114 runs for England in Tests. I was in the BBC commentary team as usual, as was Geoffrey, and through my headphones I heard the director, Keith MacKenzie, warn cameramen that he would want a shot of Boycott at the moment Gower got the new record. As David edged closer, Geoffrey was not to be found. Spies reported that he was sitting in one of the less-used commentary boxes along the roof top. The director was not pleased. Later in the afternoon, my live teatime interview on television was with Gower, already out for 73, and the former top run-scorer Boycott. After about ten minutes, I put it to both of them, 'Scoring so many runs, a lot of professionals will argue, can only be achieved by being selfish players. Is that a reasonable judgement?' Gower smiled and said that playing for oneself is mostly playing for the team, but in those moments when the team requires a different sort of contribution, he has always been pleased to do his best. Boycott was adamant: 'I am not selfish, I am single-minded.' Not many who played with him could see the dividing line between those two, but if my exercise is to hand down eternal truths from the best players, I will always turn to Geoffrey Boycott for my example of preparation and professionalism. I often wish I had been issued with a set of Boycott blinkers, but such is my love of the fuller life, I would have needed a blindfold as well.

Let me leave the subject with a Boycott quote:

Preparing the mind for batting was always vital to me. I started thinking about it the night before, but with club or occasional cricketers that might not be so easy. However, on the morning of a match, you have to give some thought to it – who you are playing against and what bowlers you will face. Then when you get to the ground it is important to look at the pitch. If it looks slow, you know the ball may not come on to you quickly. On wet ground it may even sit up and then you know in your own mind that you will have to get right forward, absolutely to the pitch of the ball if you are playing off the front foot. You deduce, though, that most of your runs will come off the back foot with pulls and cuts. On the other hand, if it is a fast bouncy pitch, you will not envisage pushing forward too often into a steep bounce, and you may suspect the ball is going to turn.

The juxtaposition of Boycott and Gower that day proves that there is more than one road to the record books. The difference probably was that Geoffrey went to work and David went to play. Both, however, stood up to the finest bowlers because that was what Test batsmen were there to do. It went with the territory they loved most, the batting crease.

THE 1977 REVOLUTION

To give Kerry Packer and his allies their full credit, the thought of the commercial piracy that turned the established administration of cricket on its head back in 1977 still gives me a frisson, a small shudder of the original mighty shock. I smile, too, because although I did not want international cricket to become the plaything of a billionaire who craved television rights in Australia, I had played out a lengthy career for Glamorgan and England for meagre financial return and I wondered if cricket could grow to match international tennis, football and golf for cash returns. Advancing the power of television and commercial rights to the game offered a tinkle of coinage to the professional player. At the time, though, it was dramatic. Old friendships were severed and lawyers swarmed all over the game.

As for Tony Greig's role, it was impossible for me to see it as anything but betrayal. He was England captain when he recruited rebel Test teams for Packer, arguing that all he wanted to do was to give MCC and the Test and County Cricket Board (TCCB) a jolt. To him, it was hard business and he has always argued the business rationale. 'You don't make dawn raids in the City by warning your prey,' he contended. I believe he cast himself in tycoon image, as an international mover and shaker, banking in Zurich, travelling by private jet – an embryo Kerry. Not surprisingly, his behaviour during the coup told everyone a lot about his play on the field. Tony Greig was a terrific scrapper and, for a captain, a joy to have in the side.

While the cricket world waited for Mr Justice Slade in the High Court in London to pronounce his verdict, I was given the chance to be in Australia for the start of this first World Series tournament. The *Daily Telegraph*'s cricket correspondent, Michael Melford, felt that his presence in Australia would give Packer's pirate ship the paper's endorsement and so I was asked to go instead.

It promised to be terrific work and on Saturday, 19 November 1977 I flew from London Heathrow to Melbourne to report the most amazing experiment in cricket. BBC Radio decided that two 'Sport on Four' Saturday morning programmes should come from Australia and my producer Dick Scales and I set off with two Uher tape-recorders, a typewriter and all the accoutrements of a couple of Scoop reporters.

Would the Packer players who were in the England side, including Greig, be banned for two years as had been proposed by TCCB? Would John Snow and Michael Procter be expelled from the county championship?

My diary records that the first friendly faces I came across in Australia belonged to Harry and Myra Secombe. We met in the transit lounge at Sydney airport. Harry loved Australia but found his patience tested by the dozens of Welsh people coming up to him and claiming him as their own – 'My auntie is from Aberystwyth, you know.' He was so pleasant to them but when he turned back to Myra and me he said, for the first time but not the last, 'You have to leave South Wales, Tony. No one will let you be successful down there. I love Wales but I am much happier in Surrey.'

Dick and I were soon in Melbourne where the sixty signed-up international cricketers – West Indians, Australians and Rest of the World – were already working in squads. We pitched camp in a hotel cheap enough to fit the BBC expenses, the John Batman Travel Lodge at 68 Queens Road, St Kilda.

In the *Sunday Telegraph* I at first represented the horror of the traditional cricket lover, explaining that Mr Packer's door, which he said was open for discussions with the established game, would quickly let in a killing draught.

Cricketers were aware of the big salaries available in other sports. It had been £200 a Test for England in 1973. For a five-month tour of India, Ceylon and Pakistan, including eight Tests, the fee for being captain was £1,300, which, I guess, was the same as everyone else in the side. Perhaps the most amusing move by the TCCB was to write to the players, inviting them to take advantage of an arrangement made to bank the tour fee in the Channel Islands, a sophistication of saving that simply did not apply to our daily lives. It was a lot less than I would have earned for freelance writing and broadcasting had I stayed at home. Yes, I would have taken out a mortgage and paid MCC just for the chance of doing that job but, at the time, the pay was a meagre return for getting to the top of the game. In sport, cricketers were comparative paupers. When Packer swooped out of the sky, TCCB spluttered statements to the effect that long-standing plans for paying more money had been on the way, but there was no proof of that and there was a lot of sympathy for the cricketers.

I knew I was stepping into a new school of professional journalism. This would be daily world sports news and front-page material. We would be as good as the importance of the people we interviewed and the strength of our questions. Dick telephoned my room at 4.30 a.m. Melbourne time to say that the High Court decision was imminent. Our work was geared to London time and so, I guess, at that same time, Kerry Packer was calling Tony Greig's room in the Old Melbourne Inn, World Series headquarters, to say, 'We've beaten the bastards and it's a whitewash' – at least, that was what Greigy told me. Mr Justice Slade had found for Greig, Snow and Procter against MCC and TCCB. 'Sport on Four' was going to air in fourteen hours; we had no time to waste. Writers can stay on the telephone all day and write an informed piece at the end of it; not so radio broadcasters. Someone has to talk into your microphone; you have to locate them, persuade them to speak, remembering that if they choose not to, you have no programme at all. There was only one interviewee, Kerry Packer. Our producers back in Broadcasting House told us that everyone at Lord's and throughout the old cricket world was devastated.

It was the third day of World Series cricket and we drove out to the Victoria Football League ground at Waverley. These rogue matches had been banned from Australian cricket grounds where the established game was played and so most of their cricket was staged on showgrounds or Australian Rules pitches. The twenty-two-yard strips for the play were being grown in concrete troughs in greenhouses behind the spectator stands. When needed, they were lifted by crane and lowered into the middle. They were set in two halves; the join looked threatening to batsmen. The grass grew quickly, its long roots wrapping round chicken wire that was laid an inch or two down to hold the surface securely together. The players were in coloured clothes. What a shock! World Series Cricket, the tournament, had to be as bold and daring as the piracy itself. Who could mastermind it? When I knew the answer, I knew it would be properly thought out. Richie Benaud and Associates, as a company, were perfectly entitled to take on this work without accusations of treachery and I can think of no one more knowledgeable and so concerned with detail and perfection than Richie. Cricket played under floodlights, in coloured clothes with white balls against black sightscreens represented a blank piece of paper for the inventor – all this would extract the very best from the Benauds. And so it did. Now I have watched British county cricket played under lights and MCC in 2002 have announced a shocking experiment – drop-in pitches at the game's headquarters, cultivated under cover at the Nursery End. So World Series, we must admit, led the way by more than twenty-five years! That is how visionary it all was.

At Waverley in 1977, where would I find Mr Packer? He was in the large Australian dressing room hoofing a narrow, pointed Aussie Rules football across a large space at Dennis Lillee who drove it back to him. He saw me with my tape-recorder and microphone but kept on

Bat or bow? The early dilemma contained in a photograph taken at home by
Peter Atherton-Galbraith

Tony Greig, one of the main protagonists in the Packer revolution

Part of the Packer legacy – floodlights over a game during the World Series. At the time we all hated it, but we couldn't see that it was the future

Around the world for the *Sunday Telegraph* – typewriter days alongside John Thicknesse of the London *Evening Standard*. How times have changed

John Arlott, the doyen of cricket commentators, and the man who gave me some of the best advice on how to broadcast

Richie Benaud and I celebrate the end of another season of cricket coverage with the BBC in the olive groves of Centinale in Tuscany. Not much about cricket was spoken at the home of Graham and Angela Chidgey

Viv Richards celebrates with Hugh Morris as Glamorgan win their first limited-overs trophy, the 1993 AXA Equity and Law Sunday League title

Matthew Maynard, one of Glamorgan's finest strikers of the ball over the last fifteen years or so, drives through the covers during the 2000 Benson and Hedges Cup final

Hugh Morris, another key figure in Glamorgan's revival

EMPICS

One of the doubtful pleasures of my presidency: handing over the Ashes trophy to Mark Taylor in 1999. How long before England regains them?

The MCC committee of 1999–2000: (back row) R.G. Marlar, M.O.C. Sturt, J.A.F. Vallance, N.M. Peters, J.A. Bailey, Sir Timothy Rice, O.H.J. Stocken, D.A. Peck, T.J.G. O'Gorman; (middle row) Lord Alexander of Weedon, E.R. Dexter, M.J. de Rohan, C.A. Fry, R.P. Hodson, B.A. Sharp, A.W. Wreford; (front row) R.D.V. Knight, D.L. Hudd, Sir Michael Jenkins, me, D.R.W. Silk, Lord Cowdrey of Tonbridge, M.E.L. Meluish

JOAN LEWIS

Frank Brache in Cape Town, the coloured administrator who fought apartheid from inside cricket – and had his house petrol-bombed three times

John Passmore on his beloved Langa cricket ground. He was very much the father of black cricket in South Africa, working phenomenally hard to bring the sport to the schoolchildren of the townships

JOAN LEWIS

JOAN LEWIS

Ali Bacher (right), evangelist of South African cricket, standing in front of the barbed wire in Alexandria township, Johannesburg. When I first visited his country in 1987, he urged me to go everywhere and report what I saw

As chairman of the Wales Tourist Board, I am signing a Memorandum of Understanding with Sam Sizman, chairman of New South Wales Tourist Board, in Sydney

About to win the Ryder Cup for Wales – October 2001: (left to right) Sir David Rowe Beddoe, me and Assembly First Minister Rhodri Morgan

1985 – many years on from our battle for a Blue, Ian Balding and I are still close friends. (Left to right) Sheyna Baig (daughter of Abbas), me, my godson Andrew Balding (now the trainer), Ian Balding, Claire Balding, Anabel, Emma Balding and Joanie

The Lewis girls at a 'Last Days of the Raj' party – Joanna, Joanie and Anabel

In the best possible company – at home on the morning I was awarded my CBE, 1 January 2002, with grandchildren Freddie and Gabriella

kicking. He made me wait fifteen minutes or so. Fair enough, I had written strongly against him. Then he turned to me and said, 'Yeah, we'll talk.' He was in shirtsleeves and perched on his head was a sailor hat that carried the message Super Tests. 'You are no friend of ours, are you?' he said. 'And I know exactly who you are.' He brushed past me and I trailed after him. 'A lot of you fellas are hopping over the fence today.'

Out in the sunshine in front of the cricket I eventually got in a word. 'Are we to chat or not?' The cat-and-mouse game was getting painful. He melted into a delicate advocate.

'We must put cricket first now. I realise they must be disappointed in England, but they are men who will accept the umpire's decision. But y'know, I went to England five or six times to hang around their door. It's not going to happen that way this time. But my door is wide open.'

We completed an interview that would be played over the whole BBC network during the next twenty-four hours. He was a businessman with muscle. He had the sixty best cricketers in the world, he had millions of dollars and he was in an international negotiating position.

Tony Greig had been in my England side touring India, Ceylon and Pakistan in 1972–73 and had led his own tour to India in 1977. He was aggressive and competitive, one of the most adaptable batsmen I have seen, a fielder who could infuriate batsmen by standing extra close at silly point and a bowler of swing and spin. Watching him bat from the other end, I saw him use his long reach to construct a sound defensive base, and play most of the attacking strokes including some cracking drives with the straightest and widest of bats. His bowling with a new or nearly new ball was whippy. He had a sharp outswing while his off-spin was something of a phantom but on line and on length. He could turn the ball in to the right-handers but often he simply got the ball to drift away in the air and go straight on along that line. Lots of top batsmen played on the inside and gave catches to the fielders ranged from point to the wicket-keeper. Above all his technical attributes was the mind of a warrior who loved the battle and hated coming second. He was inventive and up to everything.

He was easily lured to Australia to work for Kerry Packer and thereafter sought to trample over the cricket-broadcasting world with giant strides, sometimes successfully but not always. I have enjoyed his company. We played wonderfully competitive golf with Geoffrey Boycott when the three of us were working in a Sky TV commentary team on an Indian tour of the West Indies. Both Tony and Geoffrey insisted that there would be no gimme putts, not even from an inch – 'Only the ball in the hole counts.'

If I wanted to hear how poor a commentator I was, I would just have to stand behind a Greig conversation with the director or producer. All his life he has lusted to be up front, in charge and paid more than the others. I heard him not so much a cricket commentator as a salesman, shouting in a rather raucous hybrid accent from the back of a lorry. Strokes and misses and a multitude of replays were heaped into the various sales pitches. It never was my style but then, after Kerry Packer's World Series, in terms of presentation, the whole cricket world changed. 'If the ball is in the air, get out of your commentary seat and up there with it' was Greig's approach. I pointed out that seeing Curtly Ambrose loft a catch to mid-off, far from getting me off my seat, would keep my voice in the lower reaches of excitement because it was expected of Curtly to hole out there. To hear the ordinary over-hyped was switch-off time for me, but the good quality about Greigy is that you can agree to differ.

I did go to a dinner party in Sydney and was asked whether or not I would like a seat facing the television to watch 'the Wednesday game'. Channel Nine viewers had grown to love their weekly, floodlit 50-over-a-side bash. Australia meantime, the real Australia, had lost their team to Packer and had to choose a team of second-liners. Bobby Simpson, at the age of forty-one, returned to captain the side.

Jim Swanton had written to Sir Donald Bradman to introduce me while I was there and ask if I could visit him. Sir Don telephoned me at the Travel Lodge, regretting that he could not make a meeting but we spoke for twenty minutes or more. He was interested in Kerry Packer and was convinced that this was purely a television exercise. He conceded the dilemma of a young player such as bowler Wayne Prior, who was doing a menial job and could not possibly turn down a fat Packer contract, but he not only disapproved of the signing of the better players, he emphasised, 'I hate and detest those top players who could set examples for all to follow but who have now sold the game cheaply. Those who secretly talk with Kerry Packer while pretending to be something else are lower than anything I can describe.'

Before putting down the telephone, I added, 'Sir Don, I have never forgiven you for not playing against Glamorgan at Swansea in 1948. It was only when I became a county player that I understood that the visiting tour captain, if he wasn't playing against us, was probably up in London staying at the Waldorf or playing golf with Gubby Allen at the Berkshire. I was ten years old and sitting on the St Helens benches wondering why Lindsay Hassett was coming out to toss with Wilf Wooller.' I wrote down Bradman's reply: 'You didn't miss anything, Tony. It was all over by then.'

My 'Sport on Four' work continued through the weeks in Australia. I spent time at the world billiards championship, interviewed the swimmer Dawn Fraser, Harry Secombe, Wilfred Brambell and Harry H. Corbett aka Steptoe and Son, and Sue Barker after a win against Tomanova at Kooyong. There were fascinating pieces to be recorded later in World Series matches with Barry Richards and Majid Khan, who wore helmets for the first time in their lives. Imagine batting against Lillee, Pascoe, Procter, Snow, Imran Khan, Roberts, Garner, Holding and Daniel. With Dick Scales, I worked flat out for almost a month, retreating many a night to the Travel Lodge, which was licensed in the first-floor restaurant only. It was quaint and about forty years off the pace. Fifty-year-old couples did foxtrots to a three-piece band. Dick and I stared blankly at each other across the candlelit table or retreated to the land of duty-free brandy in the bedroom. We flew off to Brisbane to do interviews at the first official Test, Australia versus India, which was transmitted on ABC Television at exactly the same time as the Super Test, WSC Australia versus WSC West Indies, went out on Channel Nine.

I look at my notes on the Super Test now and laugh at my own lack of vision. I was actually seeing the future:

> Arrive at the VFL stadium to find to my amazement that the
> motif of World Series Cricket has been painted on the grass on
> the outfield, behind the stumps at each end – say twenty yards by
> ten. Three stumps in black paint which has turned out dark green
> and a red ball on top of them. It is horrific. There are only four
> hundred people here. The West Indies come out to field one by
> one each accompanied by a jazzy announcement. Sue Barker said,
> 'It's like team tennis in America. They announce you like that and
> you spring out on to the court into the midst of cockerels, cheer
> leaders and especially the one man who, as I served, was lying
> down not far behind me, looking up my skirt.' At Waverley, it was
> sad to see so many fine players performing for so few people. Yet
> the television coverage was inspired. A camera behind the bowler
> at each end was an innovation. The action replays were intriguing
> from different angles including wonderful reviews of slip catches.
> The players were better recognised than those in the official Test
> at Brisbane and the advertising breaks usually showed one of
> them in a commercial role – Lillee promoted Kay Car Hire and
> Tony Greig, Kellogg's.

There was a commentary to West Indies by that consummate professional Tony Cozier, and Fred Trueman was constantly wooing the
Channel Nine viewers with 'I can tell you Victorians that if you want
to see the best cricket in the world, you should come along to this
magnificent ground in Waverley tomorrow.'

I will always be indebted to Ian Wooldridge of the *Daily Mail* for
demonstrating how a real London sports reporter should work in the
circumstances. I interviewed him for 'Sport on Four' in his room in the
Old Melbourne Inn one morning. He said the first lesson on a hot
news tour is to get accommodation near the players and organisers.
Second lesson, with news breaking by the minute, do not become slave
to cricket-playing hours. Work according to London time to be sure
that you are not in bed after a slow dinner in the Melbourne Club

while news is breaking. Ian opened a bottle of champagne before taking me on lesson number three. We hit the Cricketers Bar in the Old Windsor Hotel at midday. He looked very Graham Greene in his white shoes and sunglasses. He was off to an elephant race in Sri Lanka, next stop. I was introduced to a gang of Australian journalists and editors, Peter McFarline, Trevor Grant, David Lord, Allan Shiell and many others; then to a press drinking club. Ian enjoyed an Aussie adulation and it was easy to see how these were the professionals ready to file the lead stories with the hard opinion. Then, as instructed by my tutor, I retreated to my bed for a sleep and composed an embryo piece for the *Telegraph*. We resumed the tutorial at a late supper with others in the Little Reata restaurant. I was back at my desk just after midnight, full of ideas for firming up my story. At two o'clock I was in a taxi to the cable office and by three o'clock the piece was filed. In London, the sports desk was just arriving for the day's work. I rang them, as per instructions, to check on the stories that others had written and were leaking round Fleet Street. I tweaked my piece and went to sleep feeling wiser. I would miss the morning's play of twenty-two stars before a spectator public of under 1,000, but I did not miss a jot in the development of the biggest sporting story of the time. Both my 'Sport on Four' programmes from Australia received a commendation from the controller of Radio Four.

Tony Greig, removed from the England captaincy, would continue as captain of Sussex. Some saw this as the first sign of a possible compromise between the warring factions but the Sussex stance was as much motivated by the High Court case, which had been won and lost on the issue of restraint of trade. Greigy could still go to work.

In the following winter of 1979, I was back in Australia with 'Sport on Four'. My script opened:

And here we are back in Melbourne two years later, on the day that peace is finally cemented. For the first time since 1977, a full England side meets a full Australian side. Meantime, Mr Packer and the Australian Board have got together; deadly opponents are now bosom pals. Packer's Channel Nine has the TV rights to cover Test matches and his marketing agency, Publicity and Broadcasting Ltd, organised the promotions of the game.

Night cricket became a fever in Australia; jingles rang out, advertisements moved quickly along the bottom of the television screen as Michael Holding moved faster on top, racing in to bowl. In fact, the World Series jingle rushed in to the top ten in the Sydney charts and climbed high in the national ratings:

> You've been training all the winter,
> And there's not a team that's fitter,
> And that's the way it's going to be;'
> 'Cos you're up against the best, you know,
> This is Super Tests you know,
> You're up against the best the world has seen.
> Come on, Aussie, come on, come on,
> Come on, Aussie, come on.
> Lillee's pounding down like a machine,
> Pascoe's making divots in the green,
> Marsh is taking wickets,
> Hooksie's clearing wickets,
> Hooksie's clearing pickets,
> And the Chappells' eyes have got that killer gleam,
> Come on, Aussie, come on, come on,
> Come on, Aussie, come on.

Some never forgave Tony Greig, to the extent that the honorary membership of MCC that is awarded to every Test player who has notched up over forty-five Test matches was withheld. Others were made to wait, decisions being taken according to their level of sportsmanship and good behaviour, or lack of both. When I was president of MCC, 1998–2000, I was happy to urge the admission of A.W. Greig, former England captain. It was ludicrous to be watching a day-night match in England without acknowledging the truth that, back in 1977, he had got a few things right.

The Packer Revolution certainly transformed the bidding for commercial rights of Test cricket. Kerry Packer thundered the power of television; it overshadowed the game itself and by 1999 the commercial rights to ICC's cricket, including two World Cups, went to a bid of $550 million. This largesse permitted the world's governing body to establish itself with a structured staff and an overriding authority. The ICC, for so long called a toothless tiger, was becoming wealthy enough to order the world game.

Other commercial rights proliferated. The televising of cricket became essential to its economic viability. In this respect, India led the way although by 2000 a friend in Bombay was constantly telephoning to complain about the amount of cricket on his screen. He loved the game but, 'What price can you put on over-kill?' he wanted to know. We shall see.

A direct result of World Series was the subsequent concentration on the packaging of cricket as entertainment. What was jokingly greeted as 'red nose and paper hat' cricket became the regular fare. Black coats for umpires, white balls, black sightscreens, pop music at the fall of a wicket – all history, long-ago touches in World Series cricket, but whoever thought that night cricket would ever settle in the United Kingdom? It is obvious that counties need to put on their shows when people are not at work, but the British summer was thought to be an unreliable companion. It may still deter counties from investing in floodlighting. In Cardiff, at the end of the 2002 season, a couple of international limited-over matches were put on under the closed roof of the Millennium Stadium. It was critically dismissed as a spoof game on a rugby pitch, but then New Zealand play Test cricket in Auckland on a rugby field with the pitch slanted, corner to corner. In 2003 we are to welcome in Britain a 20-over-a-side competition between professional teams, an evening game set up to attract the young.

There has been little new or shocking since Packer. Channel Nine television advanced miles ahead of the BBC in production and pictures, a situation that changed only when Channel 4 in Britain made its debut and set high technical standards as well as developing the magazine side of cricket coverage.

The downside of 1977 was the bitter taste of duplicity and the scorn heaped on many administrators who had made invaluable contributions to our cricket. On the positive side, it must be argued that the game of cricket in the United Kingdom was taught a lesson for a lifetime and more – to be ahead of the game at all times both in playing and commerce. Cricket, as has been stated so often, merely reflects the society in which we live. Had it not been Kerry Packer, it would have been a billionaire by another name. Cricket was there for the taking, and no one except he could see it.

RAINBOW FORMING

When South Africa played a Test at Lord's in 1994 they came as the Proteas. Apartheid had fallen, life in South Africa was officially multi-racial, and the truth was sinking in throughout the United Kingdom that the all-white Springboks who played the last Test at Lord's twenty-nine years earlier were gone forever. It was a new beginning.

During the match, Joan and I were invited to dinner as guests of the new United Board of South African Cricket, at which both the Board's president, Kris Makerdhuj, and the director Dr Ali Bacher generously thanked me for having had the resolve to travel to South Africa and to write what I saw before it became fashionable to do so. We were honoured. That evening I saw that a new relationship had been born between Ali Bacher and Steve Tshwete, Mr Mandela's newly appointed chief spokesman on sport in the African National Congress. Their relationship may have been, as Donald Woods had described it, 'the tip of an iceberg of a more widespread commitment throughout South African cricket', but I saw it representing the end of the apartheid days in cricket, more what Pakistan's General Zia ul Haq used to say when cricket bonded India and Pakistan on the precipice of war, 'cricket, a bridge and a glue'. I hoped so.

The last years of apartheid were fascinating. The world had already agreed that the laws regulating South African life according to the separate development of races were detestable. Sport was chosen as one of the protesters' targets, but, of course, it was much easier to pass moral judgement from a distance than it was for the South Africans to see themselves as others saw them. Reconciling these two poles was a painful process. South Africa was outcast from the Commonwealth. Trade sanctions had, for example, removed Cape apples from British shops, the flow abroad of Stellenbosch wines dried up and commercial investment into South Africa, although legal, began to backfire on those who toyed with it.

The original anger at the apartheid regime had turned to sporting boycott and demonstration, and it became impossible to protect sporting venues in Britain as long as Springbok tours continued. The actual cost of protecting a South African rugby match in Manchester in November 1969 was £8,985 – 2,300 police were employed, twenty-nine of them were injured and there were ninety-three arrests. Lord's cricket ground would have to be floodlit at night and ringed with barbed wire to keep out the 'ban the tour' demonstrators. I reported a Springbok rugby match in Swansea, for the *Telegraph*. Before the kick-off, a demonstrator stabbed a policeman and the pitch was 'bombed' from helicopters with flour bags and tintacks. It got more and more violent as pitch-invaders were caught by vigilantes and thrown over the low wall at the Mumbles end for a thumping by the local rugger boys. This was not because of some divine right within rugby football but because the majority of British people were ignorant of the way apartheid worked in South Africa: this was their big sporting tilt at the Springboks and they did not understand why anyone should try to stop the matches.

Certainly in South Wales, rugby was a passion. Tours by the All Blacks, Springboks and Wallabies were infrequent and therefore treated as great tests of strength. When I was a boy, I knew that Wales had never beaten South Africa and that very failure rolled up the challenge to mighty proportions for the home side. The Springboks of 1951 were my household names and all my thirteen-year-old recollections contain images of Okey Geffin, the prop who toe-kicked slowly revolving balls over the crossbar from long distances; Chum Ochse, the lightning wing, all leg muscles and dash; Basie van Wyk, the balding, marauding open-side wing-forward, born with the magical instinct of interposing his strong athletic presence between any outside-half in the world and an open space; and Hennie Muller, the captain, thundering away in the engine room of the pack.

In 1960 at Cardiff Arms Park, I saw Wales lose 0–3 in wind and rain, but we had seen the running talents of the Boks as they overpowered club and county challenges, especially the back play of F.T. Roux, Kirkpatrick, Gainsford and Engelbrecht. Avril Malan led a rough, tough team, nowhere more intimidating than at forward with the massive props Kuhn and du Toit backed by Claassen, van Zyl, Hopwood and Pelser. Pelser had only one eye but it did not appear to matter because he ran through opponents not round them. Ten years later, in 1970, when the anti-apartheid movement was at its most effective, in front of barbed wire and police patrols, for the first time in six encounters, Wales managed not to lose. Gareth Edwards led the side that drew 6–6 against the Springboks captained by his opposing scrum-half Dawie de Villiers.

There are few now who say that Peter Hain, student leader of the protest movement, was wrong. Years later, at that special dinner party in 1994, Ali Bacher spoke to acknowledge the need for Hain's work and the urgency for the most reactionary games-lover to embrace a new social order.

Then, I remember clearly one sunny afternoon in the early eighties, walking in the ground of the Hurlingham Club in London with two of the best-known South African Test players, Jackie McGlew, the former captain, and Roy McLean, the dashing stroke-maker from the middle order. I talked fondly about the old days – matches at Fenner's, games at Swansea – and we let memories flow. What was the mood in South Africa after a decade in the wilderness? Both were seriously aggrieved. The International Cricket Council had set out a list of requirements of South African cricket, particularly to make the game and its administration multi-racial, but no sooner had that challenging programme been fulfilled than the Council shifted the parameters. More requirements were made and met, but each time the parameters slid as if on an ice-rink to eternity. Jackie McGlew, a serious and Christian man, said, 'Better not to have promised at all, Tony. We are like kids who have had to crawl through ten years of barbed wire to reach Father Christmas and when we get there, he's got nothing to give us. That's cruel, man.' We exchanged letters over the following years and in one he asked me to go to his country to look around – 'No one knows what is happening here, and until someone comes, no one will truly understand. Cricket has taken a big lead. You would be proud of our cricket people.'

The more moving voice coming out of South Africa, however, was that of Mr Hassan Howa of the South African Cricket Board of Control (SACBOC). 'No normal sport in an abnormal society,' he said. It was a powerful flag to wave. A United Nations black list grew in New York; the non-white Test-playing countries began to refuse entry to any cricketer who had ties with South Africa. There were still 387 racial laws in South Africa where a person's black skin was equated with statutory crime. For the majority, Hassan Howa's word was enough, and yet I had a nagging trust in old friends and in their conviction that the social order in South Africa was changing so quickly that, in Roy McLean's words, 'It is the government, not the people, who are running to keep up.'

The most important friend, however, was Raymond White, with whom I had played cricket for Cambridge University. He played for Transvaal and lived in Johannesburg, and he implanted an interesting question in my mind: 'Do you stand the naughty boy in the corner of the classroom forever?'

I began to ask questions of my BBC Television commentary colleague Jack Bannister, who worked in South Africa every winter. He told me that no cricketer would fail to be excited by the development programmes spreading through the townships where there was no history of cricket at all. Cricket correspondents were facing crucial questions about South Africa; for example, would the Test circuit split into black and white? Thousands of words were being poured out even though no one had an idea if the likes of McGlew, Bacher and White were making important points. Many argued that they would do and say anything to get back into Test cricket. I developed a lack of respect for the sanctimonious school of political correctness. 'Above any other evil, I detest racism' was the declamation of the self-righteous, waiting for the applause before they took sadistic swipes at those who saw things differently. Who didn't detest racism? I certainly did. Very few had ever been to South Africa and most were arguing from a position of total ignorance, which can work well for a long time with emotional issues but there has to come a time when curiosity ought to win. The South African Cricket Board of Control invited me to spend some time in South Africa; the *Sunday Telegraph* was keen to lead and I was delighted to go. I went for fifteen weeks over three of their cricket seasons. Other cricket correspondents followed later.

Tales of South Africa's long exclusion from international sport and return with teams of many colours can be good, bad or ugly, depending on where you were, how you viewed events and what were your private convictions. My first visit was towards the end of isolation although the South African government had given no indication of constitutional change. I expected depressing evidence of white oppression. Ali Bacher urged me, when he met me at Jan Smuts Airport, Johannesburg, in March 1987, 'Go anywhere; write what you like.' South African international sport had been crippled by boycotts, but the playing of outdoor games in sunny weather would always fill people's days. It was football in the large black communities, cricket among the coloureds, and for the whites, the old Springbok sports of rugby football and cricket were solid pillars of national identity. If ever the Afrikaner was forced to circle the wagons again, there would be two sets of rugby posts in the middle. We were generously accommodated in Johannesburg at the home of Raymond White.

Ali Bacher asked if I would work as a commentator on radio and television while I was there and if I would take on a programme of speeches at lunches and dinners. The travel, he thought, would open up the country for the accumulation of my own information, but also cricket lovers, having been starved of contact with the game, would love to hear tales of how it was developing around the world.

On the very day I arrived in South Africa I went with Ali to the Wanderers ground. 'Superb theatre,' I noted in my diary. 'A large old-fashioned grandstand in need of a face-lift; high-rise banks of seats; hospitality boxes with balconies. Players walk out to the field down a sloping pathway alongside a wide grass bank where spectators sit in bathing costumes or shorts and sunhats. I meet Alvin Kallicharan and Glamorgan's new signing, Corrie van Zyl.' I had hardly stretched a leg before I was talking to the South African Executive Cricket Club, formed in 1986 for 'the purpose of developing cricket at all levels, particularly among the underprivileged'. Next day I was on the air, working with a memorable radio commentator, Charles Fortune. It was the Castle Currie Cup final, Transvaal against Western Province.

Charles was eighty-two years old, with upturned eyebrows, frequently flattened by a mighty pair of binoculars that looked as if they had done serious service at sea. His voice was superbly produced with occasional nasal intonations and an operatic sense of plain and pearl; he appeared to speak in a long-forgotten English language. 'You never meet a day when you cannot improve your English, do you. I am so pleased you are here. You've made me raise my game, d'y' know. And it might be my last ball-by-ball commentary. I always think that. I expect to live longer but I really cannot manage the stairs now.'

Charles Fortune was born in Wiltshire and after taking a BSc at University College London, taught in Wimbledon. He broadcast before the Second World War and, after it was over, moved to South Africa. He had done eight overseas tours as a commentator. He used language and imagery in a similar way to John Arlott. On that day of our first meeting, he let the odd ball pass by without mention but there were three winners – the game of cricket, which he never compro-mised, the English language, which he adorned, and me, lucky to share a workplace with an educated mind and a master of words.

A lot of workers in South African cricket wanted to know what Britain and the rest of the world were thinking about their exclusion and hope of return. I had an opinion, not particularly welcomed, that

Ali and the board president Joe Pamensky should drop their annual visits to Lord's. Their propaganda could not be countered by Hassan Howa because he had long been denied a passport. Ali's conviction was that only the Cricket Union could lead, especially as it was the organisation entrusted by the ICC with effecting change. I was certain, too, that the concept of rebel tours, even though they were legal, should be abandoned. I thought that the way back for South Africa was not to seek the route via Lord's or with England cricket. There could not be a return to the old days. South Africa should return, when the time came, through Asia, probably India and Pakistan.

I was opposed to rebel tours and never attended one. This was the only tactical disagreement I had with Ali Bacher but I did understand his mood of iconoclasm. He had reached the point of desperation by repeated rejection; he was content to exploit his nuisance value by recruiting top players from the leading cricket countries who would then be barred from selection for their own Test teams. The discomfort would then work both ways. Money talked. Many players, it appeared, hated apartheid but loved the krugerrand. There was a cricket reason for the rebel Tests, too. South Africa wanted to keep up their standards of play, and how could they do that in isolation? My conviction was still that South Africa should repair itself from the inside; to me, it seemed to be the only way.

It was stimulating journalism. Joan travelled some of the way with me and the girls joined us at the end of the Millfield term for their Christmas holidays. They were surprised from day one. For example, we sat in the coffee shop of the Holiday Inn, a decent three-star quality hotel, and found white girls serving the food under the supervision of a black woman. It was not supposed to be like that, they thought. On the same day, in the restaurant at teatime there was a black child's birthday party with a wholly mixed gathering of guests, black, white and Asian! It was not meant to be like that, either.

My old friend, the Indian wrist-spinner B.S. Chandrasekhar, had encouraged me to make this trip, on condition that I told him everything, especially 'whether blacks and whites walk down different sides of the road.' I could tell him that apartheid was alive but, I guessed, not as well as it had been. It certainly existed, even if not in hotels. Black labour, for example the cooks, gardeners and the unskilled, came into the wealthy white areas in their hundreds at crack of dawn, having walked miles to their work. They either walked back at dusk or waited long hours for lifts home, retreating to shanty towns to live in poverty after a day of service. That part of the white man's world was still solidly intact though it was not always a master–slave relationship. There were domestic servants who loved their jobs, adored the family for whom they worked and could argue their own fair deal; but separation by colour was shocking to see and only the world's anger had encouraged the liberal South Africans to be bolder within their own country, especially in the arts and sport. Joan and I went to the theatre in Johannesburg and sat in a multi-racial audience, and at the cricket the strict laws of apartheid were no longer being applied. The famous Wanderers Club bussed in the best cricketers among black boys from the townships of Alexandra and Soweto to play in their club nets and schoolboy matches. Not the prefect answer, but it was easy to draw the conclusion that cricket, backed by some big business, was not waiting for the law to change but going ahead of it and so I had no reason to doubt the honesty of those who had told me about change. Soon I met prosperous coloureds, mainly Asians, living in newly built but separate housing estates. It was a mixture of progress and regression.

There was space available in the *Sunday Telegraph* and often in the *Daily*. My work in the commentary box put me back in the team situation. Charles Fortune, with his long years of perspective, believed that 'nothing will prevent the melting of apartheid now it has been subjected to the heat of world censure, but it will take half a century of politics to find peace.' Another of his beliefs was that the left-wing militants, those who sought to place names on an international black list, were now the fascists, the ones who sought to destroy people's liberties.

There was good company to be found among the cricket journalists, and excellent information to be gathered. Gerald de Koch was just shaping a career in radio, and on television, former cricketer Trevor Quirk was a highly professional anchorman for SABC sport. Alan Wilkins, formerly a seam bowler with Glamorgan and Gloucestershire, had just won a media award as a television presenter. Andre Bruyns, a commentator in the Afrikaans language, had the most fascinating tales to tell as he recalled some of the efforts made by the cricket fraternity to challenge the apartheid laws. As far back as 1973, he and the former Springbok Dennis Gamsy formed the Cricket Club of South Africa on non-racial principles. It failed. Then, as much in protest as goodwill, Andre became one of four leading white South African cricketers who joined the formerly all-black Kohinoor Club in the Transvaal Cricket Council Premier League. In commentary, his words made sound cricket sense and his ideas were shaped regardless of race. He could have built an anti-apartheid podium for himself but cricket was his love and he would not see that damaged. He never told me as much but you do get to know a man and what he believes from his commentary.

Ray White had his own experiences. I remembered him from Cambridge as a superb striker of the ball and he went on to lead the side in the 1965 university match. He was the son of liberally minded parents. Originally a Gloucestershire family, they hosted discussions on racial issues over long suppers in a home that became a centre of academic debate and a focus for the suspicions of the secret police. Ray was a contradiction in the eyes of many people. In appearance, he was strong and upright, with the bearing, cars, house and golf swing of someone born to the Transvaal Ivy League. He is, in fact, thoughtful and considerate. Fathers of daughters may argue that he could be nothing else: he has three. Raymond felt that everyone in South Africa was locked in a pariah prison, therefore having no understanding of any aspect of life on the outside. 'How can our politicians vote for change?' he would ask. 'How can the people demand change? Change to what? We have no comparisons with the rest of the world because it does not admit us.' His advice to me was the same as I had received from Ali Bacher – 'Go everywhere; write what you like.'

A first visit to Cape Town is always memorable. I had seen photographs of cricket at Newlands with spectacular mountains as the backcloth, but I never imagined anything so alive and seductive as this. You can almost reach out and touch the mountains through whisps of cloud that float and shift, giving the whole land mass the appearance of being on the move. Thirty years after this first visit, my grandson, Freddie Sexton, at the age of three, pointed and said, 'Look. Moving mountain.' Two years later, back on holiday, he shocked his parents by announcing as soon as he got to Cape Town, 'The mountain is still moving, Mummy.' Wherever you are, the great, sunny and smiling, or cloudy and grumpy, land mass dominates.

The man at the top of my list to visit there was Hassan Howa, and I drove to his home where his wife provided tea and delicious cake. Hassan struck me as a thoughtful, determined man who felt that time was running out on his life's work. We talked a lot about English county cricket, which he followed and loved. Hassan remembered some Glamorgan cricketers who had been to South Africa to coach, especially the ones he called 'the wonderful Davieses', Dai and Emrys. He relived in conversation the happy memories of a young spectator watching Tests from the coloured enclosures at Newlands. He was at pains to illustrate his love of cricket in order to emphasise the firmness of his conviction that no one should play against South Africa as long as the apartheid laws ruled their lives. Hassan saw the wider picture. 'My firmness has annoyed people. A lot hate me. I have never been allowed a passport in case I preach against the South African government. Now the entire world is turning against South Africa. That is good. Soon my cry will get through – no normal sport in an abnormal society.' I assured him that it had hit its target already.

Hassan Howa was an uncompromising idealist who would not join in with initiatives along the way. Only in a world without apartheid would he come out to play. Fair enough, but there had to be progress towards that end. He did not believe he would be part of what came next and his thinking had stopped. Hassan Howa's fight had run into the buffers. The long-time chairman of the coloured South African Cricket Board was immovable in argument. Now, late in life, he had no vision any longer, no new journey to make.

When I later met Bob Woolmer, who was coaching coloured boys at Avondale, he described violence, saying that the South African Cricket

Board positively discouraged any contact with whites. They would set fire to homes, injure or even kill. 'Cricket is used for political muscle,' he believed. It meant that those who fought Hassan Howa's battles were a good deal more militant than Hassan himself. Serious threats were regularly delivered to young coloured boys who came to Bob for tuition. They suddenly withdrew from his sessions. Whites were the enemy, and youth cricket was where the real fight was taking place against the abnormal society. Cricket was one of the battlegrounds.

It was in Cape Town that Basil D'Oliveira had lived and played. He was fondly remembered, especially by his brother-in-law, Frank Brache. Frank was coloured and had decided to fight apartheid from inside cricket, not without. He had been secretary of the coloured South African Cricket Board and when it merged with the white board, he took up employment on the staff of the new union.

'We had great hopes that what happened to Basil would do a lot to crack apartheid,' he told me. 'When he was chosen by England to tour here with MCC, we thought the big day was almost with us. But when Mr Vorster said no, the protest organisations could turn to people like me and say, "There, we told you so." And they were right. It would not be a matter of cricket leading the way. Political and racial considerations would win. And yet, Tony, I have achieved more in the interests of the multi-racial cause from within the cricket authorities than I could ever have done on the outside.'

He took me on a car drive one day. 'I am so proud of Newlands. We are multi-racial in every square foot. We have boys playing cricket against each other, black, white or coloured. What is important about it is this – they will be tomorrow's negotiators.'

Frank Brache's house had been petrol-bombed three times. He put in special glass but that was blown out. Candice, his baby daughter, was saved from exploding glass only by a window blind. He picked up the pieces from her cot.

'Police slept on my premises, which was embarrassing, but the black activists warned me to stop going up the arse of the white man,' he said. 'I am a simple man but I will fight. All I want is peace in our national game. That is my dream.'

It was essential to meet the Cape coloured left-arm spinner Omar Henry, who spent the British summer working in Scottish cricket. He was full of hurried enthusiasm.

'It's 1987, and everyone here is looking for the light at the end of the tunnel. What's the mood in London? I'm sure it's just a change of mind-set now. Y'see, I say let's forget the international scene. We should not be trying to get back into Tests. We should be able to go out into the world as cricketers only when we have put our house in order and can tell them that we're ready for their approval.'

The word 'mind-set' was one of Omar's favourites and it did suggest that apartheid might disappear with the flick of a switch. Ray White, too, believed that 'great emotional issues, such as apartheid, historically collapse suddenly when the time comes'. Omar Henry wanted to reposition whites, blacks and coloureds on one great field of civilisation. He had approved of rebel Tests, agreeing with the theory that South Africa had to keep up standards, and was proud to have been selected to play in them. In fact, his premonitions of one great playing field came true and his dream was fulfilled when he played for the new South Africa, the Proteas, in three Tests against India in 1992. In my diary I have his 1987 words:

The whites did not think I could play cricket, and when I showed them that I could, they did not think I could ever be good enough. Then there were the non-whites. When I began playing with white teams, they accused me of selling out. All I wanted to do was to break the barrier, to make the whites see that non-whites could play the game well. I noticed that Cape coloured boys played on the outfields in Johannesburg and Cape Town during the lunch intervals at Currie Cup matches. I wanted blacks to do that.

Black coaches were being trained and pitches being built in townships. Omar Henry said he had decided to make himself a martyr for non-white players. Occasionally he was not permitted to stay in the same hotel as the rest of the team. 'I couldn't go to the same eating places. It was humiliating, but I knew I had to keep going in order to see the barriers of colour lifted.'

One sunny morning in Cape Town, a tall man, stooping slightly with age, came to pick up the whole Lewis family. John Passmore greeted us in the foyer of our hotel and embarked on the most courteous conversation. We were in the presence of a gentleman, seventy-five years of age, with good manners running through him like the message through a stick of rock. Ali Bacher had said it was essential to meet him. We took coffee first so that he could explain the background to his work in cricket and what he had in mind for us to visit. He was going to take the four of us past Cross Roads, and on to the township of Langa. Cross Roads was occasionally a showground of the flaming necklace, where black anger was a sideshow of sadistic murder – car tyres were forced down over a victim's head and, having been filled with petrol, set alight.

John described the heady days of Springbok cricket dominance in 1967 and 1970, explaining how successes in Test matches, especially over Bill Lawry's Australians, had proved infectious, spreading the game to Afrikaner schools for the first time. A decade later, Afrikaners took their place in sides of the highest standards. Kepler Wessels was hailed as the first of a new generation of Pollocks, Procters and Richards. I could see that John was concerned only with schools. You could see the glint of the good teacher in his eye as well as the stoicism of a man who had endured reverses and persevered unbowed. He agreed that a few months of Peter Hain had achieved more within South Africa than anything else possibly could have done, but he was worried that a continued siege against South African cricket could set back the progress of the last two years. He could see that the attention of the international cricket authorities was needed if the huge efforts to effect change were to be pursued. This was Ray White's mantra – 'How long do you keep the naughty boy in the corner?' We were talking timing here.

Meticulously, John Passmore told of his efforts to unite the cricketers in his country. His name was attached to an all-black African Schools Cricket Week. When multi-racial cricket arrived, John feared that his boys would not be good enough to break into the white Nuffield Schools competition. 'We can't get to the schools because of the ferment in the urban townships and this has a bad effect. We wanted to get to the developing schoolboys after their initial steps in the game. The problems are mainly in Soweto and the Cape Town townships. I have talked to people in other provinces and they are not as concerned about the situation there.'

This long, languid man was happy that cricket was leading social change. He had connections with government and was sure that multi-racial games were excellent test cases for wider life. There was no better communicator than John Passmore. I had made inquiries about him with two former England players settled in Cape Town, good friends Roger Prideaux, with whom I had opened the batting at Cambridge in 1960, and Robin Jackman, who was Surrey's busy new ball bowler during a large slice of my playing career. They confirmed that John Passmore was acknowledged to be 'the father of black cricket'. Back in 1970, eight years before my visit, when South Africa was expelled from the International Cricket Conference and given two conditions for its return – Test selection to be open to all races and cricket in underprivileged areas to be nurtured – it was John Passmore who loaded his car with bats and balls and bravely drove into the black township of Langa for the first time. He saw footballs kicked in all directions but nothing remotely resembling cricket. He persuaded an engineer friend to bulldoze a wide area of wasteland where he laid a cricket square and four gravel strips as bases for nets. Pausing only to go to Westpac (Western Province African Cricket Trust), he raised money and began building his dream, Langa Cricket Club.

We climbed into his ageing motorcar and on the way I asked if I could scribble a brief biography before we ventured into the Langa township. John had worked hard. Before the Second World War he lived in London for twelve years, working with the Diamond Corporation. During the blitz he was commissioned in the Beds and Herts, and was at Tobruk and in Syria before parachuting into Burma. After the war he spent forty years with Premier Wire in South Africa, retiring just before we met in January 1988. 'Now I can give cricket more time and move on to my next black township ground,' he concluded.

It was easy to understand, however, that John's efforts were seen by many to be irrelevant in the struggle to end apartheid. Many responsible for the development for non-white cricket called it window-dressing. Was his concentration on black cricket divisive? In answering that question he recalled the riots in Langa and surrounding townships in 1985 and pointed to the social value of cricket. 'There was no stone throwing at the cricket field end of town,' he said, 'and there was little crime there. My boys are off the streets and in the nets. But more than that, cricket has lifted my boys. They can talk or play cricket with anyone who shares the common interest.' That, he believed, was the necessary first step. 'Only then do you cease to be divisive.'

In 1973, John Passmore took the very first black side to a white ground, the university fields in Cape Town. The government made conditions – admittance only by written invitation, guards to be posted, no blacks in the clubhouse, no blacks in the toilets. 'Now,' he smiles, 'you can see black people in the Long Room at Newlands or playing on the outfield in the intervals of big provincial matches. There are no separate enclosures. When they play, they all shower together. We want the gradual elevation of blacks and coloureds in all aspects of life. Cricket is showing the way.'

He had his own proof that it worked. The John Passmore Schools Cricket Week for black, coloured and Asian teams produced one selected team at the end of the tournament that completed in the Nuffield Schools competition, historically the reserve of white school-boy cricketers. 'Natural progress is taking over from apartheid law,' John enthused. He was not talking window-dressing. He was talking a better future without a thought about South Africa returning to what the Test and County Cricket Board was unctuously and exclusively calling 'the family of international cricket'.

As John drove the Lewises through the townships he apologised for the squalor of life but Joanna brightly replied, 'Mister Passmore, you should see Calcutta.' I explained to John that he was in the company of three of the most travelled ladies in the cricket world. We had seen the best and the worst of Calcutta the previous year – tiny Indian children, shoeless and wearing nothing but a filthy loin cloth, trying to wash their matted hair in the dribble of brown water that came from a public standpipe, before retreating between shanty homes of cardboard and corrugated iron to find the small square yards of their family world. Calcutta was a mighty jigsaw of human deprivation; Cross Roads, the impromptu home for wandering black South Africans, looked like a minute missing piece of it.

'That is most interesting, Joanna,' John replied. 'You see, isolation does not work after a certain time. We have no gauges, no measuring rules. We need them, or rather, the government does. We don't know what goes on in other countries.' It was a serious point.

John spoke quietly and with the certainty of someone who did not have to exaggerate the claim that his Langa ground was one on which any leading club side would love to play its cricket. Apart from the main playing area, there were two more grounds within the same walls, and nets galore. It was far better than Glamorgan's ground, I noted. Who paid for it?

'The banks,' John replied, 'and fundraising and persuading all our supporters to contribute as they could, their machines or their labour.'

We went into Langa next, along streets of poor housing suddenly full of smiling faces. John slowed his car and young boys ran out to follow him. He was the Pied Piper. There must have been more than twenty boys calling, 'Mister Passmore, Mister Passmore, we need two bats. Two bats.'

'What happened to your last bats, boys?'

'Slipping, Mister Passmore,' one said. Another boy demonstrated by twisting his fists in opposite directions to show how the rubber grips on the bat handles had stretched and moved, so they could not take a firm hold. John's car was parked at the roadside. He opened the boot and handed over a replacement bat, taped round the blade but in sound condition.

When we later told white South Africans that we had spent a day in Langa, they could scarcely believe that I had taken my family there. They had never been there in their lives. One day soon, however, the famous Nuffield Schools tournament would be held there and white parents would be following the tracks of the great John Passmore, stepping-stones to a saner world.

The Langa fields were obviously the love of someone's life. The playing strips were firm, flat and well grassed. Net pitches were good and I spent the afternoon coaching some of the outstanding black players. I am not sure that I added anything in cricket terms to their techniques because they were obviously well taught. With thigh pads strapped on top of their tracksuit trousers they looked like any professional player might look in a practice session. I had found that young black boys who were novices at the game tended to chuck the ball when bowling and hack cross the line when batting, but these lads in Langa had been well coached, many by lady schoolteachers who had joined the South African Cricket Union's development programmes. It was obvious that racial harmony could only be achieved through education, and the ability to share the enjoyment of a game was a strong start. As John Passmore never tired of pointing out, 'When the day comes for all colours to sit round the same table, wouldn't it be wonderful if they already knew each other from the cricket fields?'

It was possible to romanticise the role of cricket, exaggerate it and distort the picture. All I can write for sure is that I watched the game spread, even though white and non-white children returned to their separate accommodation at night. There were pockets of resistance to change but these infuriated the South African Cricket Union. For example, the municipal councils of Brakpan and Boksburg announced their support for a whites-only game. The South African Cricket Union responded by announcing to the world that discriminating against people according to colour was against its constitution and that in the case of schools or clubs in those Pretoria towns, they would be given no cricket subsidies, all coaching schemes would be withdrawn and no players could be eligible for selection for any SACU provincial or national teams. Should local or national laws prohibit people of colour as spectators or players at public, municipal or private grounds, then no cricket under the control of the SACU would be allowed there. Ali Bacher framed the sentence for the press:

The people of South Africa should be getting together to work out a common future based on mutual cooperation and mutual respect. Anything less than this is retrogressive and the consequences will be terrible. The SACU cannot urge the government strongly enough to rid South Africa of all laws such as the Group Areas Act and the Separate Amenities Act which Brakpan and Boksburg are seeking to reinforce. Until that happens apartheid will not be dead in South Africa and South Africa itself will die if apartheid remains. The SACU is committed to do everything in its power to bring about meaningful change on and off the fields of cricket.

I pointed to situations of blatant racialism and often thought that something so endemic as apartheid would never be removed from daily life. Giant Alsatian dogs behind the high security gates of the rich white man barked wildly at passers-by if they were black. I had met the old Springbok opening batsman Eric Rowan, especially remembered in Britain for his innings of 236 at Leeds in 1951, who loudly announced that if he saw a black head appear over the fence of his property he would shoot it off. On one internal flight the young man in the next seat was in Army uniform. He pointed to the seat in front of us. 'You can smell the blacks,' he said. 'The fella in front of us will stink the plane out.'

Then again, the only black people we saw were at work. We did not dare enter the townships without guidance. My record tells me that I thought of Chicago, 1980. I was leading an MCC team and we were told on no account to turn right out of the hotel if we were white; always go left. But I did have tales to surprise old Chandra in India. One day while we were in Durban, opposite the Maharani Hotel the beaches and bathing were declared open to all colours, and big black ladies in petticoats that quickly became transparent in the sea washed away decades of apartheid in one swim. Outside Durban, buffer land was being converted into shared playing fields for cricket. I was taken to see how poor some white people were and how wealthy were the coloureds, who had shiny executive cars in multi-garages alongside acres of lawn. By reporting everything for the *Telegraph*, I hoped at least that the kaleidoscope of existing perceptions was being shaken and old patterns disturbed.

Above all, I found Ali Bacher consumed by his mission to give South Africa a cricket future and his countrymen a future of racial freedom. He was the evangelist preaching a development programme for cricket as well as the commercial entrepreneur who was leading the game to a safe financial future. He was an outstanding administrator, eternally on the telephone, and blessed with a wonderfully supportive wife, Shira, and three lovely children. He bounced into Soweto or Alexandra weighed down with kit, Bakers' Biscuits T-shirts and every possible requirement for cricket to be played in these unlikely places. South Africa was fortunate to have someone of the calibre of Ali Bacher to direct its game. His understanding of cricket and cricketers made him a wonderful leader against the most fearful opposition, a bullying government with a predilection for apartheid. Whenever he thought the enemy too strong, he must have looked back on his captaincy of the Springboks against Australia in 1969–70, when his team won all four Tests by 170, an innings and 129, 307 and 323, and drawn lessons to bolster his determination in the bigger fight. Cricket is only cricket, but Australia were a formidable challenge. Ali Bacher was a seeker of advice but single-minded once he had decided on the way ahead. He had no time for waverers and although he was sometimes wounded by the inevitable criticism of those who opposed his instinct to be in control, the vision of his ultimate goal always took him through. He played politics because only the politicians could create the rainbow country ahead. Like his batting, his administration bristled with grim determination and durability.

I sat at home in Wales, searching for the words to sum up the situation as I had briefly seen it. South African cricket was certainly sunk without hope of international contact outside the rebel tours that I did not support. At the same time, most people in Britain had no idea how the cricket community there was battling against apartheid. It was fine arguing that only politicians and governments can make change, but politicians need to respond to public pressures. In many corners of South African life, ordinary day-to-day behaviour suggested impending change.

In Britain, the holier-than-thou attitude was rampant; the completely ignorant made judgements and sang their choruses from the high moral ground. Their cries included demands to ban British cricket coaches and cricketers who were working legally in South Africa. They wanted to overrun civil liberties to condemn anyone who had contact with the devil racists, even to outlaw debate and knowledge. Turning the back on South Africa was to deny John Passmore's seventeen years of labour in the black township of Langa; and squash the hopes of Monica Magadielo, the schoolmistress in Mamelodi, who umpired in the playground at seven o'clock in the morning before school started, and coached the off-drive at lunchtime and the bowling action after lessons. It was as if Omar Henry never fought or played. It scorned the work of Freek Burger, the international white rugby referee, who became the full-time development officer for cricket in the Western Province townships. And what could Lawrence Mvumvu, South Africa's first black cricket coordinator, tell his kids? You will never play at Lord's or Port-of-Spain? Blind disapproval was wrong.

If I had looked into a crystal ball at that stage, I would have seen images of Paul Adams, Cape coloured, bowling left-arm spin for South Africa in Tests, and Makhaya Ntini, starting out in Tests soon afterwards as a fast bowler.

When the South African Cricket Union decided to take cricket to the townships it did not realise that it was starting a flow of interest that would soon become a torrent. As a cricket-lover, it was good to see. The first stage was mini-cricket. On my return, I found that black boys had been chosen on merit for the Transvaal Under-fifteen representative team. Walter Masemolo, sometimes spelt Mamesola, Keith Mahuwa and Billy Mabena lived and practised in Alexandra but their team played schools of all races, state schools and fee-paying that were open to all colours. Walter, known as Wes, could make young white batsmen hop about with his fast stuff. I watched a match at the traditional, white, St John's School in Johannesburg, between the school and the Alexandra township. Walter delivered a bruising spell to a gutsy young white boy who eventually was out for 30. I was alongside the lad under a tree as he removed his pads, and heard him say, 'I just hope that big, black boy likes to bat because I'll knock his head off his shoulders when I get the ball in my hand.' I took that to be a highly racial statement until I watched the battle between them in the next innings and saw them sitting together after the match, laughing and gulping down lemonade. That was colour without prejudice, free from politically correct claptrap.

The playing of cricket together, of course, exaggerated the separate development of the races when close of play came round and exposed the inhumanity and the immorality. The black boys still retreated to their dirty shanty towns. One evening, Joan and I were with Raymond White and Ali Bacher in a restaurant full of white people. When we were joined by a black school headmaster and his lady, I have never heard such a clatter of silence. The men stood up to shake hands when they came to our table and if it is possible to hear silence deepen, it happened then.

Mr Boloyi, the schoolmaster, was ready to join the South African Union's cricket programmes. 'When apartheid is finally negotiated out of existence,' he suggested, 'these young men, black and white and coloured, may be sitting round the table, and they will know how to speak to each other because they will have done it before, if only in appeals for lbw or to say, "Thanks for the game." ' This clearly was the growing conviction. Hylton Ackerman, formerly Northamptonshire's ebullient left-handed batsman, was involved in a massive job of tuition. He said that 60,000 black children were learning the game, and more coaches were being trained every week, seventy per cent of them women teachers.

In the township of Atteridge, near Pretoria, just before two o'clock, there was a lot of activity on the acre of rough ground that served for a playing field at Patogong High Primary School. Thirty-two youngsters, all turned out neatly in mini-cricket T-shirts, practised in two nets, one of them supervised by the young English professional Russell Cobb, the other by Charles, a senior master, wearing grey trousers, T-shirt and colourful peaked cap. The nets were excellent with flat and reliable surfaces inside perfect netting. 'Come on, Nicodemus,' urged Charles in the gutteral accent of Pretoria. 'Creeket is a sideways game.'

There was a lunch break. The boys and girls either opened packets of food they had brought from home or queued at the van outside the fence where a vendor was ladling a hot concoction on to cardboard plates – unofficial school catering. Afterwards, Charles's voice commanded, 'Now, mini-creeket,' and they rushed to take up traditional fielding positions. Play began but Charles would interrupt it.

'What eez theez?'

'Meed-on, Sir.'

'What eez theez?'

'Extra cover, Sir.'

'What eez theez?'

'Non-striking batsman, Sir.'

'And who eez theez?'

'Seely point, Sir.'

Everyone bowled two overs and the batsman had to attempt a run every time he or she hit the ball. A bowler dare not take one stride unless Charles had given the order, 'Bowl one, bowl two', like a submarine commander firing torpedoes.

In Atteridge, as in other townships, the mini-cricket league was very competitive. There are twenty-six schools, each one with two teams, Under-ten and Under-twelve. Charles was well known for persuading the best players to change to his school.

'Theez cricket,' he announced, 'I saw at Wanderers. I saw a man with a sloping walk called Slasher Mackay. I loved him. He only aimed the bat at the straight ones. I loved Richie Benaud, a great spinner.' And then, going quite soft and emotional, he almost whispered, 'And there was that Harvey. Neil Harvey. He was little and he stroked the ball so far and all the time.'

There were two conclusions here at Atteridge. First, the development programme in black townships was not entirely cosmetic, and secondly, those who worked in it were not seeking South Africa's return to Tests but the propagation of a game that might hold all of their spirits together in defiance of old statutes. It was not surprising the net pitches were good because they had been laid by Fanie de Villiers, the white fast bowler who would later play for South Africa in Tests, but no one in Britain would know that. It was not yet time to drop the formal ban on South Africa, but the bad boys were working hard for the game and they deserved recognition. The thrill of my mission in South Africa was to be able to communicate previously unknown facts and to introduce *Telegraph* readers to people working hard to make human progress in daily life. As for first-class cricket, I commentated on Graeme Pollock's final innings – ' not out' of course – in a tough game with one or two talented individuals.

In 1991, Clive Rice led his country back on to the international field, in Calcutta, with good players around him, and a name for all international batsmen to note, Allan Donald. Yes, Raymond White's words about emotional issues being resolved quickly proved to be true. The direction chosen by President de Klerk's government became clear. Nelson Mandela was released and Gatting's rebel England team, just arrived, was unnecessary and isolated. Ian Wooldridge wrote in the *Daily Mail*, 'Gatting was in the wrong place at the very wrong time.'

Those closer to the South African government than I must have felt the changing moods or else they would not have jousted with the particular statutes of apartheid that made multi-racial cricket illegal. South Africa was on the way back. I would not argue that cricket was the catalyst for change – the political and sporting exclusion was – but studying cricket's way out of the difficulties within South Africa, seeing sportsmen trying to rock the ideological totem pole of a hideous regime, remains one of the most fascinating experiences of my cricket-writing life.

Sadly, Hassan Howa and John Passmore died at the moment of victory. Peter Hain was elected a Member of Parliament for my home town, Neath, where once he might have been chased away by rugby lovers and is now Welsh Secretary in Westminster. Calcutta cheered the Proteas along the streets to a new international future. Raymond White was elected president of the now United Cricket Board of South Africa but was ousted when he opposed the selection policy, which made a quota of black and coloured cricketers compulsory in the Test team. Ali Bacher stayed to organise South Africa's Cricket World Cup, 2003, before retiring. Young Walter Masemolo, alas, died at the age of twenty-six.

WORKING FOR WALES

In 1987 I shared a car journey with Philip Carling, chief executive of Glamorgan County Cricket Club and a former Cambridge cricket Blue. He knew his game, but was by instinct a marketing man. We agreed that Glamorgan's brand name was 'failure'. For the previous seventeen seasons the county had only once finished a championship season in the top ten teams, ninth in 1975, and had been to only one Lord's final, losing to Middlesex in 1977. But, more relevantly, we had been bottom of the first-class table three times, in 1976, 1979 and 1986. Journalists made easy jokes about our lowly status. Henry Blofeld in his book about Kerry Packer's World Series cricket properly inquired how this revolution in the game would touch the pay packet of the next to lowest player in the world, the Glamorgan number ten.

Captaining in Glamorgan was a game of pass-the-parcel. Between 1977 and 1987, there had been six seasons with different captains and three with joint captaincies involving Alan Jones, Robin Hobbs, Malcolm Nash, Javed Miandad, Barry Lloyd, Mike Selvey, Rodney Ontong and Hugh Morris. It was out of that conversation of despair that I threw my hat in the ring for a place on committee, saying that I would be chairman if required but I would continue my work in cricket outside Wales for the *Sunday Telegraph* and BBC Television.

How do you go about grabbing a county and turning its fortunes around? With difficulty. Glamorgan had no ground of its own, no capital base in days of increasingly commercial necessity. We did, however, set up a much more skilled marketing committee under the chairmanship of David Morgan, who agreed to be my vice-chairman. It was not easy for either of us because we were both fully employed, I in world cricket and he in the business of marketing steel to many parts of the world. Our fax machines rattled all hours of the day and night.

While I was chairman we pruned the playing staff, removing all those who would never be regular team members. The next task was to find a captain. I went for Alan Butcher, formerly of Surrey and England, a fine player whose skills would never be in doubt, and a quiet, wise man, as he appeared to me. We needed new coaches. I asked two of Glamorgan's finest practitioners to come to the aid of the team, Don Shepherd and Alan Jones. From Leicestershire had come John Steele, first as manager but then he was transferred to the second team, not for demotion, but because he was young enough to continue playing shoulder to shoulder with the best youngsters. There were others. Glamorgan owes much to Tom Cartwright, once of Warwick-shire and England, who was the Welsh Cricket Association coach working under the Sports Council of Wales. Later Peter Walker, retired from a most successful business career, set about restructuring the wide base of the Welsh cricket pyramid.

It was interesting to discover that the presence of Shepherd and Jones was not successful with the first team. The players could not accept the authorised version of technical work: we had moved into the era of one-to-one analysis and consultation. Fair enough. Now in the 1990s, we were entering the coaching and managerial world of Bob Woolmer and the like. Glamorgan soon recruited Duncan Fletcher. We had a setback when Alan Butcher unluckily suffered a lasting calf injury and was forced to retire. The injury at first did not appear one to end a career, but as the weeks went by I saw in Alan's fate my own departure from first-class cricket: a depressing, infuriating series of efforts to exorcise the demons that had entered my right knee and had secured eternal squatters' rights. A limping, non-playing captain cannot retain presence in the dressing room nor authority. I remember hearing the former Welsh football international and Derby County player, Terry Hennessey, talk about his manager Brian Clough. 'The moment he knew my injury was serious he used to walk past me in the corridor without a look or a word. I was off the active list and so I was no use to him.' Professional sport is like that: you are off the effective strength. I felt for Alan and his most supportive wife Madeline, but in those circumstances there is little one can say.

In the technical game, both Tom Cartwright and Alan Jones were wonderful workers with players at their formative stages, and helped a very talented generation through to professional levels. Some became England Test players: Hugh Morris, Steve James, Matthew Maynard, Robert Croft and Steve Watkin. Add the overseas players, Viv Richards, Ottis Gibson and Waqar Younis, and there was enough ability available to win something. When Glamorgan won the county championship in 1997, only fourteen players were used, of which eleven had played for Welsh schools sides.

The restoration of the club's reputation in the 1990s, in fact, was not brought about by our inspirational planning, but by a tide of talent. In days when the talk is of theory and preparation there is a word that dare not speak its name, talent. Our boys had it.

Hugh Morris, a left-handed opening bat, had always got runs, from the time he was a small boy growing up in Cowbridge. Sometimes he would have technical problems born of an over-strong bottom hand, but was a real worker and always came through. If you wanted a Glamorgan player to bat you out of a tight corner, Hugh was my first choice. Steve James was developing a remarkable appetite for high scores once he had got in and Matthew Maynard was feared by oppositions as a clean striker of the ball and a man of many shots. He was also a man of uncertain temperament but a real match-winner. Much respected was Steve Watkin, a tall, zippy seam bowler with natural assets in height and high bounce that could trap the highest class of batsman. Steve had the stoical attitude to bowling of a Brian Statham – attacking but unruffled by disappointment.

Whenever the ball beat both bat and wickets, he was quickly on the turn to get back to his mark. Robert Croft had been a mature bowler from a young age, almost the finished product from the start, and in Colin Metson Glamorgan had one of the best wicket-keepers in the game.

I still do not believe that all those Glamorgan players who played for England were given a proper run at Test cricket. I recall a late-night conversation with Dennis Amiss, somewhere in Pakistan, when we discussed the number of Tests needed to shape a cricketer at the top level, relax him and develop his skills. Dennis thought eight Tests were a minimum. I thought there may not be a specific number but that selectors should look for signs of settled performance. Only Robert Croft was allowed the comfort of a near-regular inclusion in squads and tours.

Steve Barwick, another player of proven skills, had a remarkable natural talent for divining the length and line to trouble each batsman who faced him. He was also a cricketer who made me question the tenets of the new preparation for playing as advised by many who had never played the game at county level. Steve would emerge from Briton Ferry every spring, thin, white and coughing slightly. Wearing soft training shoes, he would bowl a couple of no-balls in the net, retreat and say, 'That'll be all right then.' And it was. He was simply a natural bowler full of crafty changes of pace, off-cut and off-spin, leg-cut and away swing, yorker and drifter. He reminded me of Don Shepherd, probably because he was also a new-ball bowler who turned to off-cutters and discovered a natural talent. Steve suffered a serious injury in a car crash but returned to be part of the team that won the Sunday League title in 1993.

Adrian Dale was becoming more important as the all-rounder who could glue the bits and pieces together, Tony Cottey batted with competitive spirit and from Holland came Roland Lefebvre, one of the fittest and most accurate seam bowlers, perfectly suited to the short game. Adding Viv Richards was exciting. He was the finest batsman I had ever seen in my life. Was he still that, or even half as good?

I wanted Viv at Glamorgan although the captain and players would have preferred a fast bowler. Only Don Shepherd and Alan Jones supported my contention that he could transform our chances. For many months I pursued him but could never make contact. I can recall asking Vic Marks, the former Somerset and England spin bowler and then a reporting colleague with the *Observer*, how reliable was Viv. Victor just laughed and giggled as only he can. I got the message: Viv Richards was a law unto himself. He had not acknowledged the handwritten notes I had put under the door of his room when we were in the same hotels around the world. However, persistence paid off and at last I got the answer I wanted. Viv would be throwing his hat into the Glamorgan dressing room and giving us a bit of strut and self-confidence.

Viv had left Somerset in disappointment and anger and we could feel that he wanted another opportunity in first-class cricket to show that he was far from a spent force, to prove Somerset wrong. His arrival raised the spirits of Glamorgan supporters because few of them believed that such a great player would ever come to Wales. When he did, membership increased and self-confidence grew. I felt that there would also be an effect on the Glamorgan dressing room. Richards in the field was tough on slackness. He wanted to win. Win a competition? That had not been on Glamorgan's agenda for twenty years.

Even at forty he was very special. I had been playing when he first arrived at Somerset. In fact, in my last game against Somerset at Bath in 1974, two newcomers appeared on the scene. I.V.A. Richards was a twenty-two-year-old Antiguan batting at number four for Somerset while sitting the game out on the sidelines was I.T. Botham, an eighteen year old from Yeovil who had previously been on the Lord's groundstaff. Viv came into the game like a flash of lighting. The sight of his batting had hardened old professionals sounding like schoolkids – 'Wow, you can't do that!' or 'Cor! I don't believe it!' The early movement of his front foot to the off side suggested that he would struggle against the bowler who sent the ball wicket-to-wicket from close to the stumps. Untrue. If he played round his front pad it was mostly to crack the ball to the leg-side boundary. He had amazing eye–hand coordination. Viv made nonsense of traditional field placings.

Later, when I was a commentator, I watched him play in many countries. He has left me with one special memory of beauty and sizzling power. I was one of the 40,000 at Melbourne on 9 December 1979 when he raised batsmanship to a level I had never seen before, and that includes memorable stroke play by Garry Sobers, Clive Lloyd, Rohan Kanhai, Graeme Pollock, Barry Richards, Ted Dexter, Colin Cowdrey, Tom Graveney, Greg Chappell and Tiger Pataudi. On that day, in spite of suffering injections to ease back pain and hobbling throughout his innings, Viv launched the most furious attack on anyone in an Australian sweater who cared to bowl at him. He scored 153 from 131 balls, hitting one six and sixteen fours. Desmond Haynes batted wonderfully well but looked as if he was merely keeping Richards company from the other end, like the boy who keeps a safe distance, peeping over a wall, while the real mischief-maker hurls stones at the neighbour's glasshouse.

One moment in that innings was art, not just the cricketer's craft, not just skill, athleticism or power. It was one of those experiences that Neville Cardus had long ago warned me depended on my 'receiving set'; art was the way the split-second consumed you and nothing else.

Dennis Lillee had been stung by Viv's strut and arrogant imagination as this innings raced forward, and so there was Lillee, leaning into the early strides of his familiar run, building up speed through rhythm, gathering momentum into the final sideways turn and the high, classical delivery. As he careered forward, the massed chanting thundered in time with his lengthening strides – 'Lill – llee! Lill – llee!'

They say there should be conflict in great works of art and that element suddenly appeared. Dennis was now raging in, half a dozen yards away from releasing the ball, when Viv began to advance down the pitch, bat raised, looking coolly over his left shoulder as if he was about to whack a tennis ball into the sea in Antigua. The ball flashed, the bat was swung, not exactly straight, but in the arc of a flat off-drive that sent the missile skimming about twelve feet high towards Jeff Thomson who was fielding twenty yards in from the boundary.

Thommo might catch it. I was sitting in the crowd right behind him at long off, about a dozen seats from the fence, and saw that the ball never rose in height nor dipped. I imagined myself fielding there, obeying the professional practices of eye-on-ball, feet moving into a good position to make the catch, and then I thought, 'God! How will Thommo get out of the way?' A split-second later I saw that he never had to duck or take his hand away. A fizz of red leather passed over him, still a dozen feet above ground level, until at last it hit turf and made one skidding bounce before flying over the heads of the close spectators and up, clattering among the stanchions and steps at the back of the lower stand. It was a defining moment, a duel between two great fighters in front of a full house and the television world. In the cool aftermath of a West Indies win by 80 runs, it was interesting to see that Australia used eight bowlers to complete the 48 overs required and that Dennis Lillee, in fulfilling the individual maximum of 10, conceded only 48 runs while removing Gordon Greenidge. Richards and Lillee had taken us to the peak.

It was almost impossible for me to chair Glamorgan as well as continue my writing and broadcasting career, but not quite. Vic Marks later took his Test match experience to the role of chairman of Somerset's cricket committee and continued doing an excellent job for the *Observer*. In the BBC Television commentary box, I was teased by Geoffrey Boycott about the number of mobile telephone calls I made to the 'latest scores' service.

I recall one sunny evening in June 1990, I was parked outside the rugby league club in Wigan, about to attend a sportsmen's dinner at which I was due to speak. I tuned in to Radio Wales to hear the conclusion of our match in Southampton against Hampshire. Mark Nicholas had made a bold declaration, leaving Glamorgan 102 overs in which to score 364. Glamorgan were driven to a point just short of victory by a terrific demonstration of attacking play by Vivian Richards. It was the last over and 13 were needed to win. Metson faced Malcolm Marshall. The first ball produced one leg bye for Glamorgan. Could Richards score 12 runs from five balls? It was no longer Glamorgan v Hampshire but Antigua against Barbados. The organiser of the dinner was outside the club looking for his guest speaker. I was not long. Richards' bat cracked four, six, four and he walked off; we had won with two balls to spare. He had scored 164 not out in 155 balls and had hit five sixes.

I was pleased for Viv that he was there to top-edge the winning runs when Glamorgan won the Sunday League in 1993. He had already demonstrated his extraordinary talents and given the members a big reason for getting to the games on time, and yet he was the first to admit that he alone had won nothing. Our boys were talented but, he told me, 'Even talented boys need to know how to win. I hope I've helped in that.'

There was a tempestuous side to Viv's nature, not always comfortable in a dressing room, but the only judgement I am entitled to make as an outsider is that Vivian Richards was wonderful value for Glamorgan at a crucial time when history was against us and confidence low.

After I retired, I was fortunate that my deputy, David Morgan, could take over as chairman and move the county forward to a third championship success in 1997. I was aware that I was straddling the sharpest fence, with one leg in the formal administration of cricket, representing its policies in my county, the other in the encampment of commentators and critics at the gate of the establishment, beating on the board of control with questions and sometimes accusations. I was well informed because every minute of each TCCB sub-committee crossed my desk, but my writer's edge was blunted. I never used classified information. To try to remain as objective as possible, I decided not to involve myself in national administrative affairs with the TCCB. I had originally turned out to help Glamorgan and I would stick to my patch. Other cricket writers may pass this way in the future and, I concede, there is a mighty argument for doing one thing or the other. In fact, it was not so confusing outside Glamorgan. Everyone treated me as a writer and broadcaster, not as a county chairman, and only my old friend Alan Smith, chief executive of the TCCB, would remind me, 'Now this, AR, is off the record. All right?' as if he was wondering which hat I was wearing at the time. I suppose, in the end, I concluded that cricket needed former players, and cricket writing certainly did. I had long ago accepted that the lust for as many experiences as possible in a single life was at the root of my all rounder status.

In 1993, after four and a half years, I gave up the Glamorgan chairmanship suddenly, unloading a few conclusions before I went. I thought that the democratically elected committee should resolve only those matters affecting the membership of a club, but otherwise leave the business to specialists, nominated and perhaps co-opted by the chairman and chief executive. There should be a small board setting the agenda, driven forward by the professional staff, as happens almost everywhere these days. I felt that the playing of the county champion-ship had lost its bite and spectacle. How had a once tough competition between every county, calling for cricketers to scrap hard every day of the summer as if in the football Premier League, become passive and meaningless, especially in August and September when some had no prizes for which to play? The four-day dawdle did not help this. The county system needed overhauling. Counties needed to be the new pillars of the game. They should have been encouraged to be inventive but answerable, and commercially aggressive.

I was sure that more hard work was needed on the children's game, wherever it was played. The attraction to the game springs from an individual, a coach, teacher, evangelist, rather than from any system, and if a former county player wanted to gather round himself a group of special talents, or an old club cricketer proved to be a Pied Piper and got young people crowding into a weekly net, I felt they should be supported by the board of control through the county coaching schemes. Where the embers of cricket were still glowing, it was our duty to fan hard. Times were changing quickly and the game was threatened by football, golf, computer screens and much more. My grandson, Freddie Sexton, six years old in 2002, went to football club on Clapham Common every Saturday of the year. Where was cricket club?

Chairing a county cricket club had filled up every gap in my diary with meetings, special meetings, secret meetings, attendance at din-ners, making speeches, seeking out sponsorship, understanding the requirements, or demands, of players. The daffodil on the Glamorgan sweater is a fragrant emblem of Welshness. It was fascinating to see how it was embraced by non-Welsh cricketers who joined our staff. Alan Butcher could not quite believe the numbers of Welsh media that paid close attention to the team and the club's affairs. 'There are cameras, microphones and notepads everywhere,' said Alan Butcher. 'We made television news reports only a couple of times a season at The Oval.' Viv Richards was pulled by the cause of a small country, perhaps like his home Antigua. The sounds in a Glamorgan dressing room are Welsh, the motivation for most is Wales. I enjoyed being chairman of the club but retired in a hurry, in an unexpected moment and in surprising circumstances.

The venue was the Royal Festival Hall, London, 23 April 1992. I had got through rehearsal perfectly, counting the bars of rest as diligently as I had done in the old days of the youth orchestra. My overseer was a member of the London Symphony Orchestra. I needed one because the charity concert that evening was a sell-out and I had been drafted in with about a dozen members of the Lord's Taverners to blow and bang strange instruments in Mozart's Toy Symphony. Our Taverners team, consisting of Terry Wogan, Elaine Page, Leslie Crowther, Tim Rice, Leslie Thomas, Michael Parkinson, Willie Rushton, Martin Lewis and David Mellor, stood in a curved line behind the seated orchestra. My instrument was a small metal bird filled with water, which, when blown through the tiny mouthpiece, emitted the trills of a nightingale through the spout. Alongside me was the Secretary of State for a new government ministry that he himself had created, the Department of Culture, Media and Sport. David Mellor wore a Chelsea football supporter's scarf and swung his rattle in response to the conductor's baton.

During the long wait between rehearsal and performance, David and I chatted. Initially drawn to share memories of our old college, Christ's, we ended up talking about a mutual interest in the arts and heritage. He thought I was a perfect fit for a department that included sport, the arts, tourism, heritage and media. I could offer experience of cricket

and rugby and a term with the Sports Council for Wales; membership
of the Youth Orchestra and the Association of Business Sponsorship of
the Arts; the experience of full-time writing and broadcasting; and, in
Glamorgan, I was attempting to rescue from a damp, crumbling death
a fine Georgian country house called Castellau, and had joined the
Georgian Society. Suddenly David announced, as if it was official and
therefore done, 'I want you to join my English heritage committee. I
have a place available.' I responded instinctively, 'I would prefer to do
something for Wales.' That was that.

A few days later, now at home in Llantrisant, I answered the
telephone to Wyn Roberts, a Welsh Office minister. He spoke in the
cultured tones of Old Harrovian–Conwy, a mix of former English
public school and Welsh-speaking North Wales. 'Tony, we've had some
lateral thinking. Can you come to see me in the Welsh Office?' And so,
a few days before Parliament's summer recess, I did.

After passing through the imposing façade of the Welsh Office in
Cathays Park, Cardiff, I discovered a much more modern and functional building behind. If human beings take on the personality of
their workplace, I guessed that civil servants would be as frugal as this
furniture around them, straight-lined, grey or brown in colour and
responding only to the second hands of carefully positioned clocks that
ticked away their days as they wrestled with buff files. Life in the Civil
Service appeared on the surface to be a code of conduct, procedures
noted under little 'e' or sub-section 'W', with the occasional burst into
an uplifting, emotion-charged acronym such as QUANGO – quasi-
autonomous non-governmental organisation. How did I know? My
father had retired early from the Swansea office of the Department of
Social Security in order to remove the ink and aroma of rubber stamps,
and to try to rediscover the young Swansea man he once was and to stir
the enterprising mind that had been chloroformed with procedures
handed down by Whitehall. Wilfrid Lewis retreated with my mother to
their home town, Swansea, completed the *Daily Telegraph* crossword by
9.30 every morning and all the time wondered why he had not stuck to
his original job with the London and Manchester Assurance Company
or whatever it became. His only decision for the remainder of the day

was whether to go for a pint at the Conservative Club or the Rose and Crown on Walter Road, not a hundred yards from his front door in Hanover Street.

Wyn Roberts met me in the small suite reserved for the Conservative Secretary of State for Wales, David Hunt. The 'lateral thinking' went like this: for the past nine years the Wales Tourist Board had been well led by Prys Edwards, a Welsh-speaking architect from Aberystwyth, son of a famous father, Sir Ifan ab Owen Edwards. Prys had travelled up and down Wales persuading people, especially the indigenous Welsh who needed persuasion, that tourism was good, that visitors should be welcomed and all the more so if they put pound notes into Welsh pockets. 'Prys has pumped up the ball, and we would like you to run with it outside Wales,' said Wyn. He asked me to chair the Wales Tourist Board. He did not want me to give up my BBC summer job of presenting cricket on television, which took up about fifty days a year. 'Keep the high profile,' advised Wyn. 'That's what it's about.' BBC Television cricket highlights were transmitted all over the world. Wyn was right. For three terms as chairman, I was recognised and doors old and new opened for Wales. However, after eighteen years I did have to give up my full-time employment at the *Telegraph*. The cricket network was a reliable one. As a player, writer and broadcaster, I had toured the United States, South America, Australia, New Zealand, Malaysia, India, Pakistan, Sri Lanka, Bangladesh, East Africa, South Africa, the Far East, Holland, Denmark, Gibraltar and Ireland – there had to be some visitors to Wales among that lot. As a rugby correspondent, I had made the warmest contacts in Scotland, Ireland, England and France, and there was more. 'You must be our communicator, Tony,' came the slow declamation. 'We want the broadcaster in you, too.'

What a change in lifestyle! I had to buy a couple of office suits, read bundles of papers, learn about a brand new industry and swot hard before every meeting because I was in new territory whatever the subject. In my first board meeting one of the members, Mrs Lorna Minors from Anglesey, asked my opinion of the 28-day Rule. A bit harsh on the jockey I thought mischievously to myself. Say nothing is safest, so I asked her to explain. It transpired that touring caravans were permitted to stop in a farmer's field that had only minimum facilities for up to twenty-eight days. 'Is this quality tourism for Wales or just a farmer making a few bob and getting us a reputation for cheap and nasty amenities?' she inquired.

The board was already campaigning for quality and to this day it has never let up. Wales is a staggeringly beautiful country and so compact. New sights and sounds lie in wait for the traveller round every bend in the road. The real joys are of a spectacular coastline, the main routes among mountains and valleys, tripping through a long history back to the days when Cadair Idris was the biggest volcano in Europe. Some perceptions of Wales were of a beautiful country ruined by caravan parks that ruled the skylines, scarred by old mines north and south, with a rundown coal-port capital and a stock of holiday hotels on the coast that had not moved on since the early twentieth century. One member of the board, David Griffiths, described the advance of the train from Euston across North Wales as a depressing ride through concentration camps – fields of caravans to left and right. How to improve Wales the product? What were we taking to market?

A.A. Gill's newspaper articles, skilful and entertaining, delivered regular doses of anti-Welshness as his pen jabbed and stabbed, sometimes with wounding accuracy – 'Anglesey, where pebbledash came to die . . .'

Tourism did not just involve pretty pictures, it was amazingly complex and led me deeper and deeper into the industry and its operators. I loved it. I never thought that Joan's boutique, which she ran during the 1960s, would prepare me for a real understanding of the day-to-day problems of small business. My chief executive Paul Loveluck's advice was always sound and no better than at the start: 'Take the industry with you; take the board with you.' In many minds, for all three terms that I served, I was considered to be the cricketer who had wandered off course, but not by those who knew me well.

There had to be tourist attractions, accommodation, roads and railways and hostelries, image building, communications and especially, as I saw it, training for the future. The common factor remained quality and control over it within the Tourist Board's programme of grant-in-aid schemes. The Wales Tourist Board was a sound organisation, but to fly ahead of the opposition we needed money. In spite of tourism providing seven per cent of the gross domestic product in Wales there was never a budget to half match our aspirations. It would take devolution to bring that.

Wales was promoted overseas by the British Tourist Authority. We did our best to fly our own flag but we had little money: the budget for marketing Wales all over the world was £1.4 million, exactly the same amount as Ireland spent on their sales pitch in France alone. Many politicians and several of the BTA staff did not see that the promotion of Wales made sense. Overseas visitors came mainly to England and Scotland: they were the attractions. Wales was only an afterthought, an add-on. After my very first board meeting the chairman, William Davis, the writer and publisher, the man from *Punch* magazine, summoned me to the chairman's room and warned me, in front of others, as if seeking executive approval, that he did not welcome any Welsh nationalist argument. 'England is our lead product,' he said. 'You must learn to support England.'

Those words I took as a minor affront and, while explaining that someone who had captained England at cricket in two overseas series knew a great deal about the England banner, I was pleased to assert that the promotion of Wales abroad was the statutory duty of the BTA, and any hint of non-promotion would have me leaping out of my seat. The second-guessing of Welsh tourism interests by Westminster was never going to be the answer. When devolution came, I felt our tourism would benefit but I thought the time had come to leave, happy that the constitutional change would bring new money and a surge of political support from the Welsh Assembly. This is not to write that Wales could or should always go it alone. I enjoyed working with the BTA at home and abroad; we would always feed off the volume visitor traffic that flowed into London and Edinburgh, and provide short-break holidays for the larger conurbations in England. What especially lifted the profile of Wales in tourism terms were visitations of large numbers led by events such as football cup finals played in the Cardiff

Millennium Stadium, the Network Q Rally, Rugby World Cup, European Tour golf tournaments and, in the future, the activity centred in the Millennium Centre for the performing arts in Cardiff Bay and the 2010 Ryder Cup which will be staged at Celtic Manor, near Newport in Monmouthshire.

By far the most powerful single promoter of Wales in my three terms as chairman was Charles, Prince of Wales. The whole of the world tourism industry was in a queue to meet him and they all left impressed by his understanding both of Wales and of their own countries. He was approachable and had a rich sense of humour. On some occasions he hosted parties for the Wales Tourist Board on the royal yacht when visitors would leave to the sight and sound of the military marching band performing their Welsh medley on the dock-side of Boston or Singapore or at home in Pembroke Dock. The Prince of Wales and the royal yacht attracted the major players in global tourism as they did for the Welsh Development Agency and others. British politicians were myopic and prejudiced in taking the yacht out of commission: it made no commercial sense. Change its usages, perhaps, but sink it, definitely no.

It was at Pembroke, on the yacht, that I recall chief executive Paul Loveluck grouping representatives by country and shepherding them forward for introduction to Prince Charles. I was alongside him. 'These are representatives from Sydney, Australia, Sir.'

The Prince would open up with an observation that Wales is a most beautiful country, he had done some of his painting there, but it was a shame it was so wet. After three or four groups had gone by I gathered confidence to suggest to the Prince that he ought not to open up with a negative by suggesting that Wales was more rainy than anywhere else.

He took the point and turned to the next small group, who were representing the Japanese hotel industry, and announced that he had just been given a frightful rollicking by the chairman 'who told me not to say how wet it is in Wales'. After the Japanese had moved on, he giggled, 'Take two, chairman.'

Wales is a village of under 3 million people. I felt at one stage that I was getting to know them all by their first names. One day, strolling along the new promenade at Porthcawl, I was greeted by a man wearing a flat hat and whistling as he padded along: 'Hey! Are you that tourism fella?'

'Yes, I suppose I am,' I replied.

He stopped. 'Look here mate, have you been to Tondu lately?' I had not been to Tondu, up towards Maesteg, since I was a young lad in Neath, taken to the flapping races by Sid Stevens in his Wolsley from 7 Bracken Road. 'No,' I said. 'Not for many years.'

'Then you want to, mate,' he fired back. 'The park up there is bloody filthy.'

I was soon to discover that no work for Wales is conducted in isolation: every job is another building block in the pyramid of experience. For example, I remember standing in the garden of the British High Commission in New Delhi addressing the alumni of Welsh universities, urging them to return to their student homes and to bring their families with them. Afterwards, I paid a visit to my old cricketing friend and adversary Tiger, the Nawab of Pataudi. He had played for Oxford University and India when I had been in the Cambridge and England teams. I especially wanted to talk with his beautiful wife Rinku, famous in the Indian movie world as Sharmila Tagore. My question was this: why do the Bollywood movie makers always turn to Scotland for overseas filming? It was valuable and conspicuous promotion for the Scottish countryside. Large groups were spending months there, building up the tourism figures nicely, but Wales was never considered.

'The answer is easy,' said Rinku. 'They go to Scotland because of the great golf courses. They have cameras under one arm and golf clubs under the other. They want to come home saying they have played golf in Scotland.'

At the Wales Tourist Board we had already selected golf as an area that Wales could develop with profit, and soon we began publication of an annual magazine, expertly written by Peter Corrigan of the *Independent*, who lives and plays his game in Glamorgan.

It was not long before a billionaire called Terry Matthews built an astonishing hotel called Celtic Manor in Newport and informed the sceptical hordes that he intended to build four golf courses and hold the famous Ryder Cup. I had the exciting job of chairing that bid for a year and a half. In retrospect it was the perfect follow-on, because tourism was at the heart of the matter.

Terry, now Sir Terence, was soon to prove that billionaires don't dream – they just plan to make the impossible possible. He talked continually, with the upbeat eyes of someone who has fought a lot and won everything, and after all, of the twenty-five Ryder Cups to be contended in Europe during the next century, he wanted just one. Nothing was possible without government support, and Wales was fortunate in having a First Minister, Rhodri Morgan, who enjoyed games. If he knew rugby and cricket better than anything else, he was still ready to link arms with the golfers. I made an appointment with him to say that I could not possibly run the Welsh bid for a Ryder Cup unless he considered me the appropriate person to do the job. It would be impossible without all government agencies onside. 'You are the lowest handicap we can put into the field, Tony,' he said. 'Go for it.' There were six months to go before bids were to be submitted to the Ryder Cup board, which was composed of three members from the Professional Golfers' Association and three from the European Tour. The men we had to impress were Neil Coles, Angel Gallardo and John O'Leary from the Tour and Phil Weaver, David Huish and Jim Christine from the PGA. Clearly the deepest impressions had to be made on the executive director of the Tour, Ken Schofield, and the chief executive of the PGA, Sandy Jones.

Six months' work to October 2000 and the decision near Christmas – that was our deadline. The bids were to be judged by country, not by individual golf course, and we found ourselves up against England, Scotland and Sweden.

'You can buy it,' some golfing friends said with some scorn. 'Those PGA fellas don't care if they play the Ryder Cup on a rubbish dump as long as they rake in the cash.' Many believed and still do that Europe should play the States on one of the great links courses whenever we are the hosts. 'Anything else plays into the

Americans' hands. They love places like the Belfry. We should be at Royal St George's or Turnberry or St Andrews or somewhere where we can win.' Wales has delightful links courses but not with the length, the reputation or the infrastructure to compete with the best of Scotland. Royal Porthcawl, Royal St David's, Aberdovey, Ashburnham, Conwy, Prestatyn and others are gloriously natural tests of golfing skills, but a Ryder Cup, we were informed, attracts 35,000 a day and such crowds could not be accommodated near the seaside.

The commitment of Wales was astonishing. Just for starters, £1 million a year had to be popped into the coffers of Ryder Cup Ltd for the next ten years. Tournaments had to be run annually including a Wales Open with prize money of £1.25 million. A prize fund had to be established for the Ladies European Tour of £400,000 per annum, a Seniors Tour with £500,000 at stake, a PGA National Championship with prize money of £100,000, a PGA Mastercard event worth another £100,000 and a brand new Biennial Seniors PGA Invitational from 2002 to 2012 with a starting prize pot of £750,000. The bid would include development plans for golf in Wales through the Welsh Golfing Unions with £1.2 million to cover a three-year period; a Junior trophy at £25,000 a year; and, finally, a golf technology fund requiring an annual investment of £225,000. Over three years, the commitment from Wales was £23.3 million and over the ten years, if the bid was successful, £50 million.

Within a few months, the Tourist Board would need to have 5,000 bedrooms signed up for the use of Ryder Cup Ltd at knock-down rates and all within an hour's drive of the course. On-course parking would be discouraged and it would be essential that Celtic Manor handle the huge commercial aspects, including the tented village and so much more. The maps were out on the table. It was like a scene from the old movie 'The League of Gentlemen' with coloured pins and arrows everywhere. This was a national bid and there had to be a national tourism strategy attached to the Ryder Cup and all the add-ons expected of event-led tourism.

I could see an astonishing opportunity to alter those negative perceptions of Wales, and for encouraging inward investment and attracting Welsh youngsters to the sport of golf. The golf unions began by surprising us with the information that Wales is the third oldest golfing association in the world, following Canada and Ireland. Scotland were twenty-five years later, and England twenty-nine. Did anyone else know that?

After Rhodri Morgan, I went to see David Rowe Beddoe, chairman of the Welsh Development Agency, the organisation that, in brief, offered the rest of the world an opportunity to set up in Wales, to take advantage of a hard-working labour force while gathering the commercial benefits of being within the European Community. We sat in David's office in principality buildings in Cardiff and talked through the early evening. 'Is this really as big as I think it is?' I asked. We even got round to totting up the parking fees for private aircraft at Cardiff airport and they came to £5 million for the Ryder Cup week. There was money and profile to be won at every turn; the spin-off for Wales was immeasurable. 'Yes. It's as big as you think it is,' he replied, a touch solemnly.

The 'orchestra' I was to conduct included the National Assembly, the Newport County Borough Council, the Welsh Development Agency, the Wales Tourist Board, the Sports Council for Wales, Celtic Manor, the World Sport Group led by Tim Howland, and the Welsh golfing unions. I made an immediate co-option, a person not an organisation; Brian Huggett, the former Ryder Cup captain, took his place as a full board member. Brian was a friend who had long been a Glamorgan cricket supporter and member of MCC. I wanted him on our bid committee to ensure that we never made the slightest error on the subject of professional golf. In the proposals for a Welsh golf development programme, I did not want a blade of grass lying the wrong way. Brian would have the feel for the Ryder Cup; he would understand the former players we were trying to impress with our application. Make a false move at golf and we were dead. That is how I saw it. Brian Huggett was our passport to the minds of the PGA and European Tour.

There was another addition in Anabel Sexton, head of a successful golf-specialist PR agency in Fulham High Street in London, S2 Marketing, who would ensure that our messages ran with full strength among real golf writers. She knew her golf, played well and understood Wales because she is my younger daughter and a Glamorgan girl.

In Wales, 160 miles top to bottom and 60 across at its widest, there were 201 golf courses of huge variety at 184 venues. Wales has provided five Amateur Champions of Great Britain and two Ryder Cup captains, Dai Rees as well as Brian Huggett. At the time of this bid, Dave Thomas, a popular former Welsh international and Ryder Cup player, was captain of the PGA, Ian Woosnam a US Masters champion and multi-title winner, while Philip Price, although we did not know it, was on the way to a famous day at the Belfry in 2002.

Who was against us? Scotland, with their 'Home of Golf' tag, were the favourites with five or six courses competing if they won the country bid – Turnberry, Carnoustie, St Andrews, Loch Lomond and Gleneagles. Sweden withdrew on the eve of the bid submissions. England persevered with de Vere Slaley Hall. We believed that both England and the de Vere company could be judged to be having more than their share of Ryder Cups at the Belfry.

The buzz arrived in our offices at Celtic Manor; it was Scotland for sure. How? I had an informant from north of the border letting me into the 'secret' that Sandy Jones, chief executive of the PGA, had apparently been promised a prestigious job at Gleneagles and that the Monarch course there was to be renamed the PGA National. True or false? Furthermore, Celtic Manor was 'an unplayable lump of a Welsh hillside'. But as the man on the telephone assured me, 'I'm on your side. I'll keep my ear to the ground for you.' In fact, the 'friend' regularly bringing news from Scotland told us nothing, but was very keen to hear in detail how our bid was progressing. Jock 'Haw Haw' was skilled at informing us almost daily how hopeless our chances were. We were on the way through months of mists, marshes and false Celtic trails.

Brian Huggett is nothing if not open and direct. 'You'll never win a Ryder Cup on that course, Trent Jones or no Trent Jones.' Dr John Thynne, vice-chairman of the Terry Matthews empire, was on a conference line from France and you could hear the silence. Certainly there had been criticisms by the professionals who had played in the first Wales Open on the Wentwood Hills course that the climb up from the holes in the River Usk basin to the top of the hill and the clubhouse was too steep. It would be unmanageable over two rounds a day, which is what a Ryder Cup entails.

Terry Matthews had always been planning a fourth course, but I did not imagine that the board's first recommendation would be that he take the proposed Ryder Cup course down the hill to the gentler slopes and into the curved banks of the river. By the time we presented our bid, the plans were in place for five new holes with two adjusted.

What else would be required of the resort? The hotel was enormous – 400 bedrooms with plans to double that, and below ground, massive conference and exhibition rooms. My old cricket-writer friend Martin Johnson, with whom I had chipped and putted round the world, came to look. His witty concession to Celtic Manor was that if rain fell for all three days during a Ryder Cup, it would be possible to play the match indoors in the wonderful conference and banqueting halls.

What else would we have to change in the physical presentation of course and amenities, apart from siting the new holes to create a vast spectator bank for thousands of viewers on the unpopular hillside? Our bid suggested a daily capacity of 55,000 and a wonderful view for almost everyone. No course in Scotland could match it. Priority would be given to the players with equal amenities for the two teams, so that neither felt aggrieved by inferior surroundings, as has happened in the past. A new clubhouse for teams, officials and families of players was designed alongside a new practice putting area. Most importantly, this newly designed course and luxury clubhouse would be available for public use. This was not to be a precious Loch Lomond; any club golfer would be able to stand on the tee where Tiger stood.

We were able to sit down day after day with Celtic Manor's top men, Andy Stanton and Jim MacKenzie, in charge of the building and the course respectively, and officials of the Newport County Borough Council to work out how we could manage the Ryder Cup board's insistence that there should be no on-course parking. It was at this early stage that we formed the clear view that they were looking for a location in which to set up one of the biggest sporting attractions in the world. Celtic Manor was new and our work was to help construct a theatre for dedicated usage. Celtic Manor had the flexibility over a large acreage to allow the Ryder Cup board to shape the event as they wanted, with so many thousands of feet for a tented village, and service roads in and out with one-way traffic. In my own mind, it would be like setting up the big top for a giant circus without a bottleneck or the sounds of lorries stalling or bleeping their reverse alarms as players crouched over their putts. It should be made to measure.

Getting to a Celtic Manor Ryder Cup by road was one of our advantages. Skirted by the M4 east and west and the A449 dual carriageway to the Midlands and the north, the case was easy to prove. Cardiff and Bristol airports were both about forty minutes away; Birmingham airport is an hour and a half while London Heathrow could be reached in just under two hours. Cardiff takes wide-bodied aircraft including Concorde. In the bid document there is a specific requirement that Concorde be able to fly in the American team.

By road, rail, air and sea, Celtic Manor is superbly placed. Over sixty-three per cent of the UK population is within a two-hour drive of Newport. The West Country, which has never had access to a Ryder Cup, is, quite literally, on the doorstep.

There was bad news when Corus Steel at Llanwern on the south side of Newport, announced first redundancies and then closure, but as a result the Ryder Cup bid became a beneficiary. When I was flown over Newport by helicopter with officials of the council, I was shown how rail traffic could, if necessary, be directed to the steelworks via a spur off the main railway line from London Paddington. Could the County Borough Council develop part of the steelworks into parking for the

Ryder Cup? Both chairman Sir Harry Jones and chief executive Chris Freegard nodded. It is four minutes from the first tee. With park and ride, the problem of on-course parking would be solved – there would be none except for vital services.

It was easier for Celtic Manor to meet accommodation quality and availability, sufficient space on site for media, hospitality and tented village, utility supplies, security, jumbo screens, practice areas for players, on-site office accommodation and a clean site for Ryder Cup Ltd to scoop its marketing bonanza than it would have been if we had tried to convert Wales's finest course, Royal Porthcawl, into an international venue for the week. The Celtic Manor Ryder Cup will be the first designer fixture for the great contest. Royal Porthcawl should be tomorrow's project for the R & A's Open championship.

There was one emotional plea in our approach to the Ryder Cup board – we wanted them to understand that this was a bid from everyone in Wales. We sought to popularise the bid, remove whiffs of élitism from the game itself and jolt even the most famous members' clubs into playing leading roles. So what was the golf development programme that would bind everyone to the national purpose?

The Sports Council moved forward with much imagination, embracing schemes such as 'Streets to Greens' which came out of the Gwynedd County Council in the north west. Boys and girls from the poorest families were given half sets of golf clubs to fit their physiques and introduced to the game. They thrived. What an easy game for the very young! Some established clubs supported the initiative by creating midweek memberships for the new enthusiasts.

We had a nasty feeling that Scotland's bid was a mile behind ours and they were being given an ocean of time to catch up. Decision day was postponed from January to September 2001. Initially, the Scottish Assembly was not prepared to pledge public money until after Scotland had been awarded the event. There was no such hesitation in Wales. Rhodri Morgan led from the front and Edwina Hart, finance minister, put her money where his mouth was. Jenny Randerson, sports minister, followed up through the Sports Council. From top to bottom, this was the team game to end all team games.

When eventually we won the battle, I embraced Gareth Davies, chairman of the Sports Council for Wales, a Welsh rugby international and a British Lion, saying, 'Fancy beating Scotland at golf with only half a course!' The Ryder Cup will go to Scotland in 2014, so they, too, had proved a case. Gavin Hastings, who ran their bid, sent me the most gentlemanly note of congratulations with the promise of a glass of champagne, which no doubt will precede or follow an annual rugby bash between our two countries. I look forward to that.

Tourism had meant endless public appearances, performing everything from serious speeches to ribbon-cutting but, come 1998, I discovered something about ceremony in uniform that had not touched my life as the lowest of non-commissioned airmen during my National Service. One day a pleasant, solidly built man called Byron Butler and his wife, Ann, called on me at home. He was Mid Glamorgan's High Sheriff, and he asked if I would consider stepping into that historic office. Would I have the time to devote to it? The sheriff's role was being challenged by many as a relic of the past. Did I support the shrievalty? If Byron put my name forward, it needed the traditional 'pricking' by the Queen so that I could take up the post in three years' time. Would I protect the role and try to enhance it in the county? Joanie and I thought about it for a couple of days. A new experience, we thought, an opportunity to trot off along another diversion, but only for twelve months. My year would be from March 1998 to 1999. I guessed that my Tourist Board days would be over by then because devolution for Wales was on the way and, in any case, no one served a quango for that long. As it turned out, I was still chairman of the Tourist Board and also president of MCC, but at the time, I thought, yes, I would be reasonably free. In cricket terms, I was prepared to take a fresh guard.

The post of High Sheriff is one of the oldest secular offices, dating back to the eleventh century. The fifty-five sheriffs are chosen annually by the Queen from a list drawn up by the incumbent and often narrowed to two or three candidates by a tribunal. In Mid Glamorgan, no one would choose a future sheriff without consulting the then Lord Lieutenant, Murray McLaggan. He particularly wanted the shrievalty to be classless and include representatives from all over the county, a real geographical spread. It would have been easy to find candidates every time from the larger towns, Bridgend, Merthyr, Pontypridd or Porthcawl, but the villages and hamlets north of the Vale of Glamorgan and up into the old mining valleys had to be included and that broke down any tendency to keep the job within the confines of a small social circle.

I remember reading an article in the *Guardian* newspaper two years after I had completed my year of office, accusing the shrievalty of 'institutional racism' because sheriffs were 'mostly white, male and too rich properly to represent a new Britain in which taxes are collected by the inland revenue rather than by local despots.' What a load of politically correct drivel! The work itself debars nobody. Anyone is eligible to be appointed as long as they own a home in the county except peers, clergy, officers in active service, barristers and solicitors. While I was High Sheriff of Mid Glamorgan, my fellow Lord's Taverner, Richard Stilgoe, writer and entertainer, was performing the same role in Surrey. The powers, as such, are mainly ceremonial these days but you can fill a year's diary with roles and responsibilities. If there was no High Sheriff, there would have to be someone else to fulfil the assortment of tasks, large and small. Formerly, sheriffs were responsible for the safety of judges within the county and were liable for the safe custody of prisoners as well as for the preparation of jury panels for assizes. The real value of the office these days resides in the ceremonial work. Many people are sceptical of the role but a good High Sheriff can persuade them differently.

Ceremony, the Lord Lieutenant had advised, is not easy if you have no military experience, but it is essential to take it seriously. There was the implication that a High Sheriff or two in the past had cracked up with laughter or tears at the wrong moment, as if he saw himself taking a salute for the first time in his life, as if in 'Dad's Army'. Laughter is the enemy of ceremony. However, as I dressed for my inauguration on 9 April 1998 I had to keep reminding myself of it. I must confess to having not worn tights before. What a wrestling match! I began sweating in my white shirt, detached collar with studs front and back, white silk jabot nestling under my chin, as I heeded Joan's instructions to roll up, not pull up, first one leg then the other. I had hoisted each leg of the tights to mid-thigh level when Joan turned away laughing. 'Stop! Start again,' she said. 'Don't you see, you're wearing those navy boxer underpants with the white spots. Tights will never go over them. Take the tights off. I'll get you some Y-fronts.' I could not bear to go through the agony of that again. 'Fetch me the scissors,' I said and I cut through the boxer shorts, binned them and went knickerless to my inauguration.

Court dress is a tricky little number, but sitting in the back seat, alongside the High Sheriff still in office, Ray Martin, I made myself as comfortable as I could with my sword fixed in its scabbard. Our official car snaked slowly down from my house on the hill, across the common, up into the ancient hill town of Llantrisant and on towards the church where our arrival was to be signalled by a small line of police trumpeters before we presented ourselves to the waiting Lord Lieutenant.

Unfortunately, without knowing it, I was sitting firmly on Ray's coat tail so that when he tried to get out of the car smartly on the near side to report to the Lord Lieutenant, he made a lunge out but was tugged back by my weight, like a dog making a dash for a lamp-post being yanked back on the lead. There was a reason why I was stuck on his coat tails. Trying to get out on my side of the car, I discovered that my sword was pointing outwards into the uphol-stery stabbing me in the groin and pushing me back inside. At the second attempt, in front of an expectant crowd, I played it cool, reversed the sword and I was out, but my weight came off the High Sheriff's coat at the very second he made his next effort to pull himself free. I have to report that, as the police trumpets sounded the salute, Ray Martin made a near horizontal appearance, heading towards the Lord Lieutenant like a man shot from a circus cannon. The Lord Lieutenant saved the day. With immense experience and the sangfroid that he had recommended for ceremonial occasions, he saluted the flying Sheriff. 'Good morning, High Sheriff,' he said calmly, and as I brushed up and advanced from round the back of the car, 'Good morning, High Sheriff Designate.' The show was on the road and from that moment I prepared every move when I was on official duty in court dress or else I would be a menace to the whole of Mid Glamorgan.

CHAPTER 14

THE MARYLEBONE CLUB

Colin Ingleby-Mackenzie, president of MCC, invited us to his home, close to Lord's, for informal supper. He asked Joanie to enjoy a drink at one end of the drawing room until his wife Susan could join her and then led me to an armchair at the other, obviously in a solemn though friendly mood, rather like a captain shepherding an out-of-form player into a corner of the dressing room to explain why he has been left out of the side. The questions were straight and clear. When would I be free of my complex web of professional and public work? What did I see as MCC's role in the changing cricket world? Was he considering me for the presidency? Succession is entirely in the president's gift.

We had just opened the discussion when Susan smiled her way in, first greeting Joan, then coming to give a hug, a kiss and an unforgettable greeting, 'Congratulations. You'll be a marvellous president. The Lewises? Absolutely the right team.' I had never before seen that D'Artagnan of county captains, A.C.D. Ingleby-Mackenzie, so suddenly thrust on to the back foot trying to get a defence together. Too late, his wife had smashed through it: the long interview he had planned was over. I would be president of MCC for the next two years, and naturally, would give up all professional work in cricket and clear the way to play the leading role. Immediately and above all else, I thought of my father and how proud he would have been. When I was young in Neath, he mentioned the words 'Marylebone Cricket Club' but I had no idea what or where it was. Yes, I knew the club was at Lord's, but where was Lord's? Most cricket clubs in South Wales represented towns or villages, welfare associations or works, and usually they shunned club colours, preferring badges and shields on blazers or sweaters. Consequently when, in my mid teens, I saw two orange and yellow-banded sweaters trotting through this world of club heraldry, I wondered what sort of men could be sporting them. They turned out to be Captain W.M.S. Trick of Neath, the superb left-arm spinner, and J.D.H. Riches of Cardiff, son of the Glamorgan first county championship captain in 1921, N.V.H. Riches, and himself the skipper of the Glamorgan Second XI. MCC, it was then explained to me, was a big club in London that ran everything. It was nothing to do with us.

I believe my father did conduct a piece of Christmas subterfuge in 1950 – I was twelve – by persuading a collection of relatives to pool their coinage to buy my first, and very large, cricket history book instead of socks, ties and handkerchiefs: *The History of Cricket* by Eric Parker, published in the series of the Lonsdale Library of Sports, Games and Pastimes, founded by the Right Honourable the Earl of Lonsdale, K.G., G.C.V.O., D.L. A massive indebtedness was recorded to MCC. The book was read cover to cover, several times . . . by my father.

It was not until 1963 that MCC and I had our first formal liaison on 2 May when my name was entered in the list of candidates for playing membership: proposed by Wilfred Wooller and seconded by Donald Carr of Derbyshire and England. The requirement in those days was to play ten days' cricket for the club in two seasons while the alternative route was to join a waiting list of between fifteen and twenty years. The options are similar today, but now candidates cannot be registered at birth by fond parents: mid teenage is the starting point. The scrutiny of playing and non-playing members is stringent: the Lewis girls, Joanna and Anabel, are on the list, happily padding patiently along the long road.

My ten days' cricket were easy to achieve because I was included in the MCC's club tour side to South America under the leadership of Alan Smith in 1964–65 and so completed the qualification in the most exotic locations, Brazil, Chile and Argentina.

My overseas travel before that had been limited to Europe. With the RAF Innsworth rugby team I had played an 'away' match at Ballykelly, Northern Ireland, memorable for its flight more than the rugby football. Our service transport out of Lineham flew into a flash storm over the Irish Sea when our favourite Group Captain Roberts, dutifully supporting us, shouted to the pilot a remarkable instruction for a senior officer, 'Slow down, for goodness sake, slow down.'

More rugby was played for Home Command in RAF München-Gladbach in Germany. My European cricket experiences were more memorable because of the longer stays to complete two-day matches on short tours. I played on the mat for the Combined Services in Amsterdam and The Hague and for the Air Force in Gibraltar, where I self-inflicted second-degree sunburn. With Cambridge University under the captaincy of Chris Howland I sailed to Denmark on a ten-day coaching expedition that took us to Copenhagen and Hjor-ring. Now, however, at Christmas 1964, at the age of twenty-six, I was stepping on the long-haul cricket circuit: not that the pretty island of Niteroi, a bobbing ferryboat ride out from Copacabana in Rio de Janeiro featured in your average fixture card. We were to play two matches there, a one-day contest against Rio and a two-day match against the Brazil Cricket Association with proper declarations accord-ing to the Laws of Cricket. The fame of the Marylebone Cricket Club is founded not only in a long history of major Test series, but also on the missionary work the club has performed all over the world. Cloistered by tall trees was a long, low pavilion that was both elegant and functional, harbouring memories of British naval officers at play. Plumed waiters in white tunics moved slowly to deliver lime sodas.

Over in Vina del Mar in Chile I learned that MCC was visiting for the first time since 1927, and there was the evidence before us on the pavilion wall – a photograph of the 1927 team captained by Sir Pelham Warner that included G.O. Allen, J.C. White and Lord Alexander Dunglass, later Sir Alec Douglas Home.

There was a hard-luck story from the tour at Niteroi where Mike
Griffith broke a toe, which deprived him of the honour of captaining
Cambridge against Oxford in the university hockey match on his return
home. Then farce: on the final stage of the tour, which had taken us to
the beautiful grounds of Santiago and Vina del Mar, to Lomas, San
Isidro and Belgrano, as well as the inland camps of Venado Tuerto, we
witnessed a banana slip by our skipper Alan Smith at Belgrano. The
pitch there was shiny, flat and inviting to batsmen. Bob Gale of
Middlesex and I, the tour openers, were risking a smile when Alan, best
known by his initials A.C., announced that he feared one of us might get
out to the new ball and that would be a shame, so he would open in my
place. Could this be our leader's dash for glory? He took guard, stepped a
full stride out of his crease before taking guard again then settling out
there in his stance, so indicating to the umpire that he was too far down
the pitch for an lbw. A young bowler called Vignobles ran in, sending the
second ball of the match thumping into A.C.'s front pad, which by now
was a good four yards outside the popping crease, and appealed for lbw.
It was a horror to see the umpire's finger move slowly skywards. The
skipper had been mercilessly sawn off. Number three in the batting
order, I was immediately reunited with R.A. Gale and normal service was
resumed in dream conditions. Alas, poor A.C. failed in his safety first
drill to ask the essential question in amateur cricket worldwide: is the
bowler in any way related to the umpire?

'Owzat?' Vignobles shouted.

'That's out, son,' the umpire responded.

It was the natural next thing to do for a university cricket Blue, to
become a candidate for MCC membership. Back home in the South
Wales league the number of MCC members could be counted on the
fingers of one hand. In fact, Terry Shufflebotham, a most successful
Neath captain, did play his qualifiers and joined the club, but the
colours were rare in that region.

I began serving on MCC sub-committees during the 1960s, notably
county pitches, registration and cricket. Remember, MCC ran the
whole of cricket until 1968, amateur and professional, and provided
the secretariat for the International Cricket Council. As Keith Miller

had once described his first playing experience at Lord's in wartime matches for the Royal Australian Air Force – 'every time I walked up those sprig-scarred steps of the pavilion I knew I was in the very same footsteps as W.G. Grace' – so I felt awe, a mix of reverence and fear, to be in the Committee Room where bodyline had been discussed, Test match teams selected, where the list of presidents twice included H.R.H. The Duke of Edinburgh and where Mr G.O. Allen, following his presidency in 1963, had begun his eleven-year reign as treasurer, 1965–76.

Gubby Allen, as long as he was treasurer, sat in on all meetings. He was meticulous in his preparation for every agenda item. Cogent and powerful in debate, he had an unquenchable thirst for being right. MCC, however, attracted few members of committee and sub-committees who liked to roll over and have their tummies tickled, so Gubby occasionally found himself frustrated by the specialist out-ground knowledge of Doug Insole, who could deliver the *coup de grâce*, half-smiled and half-stammered. But there was no one who frustrated Gubby more than Freddie Brown, armed with ideas not wholly thought through, but delivered in a booming voice of a vicar of good hope and everlasting friendship that reduced Allen to a cold calculator. Freddie could swing an audience and sniff out a gin and tonic several staircases away.

He chaired the pitches sub-committee and in one meeting I found myself sitting in a chair near the fire alongside Wilf Wooller. It was always an early start for us from Wales to make the morning meetings, with fitness tested further by Wilf's insistence on walking from Paddington to Lord's and back to save the taxi money. Freddie looked at me and pointed. Wilf was fast asleep. 'Wake up, Wilf,' bellowed the chairman and Wilf shot up, firing words of instant retaliation.

'Is your committee talking any damned sense yet? I've never heard such a load of cobblers in my life. Nothing wrong with the pitch at Ebbw Vale, it's just that we don't bugger up our tracks with Surrey loam.'

Freddie looked at his watch: 12.45, his favourite hour. 'Time we went up to the dining room for a gin and . . .'

Wilf interrupted: 'You've been dragging out this meeting to the respectable hour for your "first of the day". We could have finished the meeting at midday and gone home.'

It was in this committee room that I witnessed a legal battle between Barry Knight and Essex. Knight, seeking a change of county at the end of 1966 season, wished to move to Leicestershire. MCC's registration rules did not then allow such a leap without a formal playing ban on the cricketer of two seasons in the county championship. This rule was to protect Essex, who had invested time and money in Knight's development, and also to dissuade other Test-quality players from encouraging offers from one county while under contract to another. Essex entered the room with lawyers, secretary and chairman; Barry Knight came with QC and full legal team and, for the first time, I became aware of the thundering stricture 'restraint of trade'. The outcome was that MCC's registration ruling was reviewed and Barry Knight's ban from first-class cricket was reduced to one year. It still appears harsh from a distance, especially after Kerry Packer's lawyers drove restraint of trade to the summit of its importance in cricket a decade later, allowing cricketers to move in any direction outside contract.

I knew Barry well. We had played together in the Air Force and Combined Services. Many opponents were taken in by his light frame, paleness and nervous cough, but as a bowler he was nippy and aggressive, an excellent fielder and he got runs too, though he never gave the appearance of fancying anything above medium pace. He fitted in well to an England side for twenty-nine caps. I had seen him nervous at the crease, but nothing like as white as when he walked into the MCC meeting which had become an industrial court with a defendant in the dock. His eyes stuck to the floor, his clearing of the throat was now more than theatre: I expected our chairman, the solicitor Cecil Paris, to ask, 'Tell me Knight, when did you last see your father?'

The committee dining room has become one of my favourite places at Lord's, not day-to-day but in the half dozen or so winter evenings when we hold members' dinners. Guest speakers are excellent without the prompting of a fee and about sixty members pile in for an outstanding dinner prepared by the very popular manageress-chef Linda Le Ker with her French husband Alain. It is an opportunity for members to mix with presidents and committee past and present and with crucial members of the secretariat. MCC is no longer the 'them' and 'us' format that often appears to be the case at Test matches, when the president and senior officers are busy entertaining visitors important to the club in boxes and cut off from the possibility of a member's nudge on the arm followed by a complaint about the noise, the lack of parking, the remoteness of the committee and, a long time ago, the aggression of the gateman. At these dinners, low lights glow at the top of the turret above the pavilion entrance and all is well in our yellow and orange heaven.

The club's bicentenary in 1987 was a year studded with special events, great and small. There was a celebration dinner in a giant marquee on Dorset Square, site of Thomas Lord's first ground and dancing on the tennis courts to Joe Loss and his band. Storms stopped play in the concert at the Nursery End. I had been asked by the then secretary Jack Bailey and treasurer David Clark if I would write the club's bicentenary history, called *Double Century*. As well as the account of the club's two hundred years, it was virtually the history of cricket itself. 'We'll open the archives for the first time,' I was told. 'There's a mass of stuff under the Long Room.' Unfortunately, when the time came for me to explore, I was informed by the apologetic curator, Stephen Green, that there was no access to the precious store because the painters were in for many months, and all valuables were covered in dust sheets and unreachable. It proved a challenge, therefore, to my excellent researcher, Joanne Watson, a young colleague from BBC Radio sport. She soon became an expert on the development of cricket and the club by examining old newspapers now stored on microchip in the British Museum. My previous books, *A Summer of Cricket* (1975) and *Playing Days* (1985), had been well received, but neither approached the difficulties of writing a history.

Unhappily, there were only fourteen months before the copy date which, with the absence of archive material on site, made it a rather feverish run-around. Worse still, when the day came to write the first chapter, I simply could not begin. Start anywhere is the usual advice, not necessarily on the first chapter: the safe route away from writer's block. The typewriter clacked but stammered and stopped; another carbon hit the bin. I was given the generous loan of his London flat by Mathew Prichard, South Wales neighbour and friend. Then, adding to my block, came the fear of inspection by E.W. Swanton and other scribes, who would have sought the authorship in the first place. 'Any copy in yet, Lewis' became EWS's greeting. Panic set in: I was in a bit of a fix a few doors away from the Fulham Brasserie, as page after page was crunched in my fist and binned. I walked up and down the room until ankle deep in pile rising from the Prichards' new carpet. After a week, I went home again to Ewenny, near Bridgend, to my word processor: I was a pre-laptop scribe.

Early one morning I decided to doodle with my pen on a lined pad while listening to Mozart's Clarinet Quintet in A, K581 played by Keith Puddy with the Gabrieli String Quartet. Music from heaven, words from . . . Yes! I was on my way. It was 6.05 am. I could hear the office cleaners at Hodder and Stoughton in Bedford Square dust with relief, while my superb editor, erudite and sensitive John Bright Holmes, I hoped, turned in his Fulham bed, smiled, muttered, 'Lewis has started', and went back to sleep.

By breakfast on that glorious day I had written:

The story of the Marylebone Cricket Club begins in the 1780s with a few aristocrats and noblemen. Wealthy and game for a wager. Who liked nothing so much as to take a coach-ride from their clubs in the fashionable and spreading West End of London, out along the New Road, just above Oxford Street, to the cricket at Islington. They played at the White Conduit Fields.

If now, 200 years later, you want to follow the clatter and rumble of their coach-wheels on a match day, you would have to start in Pall Mall at an office block numbered 100, where most agree the Star and Garter Inn once stood. The hostelry, popular with sportsmen, was a warren of private rooms for dining clubs. The Jockey Club (founded in 1751) held its meetings there, and cricketers went there, too. Back in 1755, the Laws of Cricket had been revised by 'Several cricket clubs, particularly that of the Star and Garter'.

Out of St James's past Boodle's and Brooks's clubs, through Mayfair, past Portman Square and up Baker Street to the New Road, known today as Marylebone Road and Euston Road. It would be a bumpy trip on these northern limits of London. The roads were rough and rutted, and Edgware Road whenever it rained, for example, was deep sludge.

However, in those days it took a lot to separate the aristocracy from their pleasures. They were the men of property, affluent and glowing with the sharp rise of land prices. Some attached themselves to the new industrial surge, others to commerce.

Almost all were conscious of fashion, looking to build a house in one of London's new squares – such as Portman Square (1764), Bedford Square (1769) and Portland Square (1778) – showing off the private ballroom in season, buying eye-catching 'fribble-frabbles of fashion' in one of Oxford Street's 153 shops, and reposing among the fine furniture of the day made by Chippendale, Sheraton, the Adam Brothers or Hepplewhite. Their silver glittered on the dumb-waiter, chinoiserie too, and tea was served from the new porcelain sets. Yet, more than anything else, our own particular heroes, the precursors of the Marylebone Cricket Club, were making a serious pursuit of leisure.

Shooting birds had become competitive; fox-hunting, with horses bred specially for pursuing the packs of hounds for the scent, began in the mid-eighteenth century. From the 1770s London gentlemen could race out to the country to join the Pytchley, the Belvoir, the Cottesmore or the Quorn; so a comparatively short if bumpy ride outside the small network of street lighting, beyond the police control, did not deter them. The White Conduit Fields (hard by the modern King's Cross station) were available for public hire. It was a rough ground, skirted only by a wooden rail fence, but as soon as the bet was struck, the wickets pitched and a couple of scorers seated mid-wickets, with blades sharpened to notch the runs on a stout stick, battle would commence and the nobility and their friends were at peace with their world.

Phew! Months later, my agent and eventually fellow MCC committee member, Michael Sissons, took delivery of the final chapter by fax from Perth in Western Australia. While Joan and Joanna had slept, I wrote in our room in the Sheraton Hotel and beat the deadline by hours before strolling without a care to watch England play at the WACA.

And so to the prospect in 1998 of being MCC president for two years, the first bringing the World Cup tournament back to England and the second full of millennium celebrations. By this time most of my work was supporting Michael Sissons on the marketing committee and trying to persuade MCC to attach greater importance to the way it communicated both internally and externally. Each department of the administration appeared to be incarcerated in its own cell. Chris Rea, the marketing manager, with whom I had worked in journalism and broadcasting, tried valiantly to free and inter-relate the obvious skills within the club, but we were only half successful. The very word communications was an anathema to the administration who mistakenly believed it meant 'spin'. A happier result came from my efforts alongside Brian Thornton, the chairman of estates, in the matter of the new media centre. How we planned and plotted to win the vote for the bold design by Future Systems over the more conservative drawings! For the internal workings of the centre we took advice from Richie Benaud, Peter Baxter and Derek Hodgson, representatives of television, radio and writing. Stylistically it makes a brilliant statement about MCC's determination to be a club of long history that still seeks to stay ahead of the game: work continues in order to meet the complete approval of the working media.

Although MCC was no longer the governing body of British cricket, nor was its president the chairman of the International Cricket Conference, MCC did have one seat at the centre of the national game's management. However, the club, as I saw it, had become footloose without real power, save that it was the custodian of the Laws of the Game and its ground, Lord's, was unique. When I became president, MCC had an uneasy relationship with the England and Wales Cricket Board, not only over the commercial relationships that affected Lord's and the professional cricket played there, but also ideologically: MCC historically had been the great propagator of cricket, the teacher and developer. Now, the ECB was the sole governing body of the game, and they appeared so jumpy about the MCC traditions that they spent time and money, with a huge loss of good humour, trying to put MCC back in its box forever. How could that be when international cricket at Lord's created forty per cent of Test cricket income? How could the reputation of the club shrink when there were over four hundred out-matches each season? Can a reputation dip when up to half a dozen overseas tours are undertaken each year? The club's major tours are to countries just below Test level, perhaps on trial for Test status. MCC selects strong sides and professionals are paid. There are tours that include a few professionals alongside the very best players among the members for which travel and accommodation expenses only are paid. Then there are tours for members who pay for themselves and, perhaps more exciting, MCC tours for younger cricketers of outstanding talents. The ECB, alas, concentrated on going alone when it would have been best advised to turn the history and the strength of MCC's membership to the major purpose of developing British cricket and its players to ever-improving standards of play.

MCC, without doubt, has its critics, including some who carry the weight of social prejudice on both shoulders. They see privilege, loud mouths, misogyny, jazzy colours and old school ties. In a membership of 18,000 there are bound to be members fitting those descriptions, left overs from different days, but the club I have always known has included cricketers and cricket lovers who might be singing nightly in Covent Garden, keeping the corner shop, teaching in Singapore, selling tea in a café or wine in Tuscany, preaching in Durban or Derbyshire, coaching in schools or villages, running large city insti-tutions or the local bank. Criticism was always ignited by the Men Only rule for candidacy, but under the presidency of Colin Ingleby-Mackenzie the membership voted by the two-thirds majority required to admit women and it was my pleasure to follow up Colin's vision and hard work with the formal admission of ten honorary women members, and also to begin the life of the MCC women's cricket team.

For the majority there was relief that MCC had taken a big stride to keep up with society's changes. If there was a down side, it was that the third of the membership who had been outvoted were incensed and were likely to add their fury to any protest movement within the club.

As I arrived through the Grace Gates as president, the swords were clanging, club versus board of control, over the financial staging agreement for Test matches. There were rumbles in the jungle about the on-line rights of ECB's matches played at Lord's, coconuts were already shaken from treetops. Gradually, I tried to position MCC as the wind beneath the ECB's wings, but they were on a solo flight towards a new structure that relegated MCC and the eighteen counties, and fabricated a large, highly populated central control. However angry anyone at Lord's felt, either sitting with MCC at the Pavilion End or up in the ECB headquarters at the Nursery End, there should have been an easy compromise because the paramount aim of all involved was a winning England side and prosperity for the game at every level.

MCC's annual general meetings were becoming increasingly disso-nant affairs during the 1990s. Presidents usually managed to quell or ignore the complaints against the behaviour of the committee, but in 1998, Colin Ingleby-Mackenzie's second year, I saw real anger on the floor and a determination to challenge the committee on many subjects. A small group, basically mistrusting the committee, accused it of self-perpetuation, maladministration and dishonour – nothing trivial! There was also a battle fought on the rights and privileges that go along with membership. That sort of gossip usually went little further than the members' bar, but there was by now in the hands of many, an organ for disseminating the call to arms by new technology: members were on e-mail. One press of the button and the growing group of dissenters multiplied.

I arrived innocently, preparing my plan to realign our cricket work by repositioning MCC in the national and global context, but almost all of my time was spent fire-fighting the blazes of dissatisfaction that burst out all around me. The writing room at Lord's became my daily office where I met members arriving with criticism or succour. It was explained to me how some were still angry about the removal of Jack Bailey from office of secretary in 1987 and also about the replacement of Mr Meyer, the club's solicitor, along the way. The sharpest focus of discontent was directed at the statement by Colin Cowdrey when he was president in 1987 that no member shall ever have to pay for admission to cricket played at Lord's. Here we were in 1999, however, requiring members to pay to watch the World Cup matches at Lord's. This is not to say that the club members usually take up valuable Test match seats free of any charge. MCC makes a payment per seat to ECB for major matches, so subsidising the members in that way.

It was amazing how the answer to the original problem never sufficed. Yes, Colin Cowdrey had made that promise in 1987, but as legal counsel assured us in October 1991 'there was no legal obligation on the part of the committee to consult members before taking the steps which were taken in relation to the World Cup . . . No statements made in 1987 over-rode the power of the committee for the future to make regulations affecting the benefits and privileges of the membership.'

The committee embraced my wish to write a five-year plan and keep MCC up with and ahead of the changing times. It was easy to see that the administrative structure of MCC needed a complete review: it creaked with reactionary thought in key administrative corners. Most certainly we needed to embrace the appointment of a commercial director and set up a mechanism for decisions to be made by the week rather than monthly by the committee. We needed a chairman in regular attendance to move business forward and it was resolved that an honorary chairman would be moved to the centre and serve a three-year term. Sir Michael Jenkins and then Lord Alexander, both in an honorary capacity, accepted the responsibility. These were ideas not born out of pressure but which had been on the table for many years. Now was the time. The club and I were indebted to Sir Michael Jenkins for his work on MCC and the lines of responsibility and communication. During my two years progress was made towards turning the MCC into a business as well as a cricket club by the appointment of David Batts as deputy chief executive. We had been board members on the British Tourist Authority when he had chaired the London Tourist Board. There are sticking points, still, but the new structures have begun to work.

The hostile group did its utmost to attack the committee. So organised were they, so vociferous and disrespectful, I was forced to abandon my first AGM to avoid the committee being outvoted on almost every issue and being forced to resign, and this in spite of explaining at the outset that we had listened and were reacting where appropriate. The committee were not optimistic before the meeting and had prepared a statement as follows:

> The committee met immediately before this meeting and took the decision that it would convene a special general meeting in order that the membership as a whole should be given the opportunity of voting on a motion of confidence in the committee.

As Ted Dexter, sitting in the committee ranks, observed, 'It was like walking through the jungle and being picked off by snipers: a dart in the neck, a spear in the chest, a knife in the back.'

When the Special General Meeting came along, I better understood how to handle it. I had been put in office to be a cricket president during the World Cup year, but I needed to learn the skills of a chairman of a plc explaining to a packed hall how share prices had plummeted and the pension fund was decimated. This time the committee received a strong vote of confidence, but clearly there were friendly members who were concerned. Among them was Lord MacLaurin, who wrote to me:

> For disaffected members to say what they said was, I believe, an insult and a disgrace to the club and I would suggest a way forward. It seems to me from my days on the committee, that the

small band of anti-committee members is growing and I wonder now if the time is not right to review the total management of MCC. It is now big business turning over millions of pounds and there is no reason at all why you should not set up the management structure as a plc. I think it is totally unfair that the president should have to chair a meeting such as last evening and the situation will not get better . . . votes can then be cast by post before the meeting. You have on your committee many first-class businessmen and I hope you will be able to review procedures before next year.

In that following year we did have postal voting to ensure that the full membership could have a say. In fact, when I was representing MCC in South Africa I had a long conversation with Peter Pollock who urged the prompt despatch of AGM papers to the overseas list so that they could weigh in behind the president and committee, whom they were happy to take on trust. That was an interesting observation, because any organisation that elects a board or a committee must take decisions on trust. It is not for every member to raise a small army on e-mail because a decision does not suit him or her. Others urged the removal from membership of the most vociferous nonconformists.

Many of the challenges were legal and that is why I asked Lord Alexander QC to succeed me as president. Having worked for eight years as head of the Wales Tourist Board I knew all about accountability in public life and, although performed in an exaggerated way for the sake of civil servants, I still felt that the MCC committee could be free of false accusations if everything was open and accountable. These Bob Alexander and I agreed should be the watchwords.

There is within MCC an unstoppable desire to help cricket wherever it is played. I never tire of quoting Billy Griffith, one-time secretary, who would open every meeting with a simple statement about every decision being for the benefit of cricket and cricketers. Whether that can now apply with cash receipts growing and escalating business surrounding on-line rights, staging agreements and commercial considerations carrying such a high cash value, I am not so sure. Happiest of all stories, therefore, is the preamble to the newest Laws of Cricket which includes a piece on 'The Spirit of the Game' throwing the major responsibility for the good spirit of the game on to the captains. From tumultuous times, good practices should follow.

We had allowed the cool air of democracy to blow through the process of selection for the committee. There would be no starring of candidates unless the candidate brought specific skills to our work. There was also a resolution for voting which was intended to make a rule to establish the members' rights to free entry into the ground which they owned, though allowing the committee to act by trust in special circumstances. Roger Knight, the patient and beleaguered secretary, followed his sound instinct for keeping the club at the heart of world cricket. Good humour was restored. The game and MCC moved on, and I had lost none of my enthusiasm for the club when I became one of three trustees in 2002.

ENGLAND'S NEXT STEPS

C ricket changes in small ways but not a lot. The packaging and presentation of the professional game have made it more supermarket car park than cathedral close, but there is still bounce and swing and turn to find the edge of a wooden bat; there are sixes and fours and the ball still pitches leg and hits off. The umpire's word is law – well, at the moment it is. The difference from my own playing days, however, is in the fielding. The modern generation has proved just what can be achieved by all eleven players if a greater concentration is attached to the techniques of stopping, catching and throwing the ball. Higher fitness standards have also helped the less athletic to turn in excellent performances. In the field, the players of the twenty-first century personify the advance of the possible. There have always been brilliant fielders, as talented as any today, but the all-round competence has risen.

In 1994 I did all the interviewing and editing and most of the writing for a book and video called *MCC Masterclass*. It was intended for the accomplished cricketer, professional and amateur, who could learn something from 'the masters'. Jonty Rhodes, the brilliant South African fielder, wrote his own chapter and opened with the positive statement that comes best from him:

May I suggest that parents and teachers urge young cricketers not to think of themselves only as batsmen or bowlers? Skills with the ball in hand, requiring fast reactions, catching, stopping and throwing at targets can all be part of a small child's growing-up recreation. We had a long passageway at home and my father and I used to throw a ball to each other for hours. We broke a few pictures and windows but that was the sort of household in which I grew up. Out of doors we had a tennis court but we played more cricket on it than tennis. I had the basics drummed into me and I was always running in one direction or another. If you cannot field you are not a cricketer.

Nowadays, watching from a variety of angles round the ground, I see the technical play less clearly than I did as a commentator but still ask myself the question that will not go away: why do England find it so hard to win at cricket? The England and Wales Cricket Board was formed in 1997 at a time when England were expected to fail consistently in Tests and the game appeared to be losing its wide public appeal. These symptoms were the core of a crisis which this single governing body, known as ECB, was formed to expel.

The Board has been enterprising in packaging the cricket product and taking it into the marketplace, though not entirely successful in selling it. England has joined the jetset that is trying to establish an ICC international championship. As international games multiply, more and more players have been contracted to the board of control rather than to their county clubs. The profession of Test cricketer looks a desirable one. Initiatives have reached the grass roots too, for example the 2003 launch of a 20-over-a-side game between the professional counties for the benefit of youngsters and those who want to catch some wham-bang at the end of a day's work.

These days a National Academy is almost finished at Loughborough and the country is awash with initiatives that send the board's officers buzzing round the motorways. Six years later, however, we suffer the same symptoms: England are still losing, at least at the time of writing, leading to the conclusion that there has been more talk and more innovation than achievement. Was the original diagnosis wrong? Has the reconstruction of England cricket been wisely planned? I have argued consistently from the first day in the life of the England and Wales Cricket Board that the architects of their plan got it horribly wrong. Instead of building the house from the foundations up, they started in the attic and attempted to work everything down from the England team in Tests. I predicted reluctantly that all the army of coaches and managers and Team England committees could ever achieve at the top level was a brisk polishing of cricketers, most aged between twenty-five and thirty-five, who were too set in their methods to craft serious change. There were many advocates of everything Australian: the talk was of academies, of preparation, of toughness and we saw overseas players and coaches flow into the county champion-ship. Counties wanted two overseas players registered rather than the one.

ECB styled itself 'the sole governing body of cricket in England and Wales' and set itself up as a major institution that tried to run everyone's life within the game. There was a logic to this in that public money can help fund a sport only through the conduit of a governing body, but ECB became a control freak. Let me be fair to all concerned: it was understandable that there should be an end to the mish-mash of rule by counties who would never vote themselves a reduction of control. ECB, however, went too far in relegating all those not involved in central control and the aura of police state emanated from the Nursery End at Lord's. Six years later I am left applauding about eighty per cent of the ECB initiatives, but seeing that the urge to control every aspect of their top-down world has left them with cash-flow problems and a product in the marketplace that is far inferior to anything in Australia.

My choice would have been to start with evangelism and begin at the bottom. Then look for the magic called talent. Talent grows into a strong flower from the root upwards. I would have looked for it in groups of children taught by the old professional down at the club or by the shift-worker in his spare time. That is where I would have directed the encouragement, tried to build the recruitment to the game and spent the money to attract even more financial support from public funds, through sports councils, social exclusion programmes, the Cricket Foundation or with whatever pockets of cash I could pick. A template for geographical development becomes an artificial cage when the counties, minor counties and clubs are the ones with the close intelligence of the talents and where they lie.

I would have tried, though I would have failed, to influence government and county councils, schools and schoolteachers in order to prevent the continuing sale of school playing fields. Unfortunately, politicians are mostly those who hated team games at school and shun them later in their lives. There is one recent Minister of Sport on whose door I would have knocked hard for advice, Kate Hoey. No doubt she would have patted me on the head and told me to dream on, but a government that wanted to win the Ashes should be interested both in enabling children to play good cricket at a young age on grass and in moving the main examination term, at school and university, to the autumn, so that papers are sat just before Christmas. A strong cricket programme in schools and universities eventually dovetailing with counties and clubs in July and August during the summer would transform the game's development. Football is predator enough at the moment; it would not be as damaged as cricket if there were a major examination term in the middle of their season.

My priority would be to catch our cricketers young; introducing boys and girls to the game in an informal way and making the game competitive at the earliest possible age. Always be sure that there is a space above an outstanding youngster in the development structure so that he can progress as soon as possible. The ECB has promoted Kwik Cricket and InterCricket and sent out development officers but the operation was too self-centred and too self-important at the start to grow the devolution that the game's development requires. The eighteen counties were positively sidelined without a single message of how they were to fit in or what they were expected to contribute. All cricket cannot possibly flow from one board of control. We have 60 million inhabitants of these islands, many more than live in Australia, so why the insistence on narrowing the base? My major moves would be these, as the year 2003 begins.

Devolve money and authority to empower the eighteen counties. They understand their own geographical territory best. Only by embracing the counties will the ECB keep the population base wide. I would prune the over-populated and expensive centre. Tell the counties that they must change. For example, their elected committee should deal only with membership matters; the actual business should be the responsibility of a small board of local experts, voluntary or otherwise, who bring to the table specialist skills to make the best possible use of ECB monies. The composition of this board should meet the approval of ECB and be answerable to it. Cricket is crying out for devolution: the build-up of power and personnel has been expensive and unhealthy.

I do not subscribe to the two divisions of the county championship. True, it has added salt and pepper to the August fare, but only in the imagination is it producing better cricketers. It is more likely to result in the closure of long-established county cricket clubs and, astonishingly, the critics welcome that. We will see the haves and the have-nots and the strength of cricket will shrink. Critics talk about pruning the branches to preserve the stem, but I like Matthew Engel's response to that when he wrote the editor's notes in *Wisden*: 'I suspect it's the wrong metaphor. They would be blocking the tributaries and the river would dry up.' The counties need jolting into the modern day but they must be the reformed pillars of a winning future.

I recommend devolution, too, within Lord's cricket ground, from the ECB to MCC. I cannot understand anyone omitting MCC from serious responsibility in the national game. The ECB pretended that this mighty institution did not exist, though I did share a moment with Lord MacLaurin who told me that he thought MCC should be at the front of the efforts to enthuse and develop cricketers from the youngest age. Lord's provides forty per cent of our Test match income. MCC wants to help and, unlike other Test grounds, Lord's provides income but does not receive a distribution back from the ECB. It is a straight cash handover. MCC has a young cricketers school, women's teams, plays over four hundred out-matches a year, many to celebrate anniversaries, promotes 'the spirit of cricket', has the responsibility to develop the game in Europe, and runs mission-ary tours all over the world.

I could not look at the massive contribution made to cricket by MCC without considering it a massive ally in any restructuring. I would entrust MCC with the development of young cricketers in the amateur game. Because the club is the custodian of the Laws of the Game, give it the job of running the system of professional umpiring. I would further give MCC the task of conducting the various playing experiments that are needed from time to time, for example, Dennis Lillee's aluminium bat, Bob Wyatt's fourth-stump theory, television Hawkeye, son of Hawkeye and so much more. MCC, like the counties, would have to present its plans and be sure to nominate highly qualified people to run these schemes. They need not be MCC members. They would at all times be answerable to the ECB, but operating at arm's length. Again I say, slim down the centre, hand out the jobs and with them the responsibility and accountability.

I believe we should review the changes made in county cricket over fifty years. This is most important. Do not evaluate changes in playing conditions in isolation. How do they all add up? Is the county game healthy? No, it is not. Many true lovers of the game have reached the point of declaring four-day county cricket boring. I have. Ordinary batsmen fill their boots with big hundreds against plain bowling on dead surfaces. This conviction was put to me by Doug Insole, president of Essex and former captain, servant on countless cricket committees and a former Test player: 'County cricket is hard to watch. What do the members think?' This was not an old player's moan. He began with a fact: 'In the county championship of 1956 there were 116 centuries scored in 238 three-day matches. In 1990, in 187 three- and four-day matches the number of hundreds was 323.'

Why is it so easy to get runs? Where are the fine bowlers? Doug Insole's contention is that the board of control has failed to review the continuous changes made to the conditions of play and study their combined effect. Pitches were uncovered for almost all my first-class career. Now they are not only covered but are dressed constantly with

Surrey-Ongar loam, which eventually turns them into flat dead surfaces without much turn, similar to many others all over the world. I recall Garry Sobers, Clive Lloyd and other outstanding overseas stroke-makers admitting that they came to English county cricket to complete their education in cricket on pitches that helped the bowlers of both seam and spin. There are now commercial, corporate hospitality and sponsorship reasons why pitches are covered but no cricket reasons. I do not agree that because the four-day game near replicates Test match conditions it is sound preparation for players. Gone is the theory that four-day games would have spinners learning their tough trade and taking their skills into Tests. Where are they?

In answer to a simple question – what will make England win Tests forever and a day? I say natural pitches.

In the era of uncovered pitches, it would be wrong to imagine constant rain and a ground soaked all of the time; covers were at hand to avoid the possibility of saturation. Furthermore, there was permanent covering of the bowlers' run-up and delivery area. Batting required flexibility and an excellent technique. This is why we went for the lighter bat. Bashing sixes and fours daily with a thick blade was not possible. You had to be right to the pitch of the ball when on the front foot. Alec Stewart would still be levering the ball, on the up, through the covers at The Oval, but only when the weather was good and the pitch sound. Of recent England players Michael Atherton looked most like an old-fashioned batsman with a technique suited to the problems uncovered wickets might present: watchful, right to the pitch of the ball, bat and pad together and with plenty of punch off the back foot. Marcus Trescothick comes from a breed of British batsmen brought up on covered pitches who keep their posture upright and half-bend the front knee. Michael Atherton, when going forward, got right over the ball with the front knee well bent. I was an Atherton fan, but it appears that Michael Vaughan, breaking through to the top albeit a decade too late at twenty-seven, is now the resident model for youngsters to copy. He is a fine player.

Consider the changes to the ball. On top of covered pitches came the reduction in the number of flaxen strands in the seam of the cricket ball, causing even less movement for the faster bowlers. The ball is therefore a less powerful weapon in the bowler's hand, a fact compounded by unhelpful pitches. Link those conditions to some poor actions and you see how Dennis Lillee's description of England's bowlers as pie-chuckers was born. Doug Insole's Essex seamers got movement off firm green pitches as long as the control of length and line was near perfect. They expected to get wickets and that did much to mature their skills. Trevor Bailey and Barry Knight took some playing.

Our own tracks in Glamorgan were slow turners, helping us breed spinners such as Don Shepherd and catchers such as Peter Walker. Groundsmen could be adventurous. Not today. They fear receiving low marks and having the pitch inspector sent along to inspect their work, and so these days, even with full covered pitches, groundsmen play safe.

So I say, be bold. Uncover pitches in the county game and play matches over three days. Make it fun again and wholly competitive.

I would restore a single county championship played for prize money, each county to be rewarded in accordance with its position in the end-of-season table. That should keep the competitive juices flowing through August and September.

I would do away with players' benefits and develop an insurance scheme that rewards professional players on the merit of a career in the British professional game regardless of county and I would, as a personal whim, call the ECB the England Cricket Board not England and Wales. At present it smacks of political correctness to which I am opposed. The simple fact is that Glamorgan play in the English county championship and it is the professional pinnacle to be chosen for the England team. The Welsh will have their own board of control when we play our own Tests.

Building a pyramid of competitive cricket should not be beyond our vision. We understand the pitfalls of mindless county cricket, aimless second eleven programmes and the fixation with Under-nineteen schools cricket when the best players should be mixing with the best. Many of my friends argue that regional cricket would make a neater and more effective preparation for Test cricket. I favour a complete revamp of county cricket.

Six years of the ECB has yet to put a fine Test team in the shop window. There are whispers of good young players coming through and we must hope at this stage that the development of these will restore England's reputation. Those who have worked hard to achieve this deserve encouragement and I hope applause, but until the counties, MCC and the Board fulfil roles in the same battle plan and until the youngest cricketer can see a clear, competitive way into a full-time professional career and prefer it to life in the faster lanes, our successes will be random and our weaknesses repeated.

CHAPTER 16

MOVING ON

I was a studio guest recently in a radio programme hosted by the Welsh comedian Max Boyce. Max invited me to answer questions about my last day on earth and opened with 'Where would you like to be, with whom, and doing what?' Family excluded.

'Max,' I said, 'I want to be playing at Royal Porthcawl Golf Club and taking a rest up at Mrs Jones's halfway house at the side of the eighth green, eating one of her delicious home-made pasties with brown sauce, sipping a hot toddy, and watching Gareth Edwards putting from twenty-five feet to stay four down.'

It was the jocular response required, and indeed I believe life lived in the environs of Mrs. Jones's wooden hut is often very close to heaven, as the eye is taken over the sloping links to the wide horizon of the sea. I look across Swansea Bay to the town, now a city, where I was born, and I hear my mother's voice drifting my way from her resting place in Oystermouth cemetery, 'Not drinking whisky, are you? Never liked your father drinking whisky, y'know.' And then I can hear the shuffle of Wilfrid Llewellyn Lewis's slippers down the corridor in our old home in Hanover Street, as he whistled on his pseudo-nonchalant way for another finger of Scotch from the half bottle of Bell's in the middle room.

I can let the gaze go in along the coast for seven or eight miles to the town of Neath that never lets me go, then inland, behind the hut, rise the hills and scarred fingers of valley life. It is a thirty-five-minute drive to Castellau, the hamlet just above Llantrisant, where I live now. I sometimes knock a single ball round Royal Porthcawl, sit at the eighth on my own and reflect. I certainly wonder about life's alternatives: what if I hadn't done this or that? I cannot imagine being without Joan Pritchard, the girl who first shared with me the produce of her A-level domestic science lessons, an apple tart, a Welsh cake or a pancake, which we would eat after school near St Thomas's church, and then the rest of her days. What terrific lifelong support and advice as I took fresh guards to meet the challenges along the way! Joan was always right that family should come first, second and third. I could not have been more proud of the achievements in commercial sport of my daughters Joanna and Anabel and their playing abilities. Millfield School worked so well for them. Now the story moves on to my grandchildren, Anabel's two, Freddie Sexton, the six-year-old football fan who wants to join the Reading AFC tiddlers, and Gabriella, a three-year-old ballet dancer, permanently pretty in pink.

Now, with a sixty-fifth birthday approaching, what next? I have just accepted the non-executive chairmanship of World Snooker Limited, a delicious challenge in difficult times for the sport, and have had a first book of fiction accepted by my trusting publisher. It is all about a ladies' captain at a mythical golf club, Mrs Gruffydd-Williams, her mysteries and mischiefs, which allows my return to the golf course following the prolonged troubles of a knee replacement – purely for research you will understand. Can the metal in the right knee stop me swaying off the ball, and help create the torque and turn for a solid swing? I guess the fairways of Royal Porthcawl will struggle to keep it a secret. Handicap 12: only just starting!

INDEX

Note: 'TL' denotes Tony Lewis. Names of countries, counties, etc., are of cricket teams unless otherwise indicated.